Race and Racism

PHILOSOPHY OF RACE

Series Editors
Linda Martín Alcoff, Hunter College and the Graduate Center CUNY,
Chike Jeffers, Dalhousie University

Socially Undocumented: Identity and Immigration Justice
Amy Reed-Sandoval

Reconsidering Reparations
Olúfẹ́mi O. Táíwò

Unruly Women: Race, Neocolonialism, and the Hijab
Falguni A. Sheth

Critical Philosophy of Race: Essays
Robert Bernasconi

Beauvoir and Belle: A Black Feminist Critique of The Second Sex
Kathryn Sophia Belle

Race and Racism: A Decolonial Approach
Linda Martín Alcoff

Race and Racism

A Decolonial Approach

LINDA MARTÍN ALCOFF

OXFORD
UNIVERSITY PRESS

Oxford University Press is a department of the University of Oxford.
It furthers the University's objective of excellence in research, scholarship,
and education by publishing worldwide. Oxford is a registered trade mark of
Oxford University Press in the UK and in certain other countries.

Published in the United States of America by Oxford University Press
198 Madison Avenue, New York, NY 10016, United States of America.

© Oxford University Press 2025

All rights reserved. No part of this publication may be reproduced, stored in a retrieval system, transmitted, used for text and data mining, or used for training artificial intelligence, in any form or by any means, without the prior permission in writing of Oxford University Press, or as expressly permitted by law, by license or under terms agreed with the appropriate reprographics rights organization. Inquiries concerning reproduction outside the scope of the above should be sent to the Rights Department, Oxford University Press, at the address above.

You must not circulate this work in any other form
and you must impose this same condition on any acquirer.

Library of Congress Cataloging-in-Publication Data
Names: Alcoff, Linda Martín author
Title: Race and racism: a decolonial approach / Linda Martín Alcoff.
Description: New York, NY : Oxford University Press, [2025] |
Series: Philosophy of race | Includes bibliographical references.
Identifiers: LCCN 2025002003 (print) | LCCN 2025002004 (ebook) |
ISBN 9780197796917 hardback | ISBN 9780197796924 updf |
ISBN 9780197796948 online | ISBN 9780197796931 epub
Subjects: LCSH: Race—Philosophy | Racism—Philosophy
Classification: LCC HT1521 .A365 2025 (print) | LCC HT1521 (ebook) |
DDC 305.8001—dc23/eng/20250425
LC record available at https://lccn.loc.gov/2025002003
LC ebook record available at https://lccn.loc.gov/2025002004

DOI: 10.1093/9780197796948.001.0001

Printed by Integrated Books International, United States of America

The manufacturer's authorized representative in the EU for product safety is
Oxford University Press España S.A., Parque Empresarial San Fernando de Henares,
Avenida de Castilla, 2 – 28830 Madrid (www.oup.es/en).

To the memory of Charles W. Mills

Contents

A note on terminology	ix
Acknowledgments	xiii
Introduction	xv
1. The Historical Formation of Racial Identities	1
2. The Persistent Power of Cultural Racism	61
3. The Crisis of White Identity	108
Conclusion	188
References	197
Index	211

A note on terminology

My usage of the concept of *race* is meant to signify that it has a distinct meaning from that of *ethnicity*. Race is a form of group identity that is usually accompanied with visible markers assumed to signal lineage from a particular geographical area of the world. Its use in common speech in this minimal way does not entail the enactment of racism, even though the lineage that is assumed may be so long ago as to be irrelevant in anyone's life, and it may in fact be wrongly ascribed. I also use the concept to explore the various racist theories of race, such as biological racism or cultural racism or other theories that impute intelligence or behavioral dispositions to one's racial identity.

My use of the concept of *ethnicity* signifies a self-identified grouping that involves more than physical attributes but also belief systems and ways of life. Ethnic groups can include peoples with multiple racial identities. But these terms interact and overlap; thus it is also useful to use the term *ethno-race* to identify groups that are ostensibly given an ethnic name and yet whose identity signifies a racial meaning in their society. Examples of this can include *African American, Latinx, Turkish, Asian* and *Asian American, North African,* and many more. The distinctions that are sometimes assumed to neatly separate national, ethnic, religious, and racial forms of identity are not reliable: a religious identity such as "Muslim" or "Jewish" can convey racial and racist meanings in certain contexts, without any use of a racial term, because some associate essential features, indeed, inherent and unchangeable features, to certain religions, certain ethnicities, and sometimes even certain nationalities, who may all be thought to be identifiable by visible features. Neither philosophers nor linguists can control the circulations of meanings that are enlivened by common ways of speaking, through specifying what they consider to be the proper definitions and distinctions of terms. As Wittgenstein suggested, it is a fascinating feature of the plasticity of human languages to explode every attempt at control, so we should focus more on

X A NOTE ON TERMINOLOGY

what a given use of language does in the world and less on the speaker's conscious intent or the official definitions. This means we need a local, contextual analysis, which poses a large challenge for a book such as this, which is trying to look at concepts like race and whiteness across diverse parts of the world.

Against common usage in North America and Europe, as well as elsewhere, I do not use the word *American* to refer only to people who live in the United States. There are words in Spanish to refer to this group—*estadounidenses*, or more rudely, *gringos*—but no such words in English, and that is no accident. The restrictive reference of "America" to the United States leaves an imperial mark wherever it goes. On these pages, *America* is a term used for the Western hemisphere and includes North, Central, and South. We have to leave our linguistic imperial baggage behind.

The term *immigrant* refers to persons who are relocating permanently from one nation to another. *Migrant* is used to refer to people who relocate but intend to return or seek a home elsewhere. *Refugee* is used to refer to people who have been forced to leave their home countries because of war, violence, or persecution. Sometimes refugees are referred to as "displaced persons." Yet, in the language of nativism, these distinctions make little political or moral difference, and all are lumped into the category "immigrant."

Perhaps the most difficult terms to get right are those global monstrosities we use so often: the *West*, the *Global South*, the *Global North*. The larger the geographical area a term is meant to cover, the more it covers over. I have no magic bullets to solve this problem. In speaking about the "West," many of us, from both inside and outside this realm, put silent quotation marks around the term in our heads all the time. We mean to refer to an idea more than a reality, a mythologized representation of the vanguard of civilization rather than a simple geographical location. Even if we try to specify these terms as merely geographical, the geographical and national borders usually given are clearly ideological and sometimes racial. Why is Eastern Europe cordoned off from Europe 'proper'? Why does it need a conditional at all? Why can't we refer to Mediterranean cultures across southern Europe and northern Africa as one long-united entity? Why is New York City part of the Global North, when over a hundred languages from the Global South are spoken here? I could keep going, but there is no end in sight.

The easy answer is that the United Nations uses such terms, and this use confers their meaningfulness. But most usefully, these impossibly large terms are attempts to refer to real differences of power, attention, and wealth. Their eventual replacement will follow the eventual decline of these differences.

Acknowledgments

I have been fortunate enough to share ideas with numerous audiences in more than twenty countries around the world and have often gained insights from their questions and reactions. For about fifteen years, I have taught regularly in the DialogoGlobal Decolonial Summer School, mostly in Barcelona but also in Pretoria. I also taught decolonial courses in Sydney for three years, in Amsterdam, and in Buenos Aires. These courses had students (who were actually faculty, activists, and graduate students) from all parts of the world, who helped me to deprovincialize my own thinking about colonialism's effects as well as its reach. I well remember the moment when Salmah EvaLina Lawrence spoke up in a decolonial feminism course I was teaching, to say she'd "never seen an oppressed woman in her life." She was from a matrilineal community in Papua New Guinea, and she was not the only indigenous person to school me on the variation in "ways of existing" around the world, even in the midst of colonial incursions. Of course, I also learned much from our students about the nature of gender oppression, ethnic oppression, and racial oppression, and the commonalities these forms sometimes take in the wake of the modern/colonial world system, which has achieved ideological near-hegemony.

I want especially to thank Ramón Grosfoguel and Nicolas Kompridis and Nokuthula Hlabangane for their work to make these interactions possible. Ramón's tireless efforts together with Nelson Maldonado-Torres, to build the Decolonial Summer Schools, keep them up-to-date with theoretical developments, and keep them afloat on literal shoestrings, is a model of scholar activism.

I also want to acknowledge here a debt to Chike Jeffers for encouraging me to name and develop my position on racial identity as a theory of the historical formation of race. I also owe a great deal to Charles Mills, my friend, comrade, and interlocutor for several decades, whose strong voice I continue to hear quite clearly and quite regularly despite his passing. The small but growing philosophical

xiv ACKNOWLEDGMENTS

community of those working on race and racism, and on Latin American and Latinx philosophy, has been foundational for my ability to do work in these areas. These young people pursuing meaningful philosophical work in what is sometimes a cold academic climate give me hope that all is not lost.

Introduction

Philosophical writing, as many people have noted, is more personal than it may appear. We write out of our experience, our fears and concerns, our desires and hopes, and sometimes, our very personal needs. The connections are not always made apparent, but let me begin this book by making it clear how personal the topics of this book are for me.

My family came into existence because of colonialism, and our lives have been continually challenged by it. Colonial divisions, colonial histories, and colonial ideas have made it impossible for me to hold all parts of my family together, even, at times, to maintain communication and regular contact. My mother is from an Irish immigrant family in the United States, a family that was coerced into migration because of the resources stolen from Ireland by the British Empire. My father is from Panama, with a typical mixed heritage including Spain and North Africa, and his parents had similar economic motives for their arduous journeys across the Atlantic Ocean. Both areas experienced colonialism, and in the case of Spain, of course, it was developed with gusto and the nation continues to benefit from theft long ago. The nation I now live in, the United States, provided both arms and military training for the many dictatorships that have beleaguered so much of Central America, including the twenty-year regime that profoundly affected my family.

Colonial relationships can also create opportunities, ironically. My father was sent to college in the United States, a country that Panama had a long and close relationship with because of the building of the Panama Canal. He offered to help my mother, also a student, with her Spanish homework, and this eventually led to my existence.

I was born in Panama but raised in the United States, and feel affection and an emotional pull, as so many peoples of the world do, toward multiple nations, regions, cultures, and cities, driven by an irrational but irrepressible desire to repair the relationships that were

xvi INTRODUCTION

torn asunder. Previous ties can fray and be lost, but their imprint remains on our faces.

Today, the transnational relationships that form such familial bonds as my own often exist inside singular nations. Of course, such transnational and cross-ethnic family formations have long been the norm in Latin America. Only now is the rest of the world, if I may speak with arrogance for a moment, catching up with us. *Mestizahe* has become a pan-Western phenomenon, reaching deep into Anglo America as well as Europe, and both regions could learn about its foibles as well as its more hopeful elements by studying the many debates about its legacy in Latin America. But too often, Latin American theory and philosophy remains neglected, untranslated, unread.

The idea that 'underdeveloped' regions, or 'backward' cultures, have something to teach rich countries remains anathema. And so, such claims will come off as arrogant, that is, as an unjustified confidence born of resentment or jealousy or, perhaps, just ignorance. But transforming the world made by colonialism will require much intellectual work by those who have borne its cruelest effects.

In 2021 I was invited to give three Adorno Lectures by the Institute for Social Research that is today housed in the Goethe University in Frankfurt am Main, Germany. This was a personal thrill as well as a daunting prospect. Adorno, Horkheimer, Marcuse, Habermas, and the whole intellectual tradition of critical theory initiated by the Frankfurt School has been a cornerstone of my own Marxism since I began reading it in earnest in graduate school. Their emphasis on culture as a key element of the social reproduction of capitalism was a critically important corrective to the economist tendencies still strong in many Marxist movements. As importantly, their argument that antisemitism and the rise of fascism was enabled by broader, structural elements in liberal capitalist cultures has become a central motif of critical social theory that continues to resonate for the current challenges we face today. This tradition made it possible for many of us to begin to connect misogynist cultures and racist ideas with the workings of capitalism. No longer were the topics of sexism and racism strictly relegated to the superstructure: they began to be theorized as a fundamental feature of the social reproduction of capitalist relations of production in the modern era.

INTRODUCTION xvii

But of course, the Frankfurt School founders did not themselves pursue a theory of colonialism or of racism, although these massive systems are now understood to have structured present-day societies, especially in labor markets, resource accumulation, the flows of peoples and materials, and transnational relationships as well as many aspects of the culture industry. Only recently has serious work from the Global North engaged with the imbrications of capitalism and colonialism. I hope this book will contribute to remedying this omission.

I will argue here that, far from peripheral issues concerning only civic equality, race and racism are fundamental aspects of current forms of social and economic organization. Since I am a philosopher rather than a historian or social scientist, I will contribute to this developing project with the elaboration of an interpretive framework that can hopefully shed light on what the excellent new empirical work is showing us today about the persistence of poverty and the alarming rise of hatred and division targeting various social identities. Our identities, whether they are interpellated as racial, ethnic, national, religious, or some combination, have material effects, determining life and death. Colonialism inaugurated a transnational economic system in which labor and power and land rights were organized on the basis of our social identities.

There is no way to understand why global poverty persists and even worsens well into the twenty-first century without starting from the emergence of the modern/colonial world system, as so many decolonial theorists have pointed out. Colonialism still structures our world not only in terms of the flow of resources but in terms of the basic concepts and ideas by which we interpret, and rank, the practices, priorities, and forms of knowing of the people of the world. The current collapse of Western soft power is unintelligible to so many people only because they are still caught up in a colonial framework that sees the West as ideologically progressive and intellectually superior in comparison to everyone else on the globe.

Colonialism and our current neoliberal Western leaders have defined freedom, democracy, justice, and equality in bizarre ways that provide cover for extremely unjust pay scales, vicious unilateral invasions, covert operations that sabotage democratic social movements, and even genocides. Justice means the right to kill and

xviii INTRODUCTION

imprison, democracy means whatever vote count corporate powers can manipulate, freedom means survival of the fittest, and equality is the equal right to compete over scarce livelihoods that pit us against one another. These demented definitions are maintained in no small part because of who is doing the defining, from where, in what language, and with what experience. To break through this conceptual blockade, we need to put racism and colonialism center stage. Many people today are making this argument, as I will cite in these pages. Only a history focused on the modern era of European-instigated colonialism can explain the present and alter how we approach the future.

The three chapters that follow each provide a distinct investigation on separate though related topics: (1) the formation of racial identities within collective histories, (2) the cloak that cultural racism provides to excuse global injustices today, and (3) the current crisis of white identity that is fueling far right movements both in Europe and north America and reenforcing the move toward ethno-nationalism in parts of the Global South as well.

In chapter 1, I argue for a new way to conceptualize racialized forms of identity, by a theory of race that understands it to be an essentially historical formation.

The idea that races are not biological or natural kinds but have been formed through a process of social construction has been a useful and powerful way to counter false claims about innate biological differences, claims that have long legitimated systems of social ranking. But the approach of social construction has persistently taken a top-down approach, focusing on the mechanisms that states and elites have used to solidify racist ideas and concretize racist practices in state policy. Thus, race is presented as a nefarious invention imposed from above. The role of the majority populations in colonizing nations is then seen as simply following elite leadership. This is an historical error, as many new histories show (Grandin 2019; Immerwhar 2019; Cowie 2022; Elkins and Pederson 2012; Beltrán 2020).

Racial concepts and ideas emerged and evolved and changed through processes of colonial domination over many centuries. It started with the Spanish project of exiling Muslims and Jews from the Iberian Peninsula through 'pure blood' requirements based on family lineage rather than avowed faith. 'They' could not be trusted to convert to Christianity with sincerity, and so the first nation-state formation in Europe put forward the idea that a successfully cohesive state required homogeneity as determined by lineage. This required state involvement and oversight in order to document family lineage, a practice they continued in their colonies.

Thus, the idea of race, including the idea that race is deterministic and predictive of individual and group dispositions, clearly emerged from elite operations of governmentality. And yet the macroevents of colonization—segregation, migration, ethnic conflict, enslavement, resource theft, massacres, and land annexation—involved the participation of masses of people at all levels. In some cases, the masses of poor settlers forced governments to *respond* to their demands for land, or they violently took indigenous land themselves, or forced the formerly enslaved off land they wanted. In Europe masses of the poor participated in pogroms and massacres targeting several groups designated inferior by race or ethnicity or religion, and they also participated in colonial control. Racial ideas thus informed ways of being with others in which different groups participated differently and were affected differently, sometimes organizing to alter the terms of their treatment, sometimes rearranging the boundaries and criteria of their group, to include southern Europeans, for example, or exclude Jews, Muslims, Roma, Sinti, Sámi, Turks, and others. These experiences produced habits of embodiment and subjectivity, assumptions of entitlement, skills in violence, communities of covert resistance, and bonds of collective solidarity that made the concept of race a living, dynamic formation, always local and contextual but persistently powerful. Elites did not have uncontested power or pull all the strings. Both landless whites and oppressed non-whites had a hand in producing the meaning of racial identities in ways I will discuss.

Most importantly, when we understand racial identities as historically formed, we will understand that policy changes will be woefully inadequate to end the negative effects of racist ideas. Only changes in collective experience will alter the operations of racial concepts and diminish their power to affect intergroup trust, respect, credibility, solidarity, and understanding. Recognizing the agency of non-elites allows us to see both the positive and negative historical events that

xx INTRODUCTION

have been wrought by people on the ground, and the possibilities for future action.

Chapter 2 takes up the topic of cultural racism, a topic much explored in the early days of anti-colonial intellectual resistance but one that has lost ground in the focus on attitudinal and psychological forms of racism. Focusing on cultural racism moves us far afield from individualist tendencies or naturalized claims about the fear of difference and reveals the constitutive tie between racism and colonialism. This helps us to understand the historical processes in which animosities are enlivened by physically visible features and made into habits of perception and judgment.

Cultural racism is addressed not to people but to peoples, or the manner in which people live, dress, eat, form families, practice their religion, and comport their economic activities. It operates today as a covert form of racism by concealing itself behind the veneer of rational, liberal, legitimate critical judgment. We are not criticizing things about people that they cannot help, such as their looks or their lineage, but things about them that they can and should change, to become more like 'us.' Thus, cultural racism cannot be solved by protecting the rights of individuals but only by addressing the judgments and rankings given of group practices. When the acceptance of immigrants is dependent upon their willingness and perceived ability to assimilate to majority practices, this can be presented as a reasonable concern and a nonracist policy. But this returns us again to Spain's demand for homogeneity.

The truth is that no modern culture has ever been homogeneous. Much work coming out today by archaeologists and anthropologists, cultural historians and ethnomusicologists, linguists and historians of science is showing substantive lines of influence between groups. This is a massive scholarly project that is correcting the myths of European modernity, not ideologically driven but simply motivated by better methods of work in uncovering the past. Sometimes these cross-cultural influences can be portrayed as borrowings, sometimes theft and appropriation, but there is never an absence of significant reciprocating effects when groups are in close cohabitation, even with distinctions of rank and power. The prime advantage Europe had at the beginning of the colonial era was being a nexus of transcontinental

INTRODUCTION   xxi

interaction, and it was this that developed the region in every way, not simply its own existing ideas and institutions, which were, after all, pretty barbarian. Its technology, its political institutions, its science, its architecture, and its ethical ideas were all enhanced by contact.

Thus, a part of the response to cultural racism is to correct the story of how our cultures formed—and most importantly, Western cultures. I make use of the concept of 'transculturation' as it was developed by the Cuban anthropologist Fernando Ortiz in the first half of the twentieth century to help us find a way out of the West's persistent tendency toward cultural racism. Of course, we will need more than transculturation or an understanding of cultural hybridity to undo the existing ranking of cultures: we need to devise new ways to interact across differences. Interactions must always involve critique and disagreement, comparisons and moral judgments, as they should. Equality and respect demand the ability to raise questions and engage in debate. But for critique to be legitimate, it needs to be divested of the implicit baggage of cultural racism. And only in this way can we begin to understand with accuracy what our commonalities are as well as our differences.

Today's mainstream media in the West is replete with judgments about 'traditional' societies, 'underdeveloped' economies, and 'premodern' thinking that load the dice in favor, always, of Western ways of life. The concept of 'culture' itself has come under criticism for exacerbating the assumed existence of incommensurable, static worlds. To address this, I make use of Raymond Williams's approach as a way to understand cultures as systems of meaning-*making*, rather than closed sets of predetermined meanings. I also draw from Edward Said's insightful understanding of what can go wrong in culture-based assessments (for example, Orientalism) as well as what can go right in humanistic critique, to give us a sense of hope about a different way to interact, as well as to understand our own complex cultural lineages.

Chapter 3 takes up the most difficult topic: the crisis of white identity. In this chapter, I define and analyze this crisis and take a close look at the growing support for the Replacement Theory, which is the idea that white populations are being purposefully targeted for replacement. We need to take this theory seriously. The Replacement Theory has garnered wide support among large sectors of the public in Europe

xxii INTRODUCTION

and North America, is openly espoused by many political candidates and leaders, and has become so commonly heard on popular media platforms that journalists are calling it the new mainstream. It has even generated significant support from those who are not white, such as those concerned with the replacement of Christians by Muslims. It has an antisemitic conspiracy theory component—that Jews are behind the replacement of white gentiles by non-white immigrants, either as a means to change voting patterns or just to destroy the West. But the wildly false parts of the theory should not excuse an easy dismissal. I argue that the Replacement Theory represents a recognition of the coming end of colonial power and offers an analysis and solution of this situation for white publics that requires a serious response.

What I call the crisis of white identity has two parts: a narrative part and a legitimation part. The narrative crisis concerns the stories that are told about the formation of white-majority nation-states in the world. In light of an avalanche of historical scholarship that can no longer be ignored about the actual way these nations came into existence, what story can possibly be crafted anew that is both plausible and positive in any sense? If there are no plausible, positive narratives of the rise of Western power, then national legitimacy is at stake. This is indeed an existential threat to the ideology of Western global leadership as well as the maintenance of the status quo in terms of both wealth and power. The major narratives of European historical formation and the West in general are largely based on myths, lies, and repressed, or censored, memories. It is not clear whether nation-state legitimation, including the right to control national borders, can survive a serious engagement with more truthful histories of colonization and empire building.

I argue that the mass of white populations know and feel this slippage of the dominant narratives given in the modern era that have sought to legitimate imperial rule and the disparities of global wealth. One does not need to read academic histories to know this. The theme of nostalgia; the greatness, peace, and harmony of the past; and the attempt to counter 'wokeness,' defined as an excessive focus on unearned privilege, are signs of broad public concerns. Younger generations are quite politically divided, but there are strong currents across

INTRODUCTION   xxiii

generations, including millions of whites, who no longer believe the lies and want more truthful narratives.

The solution offered by the far right is that only an openly ethno-nationalist state can ensure white safety and security, in both an economic and physical sense. If white-majority nations cannot survive by continued rule over and exploitation of others, and cannot maintain the myths of their supremacy, there is no option left, they argue. An ethno-nationalist state need not worry about constant critical voices directed at historical lies; it need not defend itself at all but simply build its fortress. In this chapter, I look back at some of the early democratic writings that laid the groundwork for such ideas, such as those of Thomas Jefferson, who argued that the abolition of slavery, which he supported, could never lead to a functional state that included both slavers and the enslaved. Western nations have not done the groundwork to make such states possible, because leaders did not think they *were* possible.

We need to move beyond the stage of criticizing these myths, however, to develop a future-directed narrative reconstruction. I can only gesture toward a different path forward here, and I draw from many theorists working today to urge a reconsideration of paths not taken. There are some lessons we can learn from Latin America, where early postindependence thinkers like Bolívar and Martí recognized the need to address group differences (see esp. Rivera 2019). How does one create an inclusive and collaborative democratic polity, el Libertador Simon Bolívar asked, out of constituencies that include the formerly enslaved, displaced indigenous communities, and immigrant settlers from Europe? These are groups formed by different histories, not just by different cultures or religions, and creating a unity requires redressing the manner in which their interests were made oppositional. Jefferson effectively shelved such a project, and most of our political cultures have largely shared his pessimism. European nations have only recently begun to engage with their colonial crimes rather than continuing to display unabashedly the loot from these crimes in their national museums. European regionalism, some have argued, only exacerbates the problem, by displacing the importance of national identities with a veneer of a nonracial Europe. But this new Europe

xxiv INTRODUCTION

continues to carry vestiges of old ideologies about its civilizational mission, and it carefully maintains the security of its borders against its non-white neighbors, especially those across the Mediterranean, who live less than 120 kilometers away.

The Global North needs to find its way to becoming "non-orientalists," as Immanuel Wallerstein put it. This will require, he believed, a "constant dialectical exchange" in order to "universalize our particulars and particularize our universals" (2006, 49). A greater self-understanding is needed to enter into new, egalitarian intellectual relations that might achieve shared agendas. Edward Said's late humanism (2004) imagined peaceful coexistence rather than the transcendence of particularism, but Said also argued that, in truth, our current particularisms are almost all cultural amalgamations with multiple influences, precisely because of colonialism. Reconstructed narratives must refuse past lies but must also refuse reduction to the lowest common denominators, the thin articulations of our collective interests that excuse a disengagement with serious divergences of historical experience, memory, material condition, and values. The complex genealogies of national cultures, with their multiple contributors from diverse sources, must come to the fore.

We can find sources of hope in the domain of ordinary, everyday practical life in the twenty-first century. Our racial and ethnic identities operate in everyday practices of social interaction at work, home, school, and our transportation in-between. While these are vulnerable to habits and the expectation of continuity, they are also domains of openness, of new experiences, of unexpected and temporary collectivities created by necessity in moments of crisis, such as a train derailing or a wildfire or simply a blocked road, but ones from which we can glimpse a different way to cohabit a space, a town, a nation.

Mythic narratives of white supremacy continue to seek the impenetrability of closure, but the practices of communal and familial life and work have long been much more diverse and dynamic than these narratives can contain. We need to develop from these quotidian experiences the practices that can create forms of communal justice across difference. We also need to create constitutions and forms of government that recognize our plurinational and multiethnic, multiracial identities. We need to create choice structures that produce shared interests across group identities, interests concerning environmental, economic, and political conditions, but we should not assume, as Marxists did in the past, that such shared interests are natural and pregiven or exclusively material. Shared class conditions of vulnerability unite most people of the world, but these cannot be understood as transcendent of historical injustice or current social positioning along the lines of social identities. But the main point I want to make is that it is far from impossible to make change.

It should be obvious that none of the arguments of this short book are exhaustive or definitive. The broad scope that I take here, a scope that is both temporal and geographical, endangers hubris as well as terminological confusion at times, since different terms are used, and have quite different meanings, across our areas and histories. Nonetheless, we must have the courage to think globally. My hope is that this book will contribute in some way to the production of new narrative understandings of the past as well as new projects toward the future.

1

The Historical Formation of Racial Identities

Stuart Hall explained that the concept of race operated mainly as a silent partner in the mid-twentieth-century UK, and this silence even extended to its colonies such as his home in Jamaica. The very word 'black,' he writes, was "taboo, unsayable. . . . It betrayed the prevailing prejudices too openly. Race depended on a more euphemistic, coded discourse" (2017, 14). I would suggest that this sort of linguistic strategy—a strategy that enables racism by disabling race talk—has operated in similar ways throughout many parts of the world, even in Latin America, where affectionate diminutives ("cholita," "negrito") paper over racial hierarchies. The project of the critical philosophy of race has been to bring race into the sphere of the sayable, but, this time, without the reification that obscures its historically dynamic, inherently social, and contextually variable character as well as its nefarious ideological uses.

As a starting point, I will use the term *race* to mean group identities with visible markers on the body, although what is 'visible' varies according to both the viewer and the place. Perceptual practices used to identify races are learned and are taught differently in different places. Most of us see in color, and will note color differences, but the shadings that set the boundaries of racial identity vary, and there are other visible, physical characteristics associated with race that children are taught to pick out, name, and recognize as signs of racial identity. Adults can learn new modes of perception as well when they migrate or perhaps simply travel.

This highly contextual variation of perceiving race counsels against naturalizing such perception, but it is often learned in such a way that people are led to think they are simply seeing what is there in front of them, without any interpretive effort. So, some are surprised when

---

Race and Racism. Linda Martín Alcoff, Oxford University Press. © Oxford University Press 2025.
DOI: 10.1093/9780197796948.003.0001

2 RACE AND RACISM

their habitual perceptual cues do not transfer across geographical regions, nations, or even neighborhoods. And dominant groups, such as whites, often want to retain their own habits of perception as absolute, universal, and natural, and thus they resist correction. The covert nature of how racial perception often occurs—its semblance of naturalness—makes it more resistant to critical analysis and thus more powerful and more potentially pernicious, because it operates below the level of conscious intent. Those of us who inhabit multiple cultures and communities have a certain advantage here, since we experience the variation and learn to code-switch so as to function in these different spaces.

Thus, we need a definition of race that will take its contextualism into account as well as the learned nature of its perceivability. Our perceptions of race are what affect our social interactions and judgments, and these substantive perceptions of features that are visible to us do not track the thin biological basis of racial categories, as we will see. Since, in this book, we will be concerned with racist societies, we need a definition of race that will help us understand the way in which race operates in our social worlds, and this has little connection to biological facts. We also need a definition that avoids the idea that racial identities have any meaningful predictive capacity over abilities or dispositions. This is all simply to say that we need a definition of race that accords with the facts of how race operates in real, nonideal societies.

The philosophical debates

Philosophers have been debating how best to define the term *race* for several decades now, and this debate is usually pursued with a central concern over racism. In other words, philosophers have been interested in how our concepts of race can shed light on the ever-present problem of racism (Piper 1992–1993; Goldberg 1993, 1997; Garcia 1996; McGary 1999; Kim 1999; Blum 2002; Corlett 2003; P. Taylor 2004; Gracia 2005; Shelby 2005; Silva 2007; Hardimon 2017; Glasgow et al. 2019). The debates over racism itself have focused on whether it is a cognitive problem (a mistaken knowledge claim) or, more

HISTORICAL FORMATION OF RACIAL IDENTITIES 3

fundamentally, an emotional attitude (motivated by a negative affect such as contempt or disregard). And there are further debates over whether we should primarily define racism in individual or structural terms. It is obvious that what drives these debates is not simply the quest for conceptual clarity or descriptive adequacy. Those who prefer the cognitivist approach do not deny that racism involves an affective dimension, nor do those who prefer the emotivist definition deny that the concept of race involves beliefs and factual claims. The question is, what is the driver: beliefs or emotions? And this question is itself motivated by the need to understand what can be done to advance social change. In other words, philosophers and social theorists are concerned about how to draw our attention to key features of the problem of racism that will help set the priorities for anti-racist efforts.

My focus in this chapter will be on race rather than on racism, despite the many connections between the two. But we need a clearer account of the category of race itself, and we need to hold open the possibility that the concept itself can be separated from racist intent. We should not assume in an a priori way the answer to the question of the relationship between using the concept itself and racist outcomes. Also, to repeat, since it is clear that the term *race* signifies differently in different locations, and that the criteria used to designate given individuals are different as well, most agree we need a highly contextual approach rather than a universalist one (e.g., Candelaria 2007; Haney-López 2006; Guglielmo 2003). In some societies, one's family lineage determines one's race, and in cases where this has been governed by the "one-drop rule," such lineage can countermand the visual completely. In other societies, the visual, often through colorism,[1] determines one's race to such an extent that siblings will be referred to with different racial terms.

There are also arguments that we should drop racial categories and stick to ethnicity, on the grounds that the concept of race has no genetic or biological basis and will simply perpetuate false beliefs. Yet

---

[1] *Colorism* is a term used to describe the attitude of societies that prefer lightness over darkness without necessarily making rigid boundary distinctions. In colorist societies, the issue is not whether one is black or brown, for example, but *how* black or brown one is. Colorism can operate alongside distinct categories but can significantly change an individual's social status.

4 RACE AND RACISM

the debates over the biological grounds for racial categories are on-going (Kitcher 1999, 2007; Spencer 2012, 2014, 2018, 2019; Andreasen 1998; Dupré 2008; Maglo 2010, 2011). Certainly, the older biological theories that tied race to intelligence and a host of other features have been thoroughly disproved as the distinguished philosopher of biology, Philip Kitcher, succinctly explains: "the characters that divide races . . . are not significant, and the intraracial variation is greater than the interracial variation" (1999, 104). But Kitcher himself has been among those who have argued for new conceptions of racial categories based on population genetics, which would give race a different and more defensible biological basis. Thus, Kitcher opposes the "eliminativists' insistence that racial divisions correspond to nothing in nature" and argues that they do in fact correspond to our "patterns of mating," which produce physical features that can distinguish groups (1999, 104). Population genetics is the study of genetic patterns found in population groups from ancient times, and it reveals an association between such patterns and the geographical concentrations of peoples. This is what makes it possible for saliva swabs to tell an individual which geographical regions of the world their ancestors came from based on historical DNA patterns. Population genetics has ballooned new industries to provide such information for the curious, even though our ancestral geographical lineage tells us nothing about disposition, skills, or behavior, as the old ideas of biological race promised to do. Some worry that this use of DNA testing will encourage a continued attachment to these old biological ideas, and thus it is with amused satisfaction that we see some white racists discovering on the basis of a swab that their own white lineage does not measure up to the one-drop rule. Biological information, in these cases, can serve anti-racist ends.

The central point of contention in the biological debate over race is whether the population genetics and other approaches that have emerged to link biological features to racial identities, such as so-called junk DNA, actually work with the existing categories of race as they are commonly understood (Pierce 2014). As Quayshawn Spencer, another leading philosopher of biology, points out, this disconnect between biological race and social race is what disabled previous biological theories of race, since DNA patterns found in

HISTORICAL FORMATION OF RACIAL IDENTITIES 5

population genetics do not match the racial types used in common speech (Spencer 2018). There are many such examples of this, such as southern Europeans who are identified as white despite the fact that they commonly have African ancestors. And even the medical conditions associated with racial groups, such as sickle cell anemia, actually arise across a number of different groups (Maglo 2011). The corporate world of medical care sometimes uses racial categories for the purpose of marketing treatments for conditions that have long been associated with racial groups, but independent scientists have disputed the advisability of such approaches (e.g., Tong and Artiga 2021). The bottom line is that genetic patterns from the ancient world that can successfully map our geographical lineage do not explain racism or provide any correlations with significant features of human beings that would predict behavior or dispositions. And, given the movements of peoples around the globe over the last millennia, and the intense mixing of DNA today, health providers need to see us as individuals rather than simple 'types.'

Thus, what is clear is that the legitimate biological referents of race, such as population genetics, will tell us little about the everyday world of the here and now. And isn't this what we really need, an account of how and why race continues to marginalize, exclude, segregate, and devalue lives? No matter how the continuing biological debates pan out, they cannot answer this crucial question. Michael Hardimon (2017) has recently offered a minimalist account of the concept of race that accepts contextualism, sidesteps the biological issues, but is able to shed light on its ongoing usage in the everyday. He calls his approach a deflationary realism about race.

On Hardimon's view, minimalist race has three components: visible features, common ancestry, and geographical origin. These correlations are potentially benign, without inherent meanings that might veer toward social ranking or justify animosity or disregard. For racist outcomes, more is needed than just the bare fact of these three components, such as might be the case if one has notions about the civilizational status of geographical regions, a topic I will take up in chapter 2, or about the essential correlations between visible features and moral dispositions. But since this minimal definition does not necessarily include any behavioral or other commonalities within

6   RACE AND RACISM

racial groups, we can continue to use the concept in this deflated sense and identify ourselves and others racially without sliding into racism (for counterpoint, McPherson 2015, 2024).

Hardimon is making an effort in good pragmatist tradition to connect philosophical analysis to everyday speech, to moderate the hubris (or unnecessary overreach) of our quest toward reengineering the social world. His way of doing this is to say that a minimalist view that associates race simply with visible features, common ancestry, and geographical origin does not contradict the best recent science and does not entail a racist judgment. Thus, he is defending common speech to the extent it picks out actual features rather than imaginary properties. The eliminativists who argue that we should eliminate the use of racial terms on the grounds that they will still be associated with false claims reject even this minimalist approach, but on Hardimon's view, it is possible to maintain common practices of categorization based on the three components he lists but drop the social meanings that have created the fallacious ranking systems that justify discrimination. Thus, his is a minimalist approach to social engineering: an attempt to preserve what is legitimate in common parlance about race while jettisoning false claims. It is the false claims, such as tying race to intelligence, that have spread racism, not the everyday minimally descriptive associations.

The debate over how to define race has never been focused only on descriptive and scientific accuracy, but always also on racism and whether ceasing the use of the term *race* will reduce racism or simply help to conceal it, as Stuart Hall observed. And it is clear that the move to a more politically correct way of speaking—to reengineer common speech, at least in the public sphere—is not sufficient unto itself to eliminate ignorant ideas and false claims that continue to influence beliefs about various kinds of identity, from gender to sexuality to disability and so on, as well as race. In other words, whether the term *race* is allowed to be used on government forms or not, racism can flourish, so it makes more sense to redefine, circumscribe, and minimize, as Hardimon recommends, than to try to abolish it and shame those who still note such differences. Abolishing use of the term *race* also makes it difficult to track differences in the well-being of racially defined groups. Reforming wrong ideas is certainly important, but we

HISTORICAL FORMATION OF RACIAL IDENTITIES 7

also need to research the different material conditions and legal treatment that affects groups, often unjustly. To do this work, we need to gather facts about groups identified as races.

To understand racism, then, we need to understand how the concept works through deep structures that operate whether the term is used or not. The *term* "race" does not need to appear explicitly in order for the *concept* of race to be affecting the way that meanings are developed and circulated in any given social interaction, and the use to which they are put.

Like Hardimon's minimalist approach, social constructionist approaches have been developed by philosophers as a way to acknowledge that race is socially real. Even if it is not a natural kind, race is not analogous to phlogiston or ether or other disproved entities since, unlike them, race is a powerful aspect of many modern societies. The idea that races and racial identities are *socially* constructed, rather than natural, biological, or God-given, has been the main way to address the fear that talking about the significance of race will essentialize racial concepts once again.

Thus, social constructivist theories of race have aimed to unseat the pull of biological essentialism without requiring drastic changes in everyday speech or eliminating our ability to track the conditions of life for racially defined groups. They do this by explicating the biological associations in a new way. As Chike Jeffers puts it, social constructionist theorists have argued that it is "only through social and historical processes that the particular physical, biological, and geographical differences that we recognize as racial have come to gain some relatively stable significance" (Jeffers 2019, 45). The new versions of biological realism about race mentioned previously have tried to disentangle the plausible ways in which diverse ancestries and morphologies can be grouped, from the implausible claim that behavioral, moral, and intellectual attributes accompany these group identities. Social constructionist approaches are compatible with these new scaled-down biological theories. Thus, social constructionism is in general taken to be deflationary in the sense that innate moral and intellectual associations with racial categories are removed in favor of social and historical associations involving efforts at social control and social division. This means that the social constructionist view is one

8 RACE AND RACISM

that makes it easier to imagine changing the practices and the ideas involving race.

My argument in this chapter, however, is that the broad category of social construction needs a reformulation. Its emphasis has been on the production of racial concepts as a form of social engineering from above, while ignoring the collective agency of non-elites, and this leads to ineffective strategies of change. Social constructionists do more to engage with the normative questions of race talk than some of the new minimal realists, who focus mainly on providing an alternative to old-fashioned biological realism. Yet some prominent versions of social constructionism about race have led to the simplistic idea that ceasing official usage of the category will decrease racist associations.

Sally Haslanger's view is that the social construction of racial concepts was motivated by the purposes of domination and, for this reason, should be eliminated (2019, 24–25). This claim accords with the arguments of a number of prior theorists such as Ted Allen and Noel Ignatiev who base their analysis primarily on the historical formation of the category of whiteness by states and privileged elites. Allen provides evidence to show that the invention of the white race in the United States was not an evolutionary development of a concept based on shared experience but "a political act" to ensure that political and social privileges would be spread across the ethnic and national and religious diversity of European immigrants, but only to them and not to those who were non-European (1994, 22–24). Settler colonial states needed to divide the large numbers of poor and working-class, landless peoples coming ashore, or being brought ashore forcibly, since their numbers, and their significant shared interests, could threaten elite domination and elite rule. Divisions and rankings made it possible to create majority support for elite rule as long as it secured livelihoods for the majority. Thus, the concept and implementation of a pan-white social identity solved the political problem of social control and potential economic revolutions.

Haslanger makes this sort of social constructionist claim more philosophically precise and universal. She says, "A group G is racialized relative to context C" when their "observed or imagined features" play "a role in their systematic subordination or privilege in C" (2019, 25–26, 2012). Racial differentiation produces political differentiation and the establishment of hierarchies. With this view, however, it is hard to see how racial categories can be used to self-describe for liberatory purposes or to describe any group identities in a nonharmful way; eliminativism is the only option. In recent work, Haslanger has modified her view to allow that collective racial identities can be used positively by oppressed groups for survival and resistance, but she continues to hold that ideas of race are pernicious "in the long run" (2019, 30). This claim could support governments that disallow racial data collection on the grounds that we should begin now to undermine the harm that ideas of race will inevitably bring.

Races as historical formations

This chapter will argue that the social construction approach to race as it is usually formulated is misleading about the nature of what racial identities are and how they formed. As a result, social constructionism has offered inadequate solutions to racism. Rather than continue to understand race as a social construction, then, we should shift to the language of historical formation. I will argue that racial identities are best understood as formed through large-scale historical events, events that include interpellation by emerging racial categories as instituted by states and elites, as Allen and others have documented, but more than this. Races are formed not simply as ideas, or ideologies and policies that create constraints and enablements for the way in which individuals can conduct their lives, but as forms of life with associated patterns of subjectivity including, as a wealth of social psychology has shown, presumptive attitudes and behavioral dispositions (Steele 2010; Sullivan 2005; Beltrán 2020). Racial forms of life and ways of being with others are produced over time by macrohistorical events such as slavery, colonialism, land theft, and genocide, in which different groups participate differently and are affected differently. Actions on the ground affect how social policies instituted from above are operationalized, and it is also the case that state policies are sometimes *responses* to what is happening on the ground. The historical formations of race involve dynamic and ongoing processes, but these can be obscured by disavowals of racial categories as conceptually

10 RACE AND RACISM

mistaken, nonreferential, and inevitably, in the long run, morally pernicious.

Hardimon's minimalist approach usefully connects the concept of race to actual practices used in real-world contexts to categorize peoples by races. He is correct that physical features are often accurate signs of ancestral connections and geographical lineages. Yet minimalist approaches are insufficient for a full or adequate understanding of race beyond its externalities; they do not address the internal processes of self-formation or explain how lineage came to have such significant political meanings in the modern era. If minimalism is motivated by the sense of how dangerous the concept of race can be—the desire to keep it in a small box, so to speak—I suggest we can pursue a different approach that will have similarly demystifying and defetishizing effects.

As historical formations, racial identities are thoroughly social, it is true, as well as contextual, variegated internally, and undergoing constant change; for these reasons, the substance of racial identities is best understood as local, as many have argued (Torres-Saillant 1998). The view that races and racial identities are historical formations enhances our understanding of their contextualism and dynamism, their changeability, but it also points us toward better accounts of the main source of change, which is in the always contested patterns of social and material life *at all levels.* This is to say that we should stop looking only to the upper strata of societies, to policies and laws, but also to the actions and choices made by homemakers, parents, workers, farmers, soldiers, teachers, and civil servants. We need to look at the myriad forms of social organizations that 'regular people' have created and maintained, such as clubs, labor unions, and guilds as well as charitable, religious, sports, and political organizations, and the collective experiences that these organizations make possible especially when they are racially exclusionary. Some such groups have a positive effect in enhancing survival and mental health in hostile social climates, but, of course, this is not the case with all exclusionary groups. The ongoing efforts to integrate unions, clubs, and political organizations is important not simply for reasons of justice but for the purpose of creating new opportunities to experience more thoroughly egalitarian relationships across racial and other differences. Such experiences

HISTORICAL FORMATION OF RACIAL IDENTITIES 11

will not inevitably erase race but may enhance understanding of our diverse, complicated, group-related historical experiences, such as experiences in relation to current nation-states.

In this way, the view that races are historical formations will focus the debate about how to make progress in reducing racism, on the ongoing historical processes that formed racial identities in particular ways, with particular associated content, affecting choice structures and perpetrating divisiveness and racism. At the end of this chapter, I will use the concept of whiteness to draw out some concrete examples of this claim, building on the work of the new historians who are excavating the many forms of social oppression and group competition that have produced our contemporary conditions. And, following the sociologists Michael Omi and Howard Winant, among others, I argue that the historical processes that formed racial groups include not only state-sanctioned exclusions, differential treatment, and the distribution of protections and privileges, but also movements of resistance and creative forms of community building and collective expression among the stigmatized, as well as efforts to transform from within the racial group identities given unearned advantage.

Social movements have constantly challenged identity terms and created new ones: for example, changing from *Negro* to *Afro-American*, *African American*, and *Black*; from *Spanish* to *Hispanic*, *Latino*, and *Latinx*; as well as redefining such terms as *Asian American*, *Asian*, *Arab*, *Native American*, *Indigenous*, and *American Indian*. There is widespread debate today about the racial implications of geographical categories such as 'north African,' 'northern European,' 'sub-Saharan,' and 'Euro-Asian,' as well as the way continental names, such as 'Latin America,' emphasize European lineages and marginalize the indigenous (Mignolo 2005; Pitts 2021; Espinosa-Miñoso et al. 2021). Besides creating new terms, collective efforts to make social change have redefined existing terms, changing their criteria of inclusion and redrawing boundaries, with important effects especially for people of mixed heritage.

Social constructionist approaches can focus so much on the official establishment of categories that the collective agency of social movements created by the racially oppressed as well as the racially privileged gets overlooked in our understanding of the historical

12 RACE AND RACISM

formation of racial identities. To change the future of race and racial identities, I will argue, we must work from the bottom up. This is the way to change the direction of history.

The remainder of this chapter will advance my argument. In the following sections, I will sketch out a general account of how we should approach social identities of all sorts, and then, in light of this general account, I will set out an approach to racial identities in particular. I will then be able to more precisely compare the historical account to other social constructionist accounts. Finally, I show how the historical formation of race is manifest in a concrete example.

A general approach to identity categories

To begin, let us consider the philosophical attention that has only very recently been paid to group identities—such as race but also gender, sexuality, ethnicity, disability, and so on.[2] Debates over how to understand these sorts of social identities, and how to change their meanings and values, emerged in social movements of resistance from anti-slavery movements forward. As stated previously, social movements have resisted some identity terms, invented new ones, and changed the criteria of inclusion (an example of the latter is the debate among Latinx groups as to whether Spaniards should be included in the category of "Hispanics" used by the US government).

The political questions posed by activists about identity terms are not entirely dissimilar from traditional metaphysical debates over identity in the tradition of European philosophy, beginning with the ancient Greek debate over the question of the "one and the many." These latter debates have centered on the problems that beset any account of identity, whether it concerns cats, apples, or humans: plurality, internal differences, and change. Are the grounds of unity natural or only nominal, that is, justified by shared and unchanging natural physical characteristics or only by how societies interpret the meaning and significance of these characteristics? Has the unity of some categories,

---

[2] Some aspects of the following argument are developed in Alcoff 2022.

HISTORICAL FORMATION OF RACIAL IDENTITIES   13

such as gender-related categories, been coercive? (Ásta 2018). Activists and social movements push back against coercive processes of categorization but generally develop revised terms and expanded options rather than advocating for elimination, given the ongoing social significance of social identities in most current societies.

Grouping materially instantiated individual entities or beings into categories *always* entails a downplaying if not outright denial of differences. Nonetheless, the use of categories is vital to function in complex environments. With the helpful shorthand of group terms and typologies, we can guess that any cat we see may enjoy milk and that any apple is safe to eat. The fact that such generalizations do not apply perfectly across every individual cat or apple does not make them worthless, and normal category use is usually cognizant that there are exceptions. In the case of our social categories of identity for human beings, rather than cats and apples, what might seem to be purely metaphysical questions about how justifiable it is to corral distinct individuals into a single category will quickly embroil us in questions of politics and social systems as well as individual agency and free will. Category use in general is justified by utility, but we need to ask, what is the utility served by categorizing human beings into identity groups? And for whom are identity terms useful? Or better, what are the *different* possible uses in various contexts? Given the significant variation of uses, we need to consider whether the function served by a group identity category actually justifies overlooking the inevitable internal differences of its members.

The variation within categories such as 'Black' or 'Latinx' or 'indigenous' are not simply diachronic but synchronic, such that both uses and meanings vary. Social movements of resistance know that names have real-world material effects, and thus they often contest not only *the way* in which group identities have been named but also *the significance* given to one's membership in a group. Early feminists argued that gender identity is not as significant as many believed, that one's gender alone does not determine everything about one's employment potential or parenting role in family life. But even when social movements reveal the nefarious uses of social group categories, they have also introduced new uses that can create collective solidarity, support group survival, and protect traditional practices and

14 RACE AND RACISM

languages that are derided, maligned, and sometimes targeted for eradication.

Before turning to the categories of race and ethnicity, let me turn first to the categories of gender and sexuality. Feminist theory found fault with conventional understandings of gender and sexuality on the grounds that they made, or implied, specious causal and predictive claims. Some also argued that the category of gender has harmed feminist theory and practice by concealing significant differences in the forms of oppression that are experienced by straight women versus gay women, which they argue is a difference in kind, not merely in degree. Cheshire Calhoun (2000) argues, for example, that, while straight women are segregated to lower-ranked social and economic positions, there is an attempt to displace lesbians entirely from both public and private spheres, to invisibilize them and render their rights and recognition not lesser but nonexistent. Lesbians, and other noncis and nonheterosexual people, are not simply sequestered to the home as straight women were; rather, their very right to exist continues to be under threat. Monique Wittig argued that lesbians should not be included in the category 'woman' at all, since they are essentially conceptualized as male imitators or 'not-women' because they are outside the care economy that is directed toward the provision of service to males (Wittig 1981). In a similar way, there are debates over whether the category of African American should include recent immigrants from Nigeria, or white South African immigrants, or those like Barack Obama or Kamala Harris who are of mixed race. Thus, it would be a serious misunderstanding to assume that anti-racist and feminist movements are fundamentally committed to defending existing identity formations. The truth is that every social movement organized against identity-based oppression has transformed the meanings, boundaries, and actual words used to describe identities.

To further complicate the picture, Stuart Hall shows that the "struggle over the relations of representation" has necessarily led to a struggle over the "politics of representation itself.... [since] how things are represented and the 'machineries' and regimes of representation in a culture do play a *constitutive*, and not merely a reflexive, after-the-event role" (Hall 1996, 442–443). Like Foucault and Ian Hacking, Hall argued that the descriptive content of socially recognized identities

HISTORICAL FORMATION OF RACIAL IDENTITIES   15

had a hand in *producing* those identities, in the sense of producing persons with forms of subjecthood that were affected by, and conforming to, the dominant ideas about their groups. This adds a further layer of complexity to the problem of identity when it concerns not apples and cats but human beings. In defining categories of identity, we are not merely choosing which group differences to highlight, but, possibly in some cases, *we are choosing which group differences to encourage or even mandate* (Ásta 2018 and Sveinsdóttir 2013 for a philosophically precise articulation of this claim). This is one important way in which our social identities are historically formed—not simply conceptualized but actually and materially formed.

An approach to racial identities in particular

Thus far I have been arguing that in order to grapple with the question of any given form of social identity, we need clarity on the nature of social categories of identity in general.[3] There are three aspects of identity formation that must be kept in mind: (1) identity concepts aggregate through setting aside inevitable differences; (2) aggregate concepts get uptake in general populations because of their functional role either to majorities or minorities, elites or non-elites, or both; and (3) following Hall, the characteristics used to justify group concepts may have a significant effect on human behavior and the formation of subjectivity. The question of whether any given category of identity is useful or defensible will involve a number of considerations. These include its genealogy or formation, its social effects (including its effects on resistance and solidarity), and who has had a hand in the process of forming the ideas and practices that make up a given identity.

---

[3] Class identity is another crucial social identity, and as I argue in Alcoff (2006), class is almost always visible in some way: heard through an accent or way of speaking or apparent by one's manner of dress and comportment, and it can even be marked on the body given the way that health care and fresh food is maldistributed. I am setting aside the overall question of class identities here, but differences *within* social groups are critical to assessing shared experiences and the limits of shared interests. Thus, all forms of identity require an intersectional analysis.

16   RACE AND RACISM

Social identities such as race make *descriptive* claims with *normative* implications, and both elements require critical analysis. As Georgia Warnke argues, simply saying that one takes identities to be socially constructed is insufficient as a normative analysis: it cannot tell us how to discriminate "between good and bad identities" (2007, 86). Because all identities are "bound up with power," Warnke argues that all require critical and normative reflection.

Much of the significance of racial identities in particular appears to be negative: being racialized as non-white endangers people's lives and livelihoods and conscripts individuals into roles and jobs that are not necessarily associated with their particular capacities, interests, or commitments. It is for this reason that many believe social identities are inherently vulnerable to systems of ranking in a way that inhibits democracy, cooperation, justice, and peace. Surely, as Warnke, Appiah (2005), and others argue, their social significance should be curtailed.

Yet identities are also the manifestation of our connections to history, to communities, to families, and to groups with which we share commonalities. The recognition of identities does not necessarily destroy individual agency; in some cases, recognition can enhance agency by leading to greater self-understanding. Consider the approach Bernard Williams offers when he says, in regard to socially recognized identities, "something is given, even though I must choose to take it up" (1995, 10). Indeed, Williams argues that it is the *givenness* of identity, the way its meaning exceeds my will, that helps us to see "why the politics of identity should be so essential to our life now" (1995, 10). What is given is where we were born, to whom, and with what particular historical experiences, and these facts are often expressed in concepts of social identity. Thus, our identities are not something we can readily ignore or easily disavow or overcome through individual acts. Thus, to say that social identities are a mix of the natural and the nominal, or the physiological and the historical, is to say that they are a mix of the given and the way in which we, individually and collectively, take up the given, as Williams put it. To take up an identity requires interpreting its meaningfulness, the moral lessons of its history, and the degree of its significance in one's own individual life. The idea that identity categories are *nothing but* strategies of domination ignores their descriptive aspect, as Michael Hardimon

HISTORICAL FORMATION OF RACIAL IDENTITIES 17

persuasively argues, such as their capacity to pick out features of our bodies and to note our relation to specific families. My racial identification is not just about me but about my unchosen relationships to particular families and ancestors, though, as Williams suggests, I may take up the mantle of these relationships in a way that transforms their meaning and significance. I have often felt that just being a woman from Central America who does philosophy has a transformative impact on the meaning of that identity. My lineage is not eradicated, but hopefully it is stretched beyond its stereotyped limits. Conflating identities with domination ignores the fact that identities can and are manifested and taken up differently, and that we have a hand in this individually and collectively. Collective resistance movements to identity-based forms of oppression are also collective struggles over the meanings of the given.

In this light, I want now to put forward four general features of racial identity that it shares with other social identities. Some of these features have already been discussed, but it will be helpful to understand them as a systematic approach to understanding race. These four features consist of: (1) the variable way a racial category may be defined in different contexts (so that one's racial identity actually changes); (2) the rootedness of racial identities in social life (since race always involves interactions with others); (3) the subsequently limited, though not nonexistent, agency of individuals in regard to their racial identities; and (4) the ways in which every social category of identity that has been marked by negative ranking has been transformed by resistance movements and thus today are not simply the product of nefarious elites (though there can also be nefarious movements from below, as I'll discuss toward the end of this chapter).

While it is critical to understand, as I have emphasized, that social identities are always subject to variable definitions and thus best understood locally and contextually (a point that is not always understood by majority communities, in my experience), we can still develop a general methodology to define and explain what specific forms of racial identity are. The latter will include attending to the meanings, or descriptive content, accorded to a particular identity; the perceptual practices that are taught as the means to demarcate groups; the criteria used to determine membership in a group; and the political

18 RACE AND RACISM

effects of having that identity, noting that all of these elements may vary from location to location. The criteria for membership in racial groups in North America has been based on one's family lineage, while in Latin America, the criteria most often used is based on skin shades in a social practice known as 'colorism' already mentioned. Thus, in Latin America, I may be viewed as having a different race than my siblings, which is not so in the United States. Similarly, in some parts of the world, one's sexual identity is determined by the gender of one's sexual partner, but in other places sexual identity refers more to *how* one has sex or what role one takes in copulation. A man in a heterosexual marriage may have sex with men without this negating his heterosexual identity if he performs sex with other men in a certain way. Religious identity is similarly varied: it sometimes depends on self-avowal and committed practice, but in other contexts (most notably, Muslim and Jewish), it is treated as a form of inherited ethnicity entirely independent of subjective orientation or doxastic commitments. Also, the way in which one 'sees' the identity of those around them varies according to what perceptual practices they have learned. Our capacity to perceive race is a finely grained, learned skill, and the perceptual skills that are taught vary by location.

Individuals who have been oppressed by identity designations have sometimes been able to move to new cities, neighborhoods, or working environments where the *givenness* of their identity has a better set of understood meanings and associated options, in which one can be seen by others in a way that conforms more readily to one's own sense of self. W. E. B. Du Bois is a famous case of this, who spent his final years as a citizen of Ghana after renouncing his US citizenship. But others can choose to move to a different neighborhood or region of a nation to transform their daily life. Moving to New York City was particularly useful for my family: here we don't stand out but just blend in. We don't have to justify or explain our particular mix of histories, religions, and ancestries but have simply become part of a familiar norm.

In an essay on Muslim identity, Akeel Bilgrami suggests a way to make metaphysical sense of the contextual nature and inevitable variability of identity terms. He argues that taking the approach that Quine took toward scientific constructs can be helpful, for then, "the absence

HISTORICAL FORMATION OF RACIAL IDENTITIES 19

of strict criteria need no longer be seen as a sign of one's confusion" (1995, 200). For Quine, concepts like "electron" are best understood as internal to a theory. This means that when a concept like "electron" is transferred from one theory to another, we should understand that this will alter its meaning as well as its role in causal attributions and inferences. Multiple theories may make use of a term, yet it may not have the same meanings in each context. Hence, if we want to understand a concept, we need to understand it *in relation to* the theoretical system within which it appears. Similarly, concepts of social identity like "Muslim" are operational within specified contexts: once we understand them as indexical to location, we can see how they are unified and what they are meant to explain. We can then, as Bilgrami says, "embrace their locality . . . without any anxiety about losing our hold over them" (1995, 200). In particular, the racialized essentialism associated with Muslim identity in Western nations, in which individual belief is negated as irrelevant, can be understood as entirely contextual. And it may be useful for those who are seen as "Muslim" to understand what it means in those contexts rather than to simply deny that it is their identity. In the West, "Muslim" means Muslim lineage, a meaning that is not universal. What it means to say that race is local, then, is that its overt meaning as well as its informal connotations are internal to a specific context or language game. The local nature of race is not merely about ideas or the meaning of words but about one's lived experience. It is of course possible to contest these meanings, as I emphasized earlier, and to force the mainstream to alter its understanding. But this will require altering the social context in which meanings are operationalized and refashioning the power dynamics that affect this process.

The second aspect we need to understand is that our familiar social categories of identity are very much rooted in the specific contexts in which we live, work, and interact with others, in both formal and informal ways. We are identified at the moment of birth (or even before) by various categorical terms, affecting how we are treated and how our actions are interpreted. Our identities as members of specific ethnic or racial groups, as documented or undocumented, "normate" or disabled, are recorded throughout our lives and affect us in profound ways. Even without formal records, the meaning and significance of our

20 RACE AND RACISM

identities are reflected and reinforced each day in our informal social interactions as well as our media consumption. Official government forms are not the only ways that the meanings of embodied features can be conveyed.

This is a massive material system. When we look at the social world around us and observe who is rich and who is poor, who does service work, manufacturing, construction, or technology design, we are looking at the material effects of historical events and structural policies. The categories of socially recognized identities continue to yield reliable predictions of income, homeownership, likely imprisonment, and the sector of the labor market in which one works. The increasingly complex intersections of gender, class, ethnic, and racial identities, and the slowly increasing integration of job sectors, have not yet rendered identities statistically meaningless for research in economics, sociology, education, medicine, or political science. Thus, many governments as well as nongovernmental research groups continue to maintain a watch on the correlations between identity and one's economic well-being, political participation, social inclusion, health, mortality rate, and educational achievement. The maintenance of this material organization of social groups is the result of conscious and collective social efforts. Our identities are rooted in our social worlds: meaning that they are connected to our social lives and reenforced daily and, thus, very difficult to ignore.

Thus, the third aspect of identities we need to understand is the limited control individuals have since our identities are features of collective and social life. To change aspects of my identity, I need to engage with *existing* systems of meaning that interpret and interpolate me. If I attempt to enter a higher paid profession that is dominated by group identities different than my own, I cannot simply ignore the likely problems I will encounter. To succeed in a sector of the economy in which my group is marginalized, I may need to assimilate to new practices of dress, speech, comportment, even beliefs. I can also challenge current conventions, and sometimes help to change them, but to ignore the existing realm of social expectations and norms is to invite failure and to diminish my efforts at making change. If I simply ignore the existing conventions of meaning, I risk being unprepared for the

HISTORICAL FORMATION OF RACIAL IDENTITIES   21

treatment I may receive because of an identity others recognize (or believe) me to have.

In general, the meanings and boundaries and types of social identities change because of *collective* practices, some in the form of progressive social movements and some that take less positive forms, as I'll discuss later. Collective practices can force policy changes and produce new cultural forms of expression, unlike individual declarations of being a 'race traitor' (Marcano 2010; Gooding-Williams 1998; Omi and Winant 1994; P. Taylor 2004, 2016; Alcoff 2006, 2015). Social movements not only change the meanings of identities but can also create or bring into larger public awareness entirely new categories of identity such as "Chicano" and "trans." In reality, such identities are rarely new, but new identity terms can open up new possibilities for public life.

What we might think of as what is external to our self—such as the way our socially recognized identities animate prejudgments and interpretations—are, in truth, not external to who we are. Identities are items in the world, neither private nor invisible, and key features of our immediate reality that help form our selves, often from a young age. Our socially recognized identities affect the opportunities and challenges we face, our treatment by others, and all of this will affect our own self-development as, for example, confident, hopeful risk-takers or guarded pessimists or arrogant solipsists. It is therefore necessary to understand identities as the focal point of a dialectical interplay in which we have limited control. The fact that *we* have limited control comes together with the fact that the social systems that try to define us also have limited power over how individuals see themselves and over the forms of resistance creatively developed and pursued by our communities. But the social nature of identities needs to be reckoned with as beyond any semblance of our total control.

The fourth aspect of identities we need to understand is that they are not simply the product of elite control. Given the role of social movements and collectively induced cultural shifts, as well as the profound impact of large historical events, formations of identity can be the result of elements that emerge from a variety of social sectors (Omi and Winant 1994; Castells 1997).

22 RACE AND RACISM

Identities are, of course, in many cases the product of calculated and concerted efforts by state actors. Constitutions and other forms of legislation can inscribe differential rights, including suffrage, citizenship, migration, and employment conditions. Courts interpret how laws apply to specific individuals, in a way that establishes the borders between identity groups and the criteria that will be used to determine inclusion in racial categories (Haney-López 2019). Notoriously, the Canadian and US governments have operated unilaterally to inscribe the legal definition of indigenous identity, often contradicting the ideas and practices of indigenous groups themselves. States interpret identity claims based on values they want to uphold, such as property rights and the inviolability of commercial transactions. Narrowly defined rules about indigenous identity that require documentation and evidence of multigenerational ties to a region have the effect of limiting land claims, as does denying recognition of mixed peoples.

Yet, indigenous groups have flouted state laws and boundaries and redefined their own group identity. The Iroquois began to create their own passports for international travel in the 1920s and their documents garnered recognition from the United Nations. Some groups have ignored "blood quantum" demands and emphasized living in and with a community as sufficient for inclusion, even without shared ancestral lineage. Thus, it is important to recognize that resistance takes the form of an attempt not simply to escape identities altogether but to redefine, reconfigure, and assert different terms and criteria. Oppressed groups can be forcibly segregated, but they may also *prefer* to live in neighborhoods where they are the majority and where, as Tommie Shelby has argued, they can then rely on "their established social networks for childcare, transportation, and employment information" and also encounter fewer daily microaggressions (2016, 70). Whether community segregation is coercive or voluntary, it will have an effect on family formation and cultural forms of expression, with a resultant impact on identities.

Shelby argues that the agency of non-elites has too often been overlooked in the social sciences and policy worlds. His analysis of what he calls "ghetto poverty" diagnoses a persistent bias among social analysts, who tend to downgrade the agency of the poor, to "see dysfunction where perhaps lies resistance to injustice" (2016, 3). In reality,

HISTORICAL FORMATION OF RACIAL IDENTITIES   23

the conscious collective action of non-elites, as well as the aggregation of individual choices, can shift both the meanings and political effects of social categories of identity across time. As Allison Weir puts it, "identities are not simply effects of a single binary logic of subjection through exclusion, but are produced through multiple contesting relations" (2013, 3). She goes on to argue that "*no* identities are produced *only* through subjugating regimes of power" and that theorists need to attend to the various "we" relations in which one enacts agency (2013, 8). This is not to downplay the *longue durée* of colonialism but to remind us of the successes of everyday acts of resistance and struggles to maintain a positive sense of self. Elite projects can sometimes have unintended consequences that enable new forms of agency, create new solidarities and motivate political participation toward new ends. Within the United States, the management and consolidation of ethnically diverse immigrants from South and Central America by use of a single category—"Hispanic" or "Latino"—has created overlapping experiences and a potential for new collectivities, although most of us abjure such terms as a meaningful recognition of our identity. Most consider their (or their family's) national identity to continue to be relevant.

Of course, just because non-elites exert their agency over the terms by which we are categorized does not mean we are always correct. In other words, determining the genealogy of terms is not sufficient for normative analysis. All identities, of whatever provenance, pose ethical questions for how we inhabit them and how we interpret them, how they expand our societies and inhibit or enable relationships with others.

Weir has been among the many feminists arguing for relational accounts of the self that may give us some normative guidance on the ethical questions posed by identity. As Weir puts it, identities are "*connections* to our ideals, to each other, to places, to our bodies, to ourselves" (Weir 2013, 10) Which of these connections will be ones we wish to nurture and cherish or to transform? A relational approach to the self will recognize that we cannot act on our given identities in the absence of others. Relations with others close to us can sometimes be stifling, but they are also the means by which, by and large, we achieve productive forms of self-understanding, deliberate over goals, resist

24 RACE AND RACISM

noxious conventional or mainstream ideas, and in these ways, *maximize* our individual autonomy. Identities thus represent the givenness of our material and historical contexts, but they also enable knowledge and action.

In this way, we might rethink how we understand the complicating intersections of identity terms. My connections to and relations with others are grounded in the material particularities of shared locations and shared experiences as well as the interdependence of families, coworkers, and affective networks of care, and not simply on the stipulative identity categories of the state. This suggests that the central relations that affect my own self-formation will never simply involve those who share a straightforward form of social identity with me: I may share a location with a neighborhood of diverse people or share experiences with people with whom I only share a similar form of disability or some specific history of migration. My complex, partial connections to these diverse types of people are also very much a part of the *givenness* of my identity.

This approach shifts the normative question from *whether* we should have identities—whether states or other political organizations should recognize and affirm identities—to *how* we inhabit, and name, our connections to others, to places, and to historical events. What obligations do our identities incur? What social understanding can our identities engender? Exploring the social ontology of identities reveals their constructed and fluid character, the complexity of their multiplicity and intersectionality. Acknowledging both the natural and nominal elements of identities can remind us of the inevitable limits to individual freedom as well as what is at stake *for others* in the way in which *we* interpret and inhabit our identities. And investigating our complicated connections and relationships will no doubt suggest many critical moral questions: what are my obligations, and to whom? What are my possibilities?

To deepen this analysis, I want to turn next to look more specifically at the question of race in relationship to the self, and to raise doubts about the adequacy of the language of "social construction" to represent this relationship. As Charles W. Mills put it, the assignment of racial identity "influences the socialization one receives, the life-world in which one moves, the experiences one has, the worldview one

HISTORICAL FORMATION OF RACIAL IDENTITIES 25

develops—in short . . . one's *being and consciousness*" (1998, xv; emphasis in original). He concludes from this that we need to alter basic philosophical methods of analysis, since abstract approaches that pare away particularities of our identities such as race risk producing theories and norms about human beings that tacitly assume a form of being and consciousness marked by whiteness, given the white predominance in the philosophical profession. What is experienced as neutral or taken as a universal is not necessarily so, but this becomes indiscernible if the basic approach to self-understanding sets social context aside.

Social construction and the historical emergence of race

To have a socially recognized racial identity is itself a historically and culturally specific form of human experience, rather than a universal one, and it is this fact that has created the academic consensus that race is a social kind rather than a natural kind (Gossett 1965; Hannaford 1996; Augstein 1996). Boundaries and criteria even today shift from community to community, and immigrants from other parts of the world can find their prior identities upended. This variability contradicts ideas about natural perceptual markers that ground the categories and concepts.

There is also diachronic variation. As the historian of racism Francisco Bethencourt (2013) argues, although ethnic preconceptions that have motivated systemic discriminatory action can be found in the Western world prior to the Crusades, it was the Crusades that "adapted ethnic assumptions developed within the different contexts of classical antiquity, barbarian invasions, and Muslim expansion" into useful motives and justifications for European imperialism (2013, 11). This language was later augmented with the Christian reconquest of the Iberian Peninsula and the expansion through the Mediterranean, to create the concept of "limpieza de sangre," or blood purity, a concept in which one's family lineage was all-determining. And this became the principal way in which identity was classified for political purposes, according only to those who could prove their purity the right to remain in Iberia and, later, Spain.

26   RACE AND RACISM

Many of today's Christians take the teachings of a universal Christian brotherhood to counsel against ethnic hatreds and racism. But the practice of Christian universalism has long had a limited scope, with fulsome exceptions: it was not even extended within the Christian world itself, as evidenced by the bloody competitive wars between the Roman Catholic, Orthodox Greek, and Eastern Christian churches that began in 1054 and sparked intermittent wars over the next several hundred years (2013, 37). Thus, universalist ideas about 'one God' for all not only accommodated ethnic conflict and imperial projects but sometimes provided cover. Bethencourt portrays the medieval era as a time of transition, in which ways of classifying one's enemies led ultimately to "typologies of humankind" (2013, 48). All of humanity might come in for Christian teaching and Christian judgment, but not all of humanity need be afforded the same political rights.

Skin color was not the central issue in all cases. Dividing lines concerned "styles of house building, food habits, use of animals, codes of conduct, and court ceremonies" (2013, 54). Thus, stigma could be animated by practices more than embodied features. Muslim rulers who came from the territory today called Senegal were well respected by the Portuguese kingdom in the late fifteenth century, and "received in state like a European prince" (2013, 83–85). In the early seventeenth century, the Dutch geographer Olfert Dapper described the highly variable physical characteristics of black Africans, characterizing some as beautiful, but he also began to link character traits to ethnic identities. Again, the associations were varied, ranging from his praise of Hottentots for their "lack of greed and sense of honor" to his simultaneous condemnation of the people of Madagascar as "flatterers and liars" (Bethencourt 2013, 88).

But the emerging association of shared physical types with *inherited, stable dispositions and capacities* gained wide acceptance within Europe during its era of global empire building. And the variations began to give way to cruder and simpler typologies of five racial types or sometimes only three. The ranking of human differences based on permanent features motivated and rationalized state policies governing a variety of social protections, inclusions and exclusions, from suffrage to immigration to property rights. White supremacy slowly became an ideological system that allowed rankings over every region of the globe.

This history may also make race appear to be something located outside the self, something that has a powerful effect on our lives but is essentially exterior to the basic capacities of human consciousness. The idea that race has been socially constructed is sometimes presented in this way: that external forces have constructed our societies in order to divide and rank, and ultimately exploit and oppress. On this view, while the individual has been categorized and grouped by such political systems, with their agency subsequently curtailed or magnified, we are still essentially individuals free to engage in self-making, including rejecting the salience of such concepts for our own lives.

If we accept a top-down, externalist version of social construction, two problematic ideas follow. The first is that philosophical treatments of the self, moral agency, personal identity, linguistic capacity, normative practices of cognition, and so on can be pursued separately from, or prior to, an engagement with questions of social identity such as race. If race is external, we can fashion an abstract concept of the self as unraced and imagine ourselves to be fundamentally decontextualized in time and space. And this accords with the unfortunate reality that philosophical treatments of the self and identity formation are typically pursued as if race or other significant forms of social identity can be ignored. In other words, business as usual in philosophy can proceed, with issues of race and racism sequestered to political philosophy and ethics, irrelevant to metaphysics or epistemology. I suggest that this form of abstract metaphysical universalism has fared no better than Christianity in blocking the typologies of humankind that the modern world has invented.

The second implication of the externalist version of social construction is that the most liberating approach to race will be one that deflates its spurious significance and eliminates it from social life. If it is only contingently related to our identity and has been used to legitimate domination, we should certainly strive to reduce its power, as Haslanger and Glasgow argue (Haslanger 2012; Glasgow 2009; Glasgow et al. 2019). Some states, such as France, use such arguments to disallow the gathering of statistics that involve racial as well as ethnic

28 RACE AND RACISM

and religious identity. By withholding official recognition, they hope race will wither away of its own accord.

As explained previously, the theory that race has been socially constructed was meant to replace biological essentialism, open up the possibilities for reflecting on the genesis and current function of racial categories, and help lead to change in the way we categorize and judge ourselves and others. Philosophers of race as well as historians and other theorists have put a lot of work into showing how the concept was built on the colonizing ideologies and practices that served economic as well as other ends (Allen 1994; Harris 1999; Mills 1997, 2017). But those who advocate eliminating race categories entirely have to do more than reveal the problematic genealogy of the concept: they must argue both that elimination is *possible* in the present or near future and also that it is *desirable.*

The subfield of philosophy now known as the critical philosophy of race has generally taken issue with eliminating the category of race and argued instead, following Hall and Mills, for making what is latent more visible.[4] I want to add to this that eliminating race will encroach on our ability to retain an effective historical consciousness, which Hans-Georg Gadamer described as central to the capacity to reason well (Gadamer [1960] 1991, 1976; Alcoff 2006). Understanding ourselves requires a "hermeneutical reflection" in which we recognize the "constant operativeness of history" in our own consciousness (Gadamer 1976, 28). We are products of our histories whether we acknowledge this or not. However, the dynamism and open-endedness of our hermeneutic horizons counsels against viewing this fatalistically as a limit on the possibilities of transformation. Rather, hermeneutic self-awareness, what Gadamer calls effective historical consciousness, can motivate us to transform ourselves and our societies.

Eliminating the topic of race disables self-reflection and self-knowledge, and is sometimes motivated by a form of bad faith that seeks to avoid individual and group responsibility. For phenomenologists such as Sartre, the self is the product of a dialectical interaction between the particulars of one's social situation and

---

[4] See my (2021a) *Stanford Encyclopedia of Philosophy* entry on the Critical Philosophy of Race, from which some of the following section is taken.

HISTORICAL FORMATION OF RACIAL IDENTITIES 29

the choices one makes as an individual. As Donna-Dale Marcano explains, Sartre's model "enables us to explain how and why members of an oppressed group positively assume and create an identity for ourselves" that includes concepts and terms that have been used against us. We want to acknowledge this history and the group ties and forms of resistance that have had a hand in shaping our identities (Marcano 2010, 25). The motivation to forget varies across groups: some may be motivated to forget atrocities that played a role in their family enrichment, while others may wish to forget the traumatic humiliations of group mistreatment. Still others wish the world to remember the lessons of the past as well as the history of collective resistance and survival. Clearly, forgetting is not a valid philosophical option, whatever its motivations. If our selves are indeed the product of dialectical engagement, a philosophical treatment of identity and the self will need to incorporate the situated and relational elements that play a role in constituting us, without assuming a priori that the modes of self-constitution are themselves universal and exempt from social contexts.

Social constructionists about race are not uniformly committed to eliminativism. But while historians and other social scientists have been producing rich ethnographies that reveal the multilayered processes of social construction, too many philosophers focus on elite agents, downplaying, as Shelby put it, the agency of the oppressed.

Historical accounts of the formation of racial ideas and practices helpfully reveal their fundamentally social origin and the many nefarious uses to which the concept of race has been put, but by themselves, these histories cannot reliably predict the reach of the concept's political transformability. Although race is an important element in our histories, the historical accounts also show similarities across racial groups, differences within groups, and the instability of racial terms and meanings. Yet still, as Mills emphasized, race has such a significant impact on our lives it cannot but affect some of what we know, some of how we know, and also, how we understand ourselves in relation to our worlds (Mills 1998). Thus, a historical approach will both complicate, and de-essentialize, race even while it demonstrates its importance.

The social constructionist approach can sometimes lend itself to the idea that societies can bring races into existence simply by the formal use of the category in official legal documents. This view, in turn, can

30 RACE AND RACISM

give rise to the belief that races can be deconstructed by reversing this process. The historical approach to racial identities offers a different, though not entirely distinct, approach. Racial groups exist within history and are formed by historical forces, but these include not only top-down machinations of states but also the collective agency of those so designated. It is not just state policies that construct identities, but social movements and collective action, both progressive and reactionary. This explains why the meanings of race, and their political valence, can change across historical periods (Jeffers 2019; Omi and Winant 1994; Alcoff 2015).

Historical debates

The debate over the political genealogy and meaning of the concept of race is hardly new. W. E. B. Du Bois took a Hegelian approach that understood African peoples in the post-slavery diaspora as engaged in a dialectic process of self-formation in light of their racialized treatment. Enslaved people had been violently dispossessed of their languages, ethnic cultures, and religions, as a means of domination and control. Yet, rather than simply assimilating to the Anglo-European culture of North America, Black people even under slavery were creatively producing new forms of cultural expression and communal forms of life that gave voice to the sensibilities of their unique and shared historical experience as well as their group aspirations (Du Bois 1903). Abstract individual conceptions of selfhood could be helpful in withstanding racist projections but did not shed much light on the group-related experiences Du Bois described or the specific forms of cultural life and artistic expression that emerged from slavery. Historical forces of varied sorts shaped the conditions in which Blackness became a feature of the self, albeit a dynamic and variable one.

Similarly, in the southern part of the Western hemisphere, theorists such as José Vasconcelos in Mexico and José Carlos Mariátegui in Peru were analyzing the specifically racialized forms of social identity in their societies and imagining how, given this, social progress and liberation could be achieved and what it would concretely look like

HISTORICAL FORMATION OF RACIAL IDENTITIES   31

(Vasconcelos 1979; Mariátegui 1971; von Vacano 2014). Vasconcelos understood racial identities as the product of both biological and social forces, but he saw racial *rankings* as simply tools of "imperialistic policy" (Vasconcelos 1979, 33). As the first minister of public education appointed after the Mexican revolution that lasted from 1910 to 1920, Vasconcelos was tasked with reforming a racist system that had slowly developed over four centuries of colonization, while creating a feasible educational approach that could serve civic participation in the new democracy. One of the ways Vasconcelos sought to overcome racism was by defending racial mixing, a widespread practice in Mexico as well as the rest of Latin America. Unlike his neighbors to the north, who had outlawed and vilified miscegenation, Vasconcelos saw nothing wrong with mixing. The criticism of mixing, or *mestizahe*, was sometimes based in European modernist ideas that saw mixing as a form of decline. If Europe's global superiority was based in its cultural essence, a Hegelian idea, then it was a danger to dilute it. Vasconcelos argued that such claims ignore the fact that all races and cultures are in a constant process of dynamic change and mutual influence. Moreover, diversification improves humanity, he argued, and will have the political benefit of leading to the formation of a *more* highly developed and unified race, what he called an inclusive 'cosmic race,' assuredly stronger than any segregated 'pure' race. Yet, while advocating for mestizahe, Vasconcelos reproduced a new form of racial ranking in which one of the benefits of mixing would be the reduced numbers of 'pure' Black and indigenous people.

In contrast, Mariátegui criticized the way in which mestizo and criollo elites defined the "problem of the Indian" as a problem of resistance to assimilation. As a forerunner of societies such as Ecuador and Bolivia that today define themselves as "plurinational," Mariátegui argued that political systems needed to recognize the legitimacy of native group identities and of their political and territorial claims. Indigenous groups in Peru had distinct ideas and long histories of practice about communal land stewardship, religious practice, and aesthetic values, and these had produced many flourishing societies prior to the Conquest that not only functioned well in terms of food and housing but also had some measure of social justice, by the standards we use today (e.g., Garcilaso de la Vega 2006). Hence, Mariátegui

32 RACE AND RACISM

(1971) argued that the indigenous simply needed land, not projects of assimilation (Mariátegui 1996; O. Rivera 2019). But land rights were formulated not in terms of individual property ownership but as group rights, and this was predicated on their own self-understanding of their group identity as distinct from the Peruvian national identity.

In Latin America and the Caribbean, theorists engaging with the new racial concepts of identity that organized and stratified their societies tended to hold that the Conquest and transatlantic slavery altered and realigned but did not erase prior values, practices, or beliefs (Henry 2000). In other words, the new racialized group identities carried vestiges of earlier practices and cultural ideas even though they realigned groups, sometimes displacing prior religious, linguistic and ethnic lineages (Jimeno 2014; de la Cadena 2015). A number of indigenous groups were forcibly realigned by colonial annexations of land, and their response was to create new communities with new identity terms. Liberation from formal or de jure colonial control, and emancipation from slavery, also created new political constituencies, sometimes with shared aspirations for the creation of new forms of sociality in which they could chart their own futures. Thus, while these constituencies maintained some continuity with the pre-Conquest, pre-slavery past, they were also dynamic responses to new conditions and possibilities.

The contrast between political philosophy coming from Latin America versus Europe is instructive here. The project of the democratically minded Latin American political philosophers such as José Martí, Simon Bolívar, Mariátegui, and Vasconcelos was never to create ideal political institutions for any given collection of random individuals but to create workable institutions that could overcome the devastations wrought by colonialism, land annexation, cultural imperialism, language oppression, racism, and enslavement. This required addressing group differences and group histories and thinking beyond the approach of classical Liberalism emanating from Europe (Hooker 2009; Rodo 1988). For Mariátegui, the Indians of Peru deserved land rights not as individuals but as specific historical peoples whose land had been stolen. If Peru treated its citizens as essentially fungible individuals with uniform rights and duties, only injustice could result. Classical liberal formulations of individualism have

HISTORICAL FORMATION OF RACIAL IDENTITIES   33

proved spectacularly deficient in redressing group oppression, and this is a lesson applicable to all regions of the world. Like Vasconcelos, Martí was interested in devising an educational system that could work for Latin America's liberation from colonialism and imperialism, and here, he tempered his own universalist dispositions with strong doses of contextualism and historical consciousness. He was very concerned that the Eurocentric universities of Latin America offered no "analysis of all that is unique to the peoples of America" (Martí 2002, 291). As a result of their European or US–based curriculum, "the young [Latin Americans] go out into the world wearing Yankee or French spectacles, hoping to govern a people they do not know" (291). He asked how the new American nations could produce good governments with the ability to resist tyranny, when the European-modeled university's disciplinary divisions and curriculum were transported "to the American university" (291).

Martí despised the concept of race, held that racism was a sin against humanity, and sought to undo the racist projections the Spaniards made on Black people and Indians (Martí 2002, 296; Schutte 1993 and O. Rivera 2019). But he also held that new societies must come to understand and address each group that exists within the new nations and recognize these as having distinct histories with new condensations of "vital and individual characteristics of thought and habit" (Martí 2002, 119) Writing some decades later, the philosopher Leopoldo Zea echoed Martí's warning, in his diagnosis of the sad state of the philosophy curriculum throughout Latin America, which had largely adopted European frameworks without investigating its own cultural context. The result is that "the Latin American man who had lived so comfortably found that the . . . ideas in which he believed have become useless artifacts, without sense" (Zea 1986, 220; Zea 1992). In Zea's view, a philosophy that seeks to escape historical and cultural specificity will lose its relevance and utility.

In many post-liberation, post-slavery writings, racial identity began to signify differently than it had for the colonizers. As Du Bois (1903) recounts, it began to mean group identities and forms of life that had been forged by historical processes involving, most centrally, colonialism, enslavement, and oppression but also the agency and forms of resistance devised by the colonized. Generic terms like "Black" would

34   RACE AND RACISM

change their meanings to signify new group formations whose content or unifying elements referred both to the diaspora enforced by slave societies as well as new forms of collective unity and resistance. The generic term *Indian* itself was initially unified only in that it was used by settler societies to project negative attributes on all local peoples. In this sense, the term had elements very similar to other racial terms. Yet indigeneity, and in some places, *Indian*, began to signify something more substantive as well as something more positive: a broad and diverse grouping that yet shared certain historical experiences, values, and practices of relationality that cut across many particular differences between indigenous groups. There is ongoing debate today about the validity of the term *Indian*, and the diverse and negative connotations that the term invokes in different parts of the Americas counsel against its broad adoption (esp. de la Cadena 2015) There is also ongoing debate over the application of the concept of "indigenous" to various peoples in Asia, Africa, and the Pacific Islands. But there is widespread agreement that such terms as *Indian* and *indigenous* signify more than what was *done to* peoples by their oppressors but also point to broadly shared forms of religiosity, community, and relationality (Teuton 2008; Pratt 2002; Burkhart 2019).

What becomes clear from the political history of ideas about race is that the concept has enabled many different purposes in its historical usage, from political exclusion to recognition of new forms of social identity created by colonialism. We must also remember that variations of the concept coexist within very different boundary conditions and criteria of inclusion. Racism can find habitable quarters within multiple ways of defining race, but it is important to recognize that different meanings produce different political challenges. When racial mestizahe is the norm, and purity is no longer seen as the necessary cornerstone of a cohesive society, the historical transformation of social identities may no longer be viewed as an inevitable loss.

Race and culture

This history of the concept of race raises the question of how we should understand the connection between racialized identities and cultural

HISTORICAL FORMATION OF RACIAL IDENTITIES   35

differences, a topic that chapter 2 will address more fully. Here I want to explain the way in which an exploration of culture can help to understand race as a historical formation.

As the philosopher Leonard Harris reminds us, "Civilizations and peoples are not . . . coterminous with races" (Harris 1999, 445). In other words, cultures and races are not identical, and yet, there are links. For the early twentieth-century theorist Alain Locke, as Harris explains, socially created races should be understood as having a relation to "beliefs, habits, customs, and informal institutional regulations." If this is the case, races may be associated with distinctive ways of life, even though this will surely remain partial. But the crucial point is that the "beliefs, habits, customs" that Locke is referring to are, for him, the products of collective *agency*: it is civilizations and peoples that decide what traits to support and encourage given particular contexts and historical circumstances (Harris 1999, 445; Locke 2012). Thus, Locke rejected the idea that race can be a *cause* of culture; this is a central motif of racism. But Locke argued that it is also a mistake to assume that historically formed racial groups play no role in the "beliefs, habits, customs" that are selected and reinforced, perhaps because they play a role in surviving adversity or, on the other hand, in conquering. His influential argument in his 1916 lectures on race and interracial relations holds that, as Jeffrey Stewart puts it in his introduction to these lectures, "race was not a biological but a historical phenomenon" (Stewart 1992, xx). In other words, races are historically formed, and in a way that involves collective agency. To the extent we associate races with ways of life, this is a historical phenomenon.

Perhaps the most philosophically rich discussion and debate about the relationship between race and culture came out of the anti-colonial movement in the French Caribbean and Africa. One idea that was put forward to connect race and culture was the concept of *negritude*, a word used to denote "Black culture."

In the writings of Léopold Sédar Senghor, biologically caused racial identities always have associated forms of cultural expression that, because of their biological origin, have limited transformational potential. For Senghor, Black culture is, then, both unified and fixed, at least in its general and broad forms. But for other theorists, Negritude is essentially historical, a Black culture, yes, but created within and against

36   RACE AND RACISM

the conditions of colonialism. And it is also constitutively plural as well as dynamic (e.g., Mosley 1999, 75–86).

Suzanne Césaire, for example, imagined a Negritude that would recognize "the racial and cultural *métissage*" of Martinique, where there was a "continuous intermingling" of Europeans and Africans (quoted in Sharpley-Whiting 2003, 117). As T. Denean Sharpley-Whiting explains, because the Martinicans were seen as French yet never given the right of citizenship, either formally or metaphorically, they created their own culture and formulated a way to conceptualize their own identity. Suzanne Césaire, together with her husband, Aimé, saw negritude as the cultural fruit of a historical process that could offer intellectual nourishment to the developing social movements striving against the racism of the French state. By signifying this cultural formation with a racialized concept, the Césaires emphasized a post-slavery experience that unified a people by their visible difference. But the term also evoked an attitude, an unapologetic boldness, and thus an assertive form of collective consciousness.

The Césaires' project was to document the creation of a new amalgamated culture by and for the formerly enslaved, attesting to their collective agency despite the efforts of the French colonizers to assimilate them as subordinated colonial subjects. And just as importantly, they wanted to show that colonized spaces such as Martinique could not be understood as simply European. Despite ongoing colonial influences, mandated in the educational curriculum, the French Caribbean was something new, and something distinct.

> "We are not men for whom it is a question of 'either-or.' For us, the problem is not to make a utopian and sterile attempt to repeat the past, but to go beyond. . . . It is a new society that we must create, with the help of all our brother slaves, a society rich with all the productive power of modern times, with all the fraternity of olden days. (Césaire 1972, 31)

Thus, the concept of Negritude provided a name for the norms and values that were developed by a people determined to depart from Europe's barbarism. Europeans claimed to uplift their colonized African subjects through cultural assimilation, as if progress required

HISTORICAL FORMATION OF RACIAL IDENTITIES   37

turning away from the historical tie to indigenous African cultures. The Césaires argued instead that this was a productive tie, especially for anti-colonial agendas, since these cultures were neither modern nor liberal by Europe's lights but communal, cooperative, and anti-capitalist, with their own forms of democracy (Césaire 1972, 23). The broad African legacy that the enslaved brought with them should be affirmed and defended against the misrepresentations of racist cultural supremacists. Decolonization required more than merely attaining formal political independence: it also must involve reassessing derided cultural forms from which might be drawn new ways to live (Getachew 2019).

The concept of negritude was the name given to this endeavor, signaling unity between the formerly enslaved with the continent of Africa but maintaining their capacity to create something anew. To be sure, the concept has sustained decades of critical debate concerning both its political effects as well as its claim of a cultural grounding for a racial identity (Sealey 2018; Appiah 1992; Wilder 2015; Mosley 1999). One point of critique concerned whether the emphasis put on 'emotion,' 'intuition,' and 'myth' long associated with indigenous cultures only played into the hands of white supremacists. For Senghor, the point was to redefine and reunderstand the sphere of emotion and the importance of myth, without the baggage of the European Enlightenment quest to escape all realms of affect, embodiment, and spirituality. The intellectual value and integrity of these derided spheres could then be reclaimed, not as the premodern holdover of less rational societies but as features of every vital culture. European definitions of rationality that excised affect and emotion and imagined Europe as having overcome its myths of origin only hobbled its self-understanding and, by the mid-twentieth century, these new myths, put forward by the Enlightenment itself, were being criticized within Europe, often from its own minorities, as with Adorno and Horkheimer. And in his 1903 book, *The Souls of Black Folk*, Du Bois also ventured beyond Enlightenment ideas of rationality, to express and affirm the intellectual and political importance of a specific form of spirituality and historically engendered affect that fueled a *reasoned* resistance, even while making creative use of Hegel's philosophy of history to do so. Eventually, Du Bois's approach would resonate in the

38   RACE AND RACISM

idea of "soul" as the cultural form of a people, becoming a conception with an indelible racial connotation.

Negritude was motivated by the project Aimé Césaire named "disalienation": the effort to overcome the forced denigration of one's African lineage along with the forced assimilation into the culture of the colonizer. The formerly enslaved were taught that their cultures of origin were deficient and that the only way that intelligent individuals among the colonized could achieve significant cultural or political accomplishments, even in service of their own group advancement, was to absorb the intellectual traditions of the West and become a part of these more enlightened societies.

Yet interestingly, disalienation for Césaire did not require a repudiation of *métissage*, as it seemed to for Senghor. Césaire continued to maintain that his writings were influenced by the French poetry and literature he had imbibed as a student, even while he insisted that his project was to "create a new language, one capable of communicating the African heritage" (Césaire 1972, 67). In the colonial context of Martinique, the French language was ubiquitous, and its use was not an issue of debate. But it remained important to recognize the "new means of expression" that reflected the creation of an "Antillean French, a black French that, while still being French, had a black character" (67).[5] Thus, the Césaires' articulation of cultural métissage aimed to express what the colonizer's assimilationist project had attempted to smother, and to reveal the truly inventive and creative work that could showcase what Martinique brought that was new and not a mere replication of France. They identified this new element as incorporating a Black diasporic experience that included memory, affect, orientation, and sensibilities across the domain of many diverse ethnic, religious, and language communities from which people were taken. Thus, the Césaires believed that the Caribbean brought about something culturally new because it incorporated multiple ways of understanding the world.

Many traditional Western conceptions of rationality have difficulty in making sense of such ideas. The abstract individual who serves as

---

[5] Note the difference from the African continent, and the famous debate on the use of non-European languages between Achebe (2009) and Ngũgĩ (2023).

HISTORICAL FORMATION OF RACIAL IDENTITIES   39

the unit of metaphysical analysis, whether in reference to philosophical problems of the self or political problems of how to formulate and ground rights claims, is conceived in a way that sets aside the historical particularities that the Césaires as well as Martí, Mariátegui, and others invoke. Abstraction produces a core/periphery model of the self, in which a minimalized core is the same for all while only the periphery varies by context and historical time period. This allows theories of the self, including theories about how we reason, make aesthetic judgments, and so on, to be approached in a generic way without consideration of historical difference. It conceals variability in a way that can lead to racist (and sexist, ableist, etc.) outcomes. When another person reasons in a different way, by avowedly trusting their intuitions and emotions, or making important life decisions in a nonindividual way, negative judgments can follow.[6]

The emphasis on the role of historical events in the construction of cultural differences and practices of reasoning can help us to avoid thinking that differences can be easily eliminated but also to avoid a cultural determinism that can slide easily into racism. Historical events produce collective trauma, differential material conditions, and forms of collective self-consciousness that have an impact on our experience of temporality, including the relation to futurity, the felt presence of the past, the relevance of the past to the present, which elements of the past are foregrounded, and thus many value judgments. Historical events alter the way we understand and feel about family lineage, when it involves sexual coercion under conditions of oppression, for example. Historical events create substantive material and psychological conditions that can persist for centuries with intergenerational wealth transfers, geographical dislocation, linguistic disruptions, and so on, which can create collective cohesiveness as well as conflict and alienation in the present and alienation. As Ella Myers argues in her study

---

[6] The philosopher Olúfẹ́mi Táíwò has argued in a number of books that African cultural differences should not be seen as a rejection of rationality or of modernity and that Africa was already in the process of becoming modern when colonialism thwarted these efforts. See esp. Táíwò 2010. His account, as I read it, is not in contradiction to the critique of Enlightenment concepts of reason discussed here but is an avowal that some liberal values, such as democracy and the rule of law, were not something the colonists brought to Africa but something they attempted to thwart.

40 RACE AND RACISM

of Du Bois's thought, the abstraction and historical decontextualization of the self makes it possible to ignore the "material, psychological, affective, libidinal, existential, and spiritual" elements of whiteness today (Myers 2022, 7). History produces a habitus: ways of perceiving, reacting, and interacting as well as judging, knowing, and discerning (H. Morgan 2021; Sullivan 2014).

Yet the lessons of history for the way we understand the construction of cultural differences and social identities is subject to debate, as a famous exchange between Sartre and Fanon reveals. Sartre came to defend the concept of negritude against its detractors, but he altered its meaning. In "Black Orpheus," Sartre suggested that negritude was a transitional stage in a Hegelian dialectical moment that would lead beyond itself to a future without racial differences (Sartre 2013, 149–186; Bernasconi 1995, 2006). Such a future free of racial identities is one that many anti-racists, people of color among them, aspire to (P. Williams 1997; McPherson 2024). But the problem Fanon saw was that Sartre was wielding a universal historical teleology in which a repudiation of collective identities, sensibilities, and historical memory were disproportionately distributed (Fanon [1959] 1967a; 1967b). It is the Black man who must "renounce the pride of his color . . . [accept the] future universal that will be the twilight of his negritude" (Sartre 2013, 184). But such a formulation, with its goal of a race-less universal, is in fact a continuance of certain ideals articulated by many Europeans, the French colonizers in particular. And these ideals were used in colonial ideology to rank groups. Fanon retorted that "it is the white man who creates the Negro. But it is the Negro who creates negritude" (Fanon 1967b, 47). Neither the future nor the meaning of negritude can be decided by philosophies born of colonialism, such as Hegel's.

An effective-historical consciousness, as Gadamer suggests (1976, [1960] 1991), need not stabilize historical interpretation or calcify cultural meaning. I should develop a consciousness of my own situatedness within a particular cultural tradition not as a means to escape it but so that I can understand how this affects my interpretations and judgments. Intensifying our historical consciousness can certainly change the way we see the world and the way we imagine desirable futures. But it should also disabuse us of the idea that we approach our projects of inquiry unencumbered by particular historical horizons.

HISTORICAL FORMATION OF RACIAL IDENTITIES   41

Gadamer's own monolingual hermeneutics needs to be reformulated, however, to accommodate our postcolonial pluritopic horizons, which are increasingly characterized by métissage. As I will argue further in chapter 2, we need to see the multiple and conflicting narratives at work in the interpretive sources our biographies have produced. Whether mestizahe or métissage is normative or not, visible to the mainstream or not, colonial societies have produced an array of cultural differences that inform historical consciousness and subjectivity. Another theorist from the French Caribbean, Édouard Glissant, applied the concept of métissage to the way in which we approach historical understanding of all sorts. He argued that there is a danger with historical approaches that assume a singular meaningful history that unifies us all (Sealey 2020).

> One of the most disturbing consequences of colonization could well be this notion of a single History . . . The struggle against a single History for the cross-fertilization of histories means repossessing both a true sense of one's time and identity. (Glissant 1989, 93)

As Kris Sealey powerfully argues, homogenized and universalist teleologies, such as Sartre presumes in the developmental political narrative he applied to negritude, put a stranglehold on the political imagination, limiting the possibilities of future alterations of the nation-state formation or any liberatory political formation: "The political effect of alternative, creolizing imaginaries is in the rupturing of existing structures, in the ways those imaginaries contest the directionality and telos of existing power" (Sealey 2020, 173). There is a *newness*, as she puts it, an *otherwise*, in conceptions of the future beyond coloniality. Drawing from the extensive archive of mid-twentieth-century anti-colonial theorists, Adom Getachew has similarly argued that there was a much broader conceptualization of future "worldmaking" after colonialism, and one that went well beyond formal independence. She writes: "Even when anticolonial nationalists appropriated key principles, such as self-determination and sovereign equality, they redefined and reinvented their meaning. For instance, anticolonial self-determination always included economic as well as political independence" (Getachew 2019, 25). Sartre was undoubtedly concerned

42   RACE AND RACISM

to connect anti-colonialism with socialism. But his assumption that, for this to occur, racial identities would have to be set aside, betrays a French conception of unity. This is not a neutral universal but a concept engraved with its cultural and historical particularity.

Yet we should not dismiss the concerns many have raised about the tendency of movements to essentialize and calcify our racial and ethnic identities. These concerns are shared by many today in a way that echoes the worries that both Fanon and Amilcar Cabral had about negritude itself, that, in some formulations, it tended to downplay dynamism, internal conflicts, and the heterogeneity of the diasporic experience. Both Fanon and Cabral suggested that the imaginary projections of homogeneous cultural identities, even when these were understood to be based on historical experiences of shared racialization, were the product of alienated middle classes seeking an authenticity they had lost (Cabral 1973). Cabral suggests that negritude and pan-Africanism are the inventions of frustrated and deculturated petit bourgeois activists seeking to rediscover their own identity, and these failed to center the precarious lives of the majority. And certainly he was right that too many midcentury revolutionary narratives downplayed cultural métissage in favor of oppositional binary struggles that imagined unified cultures.

However, as we've seen, the idea of Negritude was not understood by the Césaires as a return to tradition or to an unchanging cultural essence rooted in the pre-slavery past, and here, their intellectual and experiential genealogy in the Caribbean is no doubt important. The concept of negritude was not a return but a way of naming the present, which was a specific cultural formation with African influences but one that was mixed and a historical innovation. The concerns voiced by Fanon, Cabral, and others are important, but Sartre's concept of a de-raced future universal is premature at best, as Fanon's stern criticism makes clear.

We need concepts of culture, of race, and of ethnicities that maintain a sense of their dynamism, and we can do this best if we understand them as products of historical experiences. Recognizing the historical specificity of identity formations will open up collective imaginaries about multiple future possibilities.

The relationship of race to culture, then, lends solidity to the idea of racial differences as a functional interpretive category. If our

HISTORICAL FORMATION OF RACIAL IDENTITIES   43

judgments always involve an interpretive process of assessing meaning as well as significance or relevance, then the hermeneutic horizon that informs interpretation will have an important effect. As individuals we have significant epistemic agency in regard to our beliefs, but there will be a group-related aspect of our horizons, related to our racialized identities, that will affect what background knowledge we have ready to hand, what inferences we find plausible, and how we assess significance and relevance, and of course, will also be relevant to the spheres of motive, affect, and self-interest (Alcoff 2010).

Race can make a difference, which is why diversity can lead to equity in juries as well as scientific research teams. But diversity is also essential in scientific research teams that aim for reliable knowledge (Harding 2015). This excursion into the decolonial theory of negritude should show support for these claims, despite the fact that it opposed the belief that either races or cultures are solid or uniform. Following the Césaires, I suggest we see cultural and racial formations in the modern era as pluriversal and internally complex entities, in which diverse elements generate innovation. Racial identities and experiences are critical elements of expressive cultural formations and cultural problematizations, and yet it should be clear that the long period of colonization has rendered purity and coherence an illusion. I will discuss Fernando Ortiz's concept of transculturation to further this last point in the next chapter. To acknowledge métissage is also to acknowledge our significant commonalities.

In the remainder of this chapter, I will further flesh out the concept of race as a historical formation and make use of a concrete example. The function of a historical approach is not only its descriptive and explanatory value but also its political value as a means to formulate the mechanism of change in light of our complicated multicultural formations.

Race as historical formation

On the face of it, the idea of race as a historical formation is simply a token of the idea that race is a social construction. Certainly, to say that race is a historical formation is to reject biological essentialist accounts

44   RACE AND RACISM

that would make race independent of human activity. So why make a distinction between social construction and historical construction?

The idea of race as a social construction is today large and vague, encompassing semantic causal accounts, institutional causal accounts, as well as cultural and historical causal accounts. Yet we can make a useful distinction between two broad types of social constructivist claims in a way that will help us understand the theory of historical formation. One type of social constructivist says that social events and policies have caused the *ideas and ideologies* of race to come into existence, while a second type says that historical events have brought into existence racialized *identity formations* as ways of being, habits of action, and forms of life. So, the first view sees social construction as constructing our ideas and ideologies about ourselves and others, as well as our categories and concepts about human types, while the second view sees social construction as actually affecting the formation of ourselves and others. On the first view, it is easier to argue that racial identity is a mistaken belief I should be weaned from. Ideas about race were introduced to support domination, not to provide ways to describe social realities already in existence, and those attached to these ideas either have suspect motives or have been victimized by those in power. On the second view, to believe that I have a racial identity may well be an accurate view, a true belief, at least in some contexts. But it's also the case that our identities are complex, dynamic, and changeable, so saying "I am ___" must always carry qualifications, such as "for now," or "in this location," or "in this sense though not in that sense." Importantly, if we understand our racial identities as the product of historical events and forces, we have a hand in changing these identities, perhaps even eradicating them in the future. But for this to happen, we have to take action, on the ground.

I would also argue that the historical formation view of race is what we might call, following Ian Hacking, a form of dialectical realism or dynamic nominalism, in which the nature of the real is understood to be perpetually under interpretation (Hacking 2002, 2). The idea of a historical ontology is that the categories of things that exist, including categories of identity, are affected, as critical theorists argue, by the categories themselves. Race is certainly a species of historical ontology. But Hacking's Foucauldian-inspired idea of historical ontology puts the emphasis as much on ontology as it does on history, which is to say that historical discourses and practices bring things, and not just categories, into existence. Dialectical realism is not a mere matter of language, or getting our terms correct, while what we take to be 'reality' remains stable. Thus, we can only transform ourselves through transforming our social contexts, which includes but is not limited to our language. This approach should help to show why the elimination of race terms will not so easily disappear race itself, nor lead to the transformations we want.

Chike Jeffers suggests a further way to divide social constructionists that helpfully illuminates the issue of causal agency I want to foreground. Jeffers divides them into those who have a theory of *political constructionism* and others who have a theory of *cultural* constructionism. He takes Haslanger to exemplify the political constructionist view, that races are the product of political policies and practices that have created social hierarchies and exclusions based on the idea of race. As Jeffers puts it, the political constructionist view is that "race is made real *wholly or most importantly* by hierarchical relations of power" (2019, 48; emphasis added).

The cultural constructionist view that Jeffers himself defends holds that "participation in distinctive ways of life, rather than positioning in the hierarchical relations of power, is what is most important in making race real" (2019, 50). He argues that Du Bois held such a view, "explicitly distancing himself from the political approach" (2019, 50; Bernasconi 2023, 157–175). For Jeffers, however, the sphere of the political and the sphere of the cultural are both important in understanding racial identities. He also distances his position from a version of cultural nationalism that would take a prescriptive approach to how one should live one's life, in the sort of way Paul Gilroy and Cristina Beltrán are concerned about as I will discuss in chapter 2. Jeffers's cultural constructionist view, as I understand it, is less prescriptive than descriptive. The point is to acknowledge our differences without fetishizing or essentializing them, and also to critique the ways that racism has ranked differences. While racism surely created some group differences, he argues that it also regularly "disparages and suppresses difference where it ought to be respected" (2019, 71).

46 RACE AND RACISM

Jeffers accepts the tenets of political constructionism up to a point. He agrees that "races emerged out of political conditions that divided people into groups unequal in power" but argues that this is only the beginning of the story, for social categories so created shaped "the identities of those who are included in them in such a way that these members may plausibly view these categories as culturally significant" (2019, 62). Thus, he argues that the political constitution of races produced cultural shifts, forms of socialization, and "novel forms of cultural difference" (62). Thus, racialized cultures were created not only by laws and policies but by historical events and social relations in which people took things into their own hands.

I share Jeffers's view that history plays an important role in racial formation. And I take it that his account is not meant to downplay the importance of embodiment but to note how the current meanings associated with embodied features (meanings that can be quite diverse) came into being and have been sustained. He does not presume "a uniformity of experience across individuals" or "uniform cultural experiences" (2019, 65). Jeffers's theory is about the manner in which races were formed, but it is also about what it means to be a person with a racialized identity: that one can trace some aspects of one's self to certain significant historical and political events and conditions and the forms of cultural life that were created in response.

One of the principal divergences of emphasis within varied social constructionist accounts is whether or not shared experience is given a causal role. Some argue that those experiences that can be associated with race are too thin and too fractured to be of any use in understanding identity terms. Against Shelby and others who cash out shared experience in a minimalist way that includes only shared racist oppression, Jeffers holds that there is also a shared experience of creating forms of life under common external conditions (Shelby 2005). Shelby's account is surely overly minimalist. It helpfully directs us away from assuming political or cultural uniformity within racialized groups, the sort of assumption that leads some people to be surprised that minority groups don't all vote alike. But it does not offer a way to understand the divergent perceptual, doxastic, relational, and cultural practices and formations that are group-related. An account that will help us achieve a better understanding of the historical effects on subjectivity, and associated manners of perception, judgment, and reasoning, will require that we enlarge our understanding of how experiences shape us.

I am in general agreement with Jeffers in these debates, but I want to encourage more attention to broad historical events, not just those that corral peoples and exert external coercions in various ways but those that involve significant collective agency and reveal the effective praxis of non-elites in fashioning racial identities. If the political construction of race explains the connection between race concepts and oppression, the cultural construction and historical formation accounts explain survival. So perhaps we need all of the above. Our diverse forms of life, relations to the past, modes of social interaction, and approaches to economic activity are affected by history, or what Williams would surely call 'the given.' Out of this given of group conditions, collective racial projects, as Omi and Winant define them, are created with intentional goals. This is not a story of simple imposition from above or of mistaken attachment to false beliefs.

Jeffers does not close out the possibility that in the future, racial concepts and racism may meet their end. But he argues that "race as a social construction could live on past the death of racism . . . given that racial groups could continue to exist as cultural groups" (2019, 57). There would be no way to posit such an eventuality if races were simply the products of political domination.

The theory of the historical formation of race must operate with elements of political and cultural construction, but it rejects the claim that either of these, or both together, are sufficient to understand what we have before us today. Race should be primarily understood not as a belief but as a practice with accompanying affect, sense of entitlement, self-understanding, and attitude toward the social world. It cannot be so easily eradicated; hence the jokes about white liberals who espouse anti-racist beliefs but cannot seem to let go of their sense of noblesse oblige, entitlement, or habits of social superiority. Our practices are not solely determined by our beliefs.

We will be able to see more fully the importance, and fruitfulness, of the theory of race as a historical formation with a concrete example. While Jeffers focuses on the cultures produced by the oppressed, I want to focus on the subjectivities of one particular form of identity

48   RACE AND RACISM

that has had dominance in the West, and of certain practices that have long been associated with it: violence and theft.

The formation of whiteness

By considering the historical emergence of white subjectivities, we can view a complex assemblage of affects, habits, motives, and aversions that have been the effect of sustained, legitimated, ongoing practices of violence against those who are racially stigmatized and portrayed as having inferior cultures, creating, as Beltran puts it, a form of citizenship coterminous with cruelty (Beltrán 2020). Hagar Kotef has argued similarly that, in some historical cases, violence has become "an explicit part of collective identities," rendering it not exceptional but everyday (Kotef 2020, 5). The belief in the right to violence, and the desire for violence, becomes stitched into one's socialization to such an extent that the removal of this right feels like a violation, a loss of self, a reduction to the disreputable status of victim or prey. Thus, Kotef argues that the "we-self" assumed in liberal societies is mistakenly taken to be distinct from the violence the society perpetrates, as if there is a gap between the self and the mechanisms that produce ongoing atrocities. She writes that the "framework of subject formation" can show that "subjects in positions of privilege are likely to be attached to the conditions allowing these privileges to endure, even when these generate, sustain, or are themselves a form of violence" (Kotef 2020, 48). Her view does not counsel pessimism about social change but argues for a different approach that focuses on practices and the conditions of life more than simply beliefs or ideas.

Kotef and Beltrán help to show why the historical formation approach to race can be more thorough: because it extends well beyond categories or concepts of language to reach, in a Foucauldian sense, the production of a certain kind of self, with associated affects, motives, and orientation toward social relations and the world in general. My example will be whiteness formed within settler colonial societies as well as societies engaging in transnational colonialism, but this is far from the only dominant group to which this approach will apply. I want to stress that this approach does not imply uniformity or sacrifice

HISTORICAL FORMATION OF RACIAL IDENTITIES 49

dynamism; like Foucault, I see historical formations as always riven by conflict and always productive of new articulations and practices. Resistance is a permanent feature, always enabling new assemblages. The point is that we need to understand how racialization works at the ontological level, to affect not just what we know, perceive, and believe but what we are. The diversity and dynamism of these ontological effects cannot justify ignoring the significant patterns that exist, some of which have proved to be quite recalcitrant to change.

While white racial identity has transnational forms of both ideas and practices, it is also local in important respects. The criteria and boundaries of whiteness vary by location as well as time period, and there are significant differences between European formations of white identity and those in the Americas and Australia, given the effects of settler colonialism and different national histories.

In this light, it is important to note that the history of the formation of whiteness as a category originates, as a number of historians and theorists now argue, in a relationship *between* Europe and its colonies in the Americas, particularly in the seventeenth and eighteenth centuries (Jordan [1968] 2012; E. Morgan 2005; Beltrán 2020). Whiteness emerged in a way that eventually linked diverse ethnic and national populations across the Atlantic, even though the distinct practices and experiences on either side created distinguishable forms as well as degrees of whiteness. England's early colonization of North America relied heavily on a system of indentured servitude, mostly from Europe, that could provide a helpfully constrained labor force. The plantation economy in what is now the state of Virginia, for example, was initially organized with the use of labor by indentured servants before the system of slavery was put into place. Indentured persons were housed separately, underfed, poorly clothed, ruled by overseers, and whipped, creating a structural and material organization of labor that was helpfully already in place when slavery emerged (E. Morgan 2005). The historian Nell Painter (2010) has no trouble describing such indentured people as enslaved, given their limited freedom and poor treatment, but this system should remain distinguished from the system of chattel slavery that developed later, which was imposed over the entirety of one's lifetime, was hereditary, and was organized by race. As the historian Robin Blackburn explains,

50 RACE AND RACISM

beginning with the nineteenth century, the "chattel principle" bonded together slavery and race, and the prerogative of all whites to escape enslavement became a central feature of racial capitalism (2024, 127).

The inauguration of chattel slavery broke down some of the boundaries that had previously existed between the indentured and the gentry. Indentured whites could feel this boundary diminish when state law ensured that they would escape the system of enslavement visibly growing around them in their towns, cities, and states. Indentured whites in the United States were singled out *by race* to escape this fate, while enslaved Africans and their offspring were treated by the new laws as locked into a hereditary system. Native peoples could also be enslaved, and there were further laws about what racial groups could do the enslaving. African Americans and Native people could themselves enslave others, but they could not enslave whites. In this way, the state structured cross-racial relations and enforceable hierarchies.

It is important to understand the historical moment prior to chattel slavery. Indentured servants, largely from Europe, could not move about freely, nor were they allowed to leave their employers, even after beatings and abuse. They could also be sold. Yet the system of indenture had a time frame, allowing the indentured to eventually become free, although many lived under such deprivation that they did not survive long enough to achieve their freedom. Thus, it is no surprise that prior to chattel slavery, servants and the enslaved sometimes made common cause, organizing collective escapes and rebellions, stealing food, or simply enjoying some alcohol-infused revelry together on a Saturday night, as historians Peter Linebaugh and Marcus Rediker recount.

The European poor, especially the poor of certain ethnic groups such as the Irish, had long been subject to a form of essentialized representation that imputed their biological features as signs of their animal-like nature and inferiority. Their poverty, ignorance, and destitution had long been explained through varied scientific claims as due to inherited characteristics. In this way, the abject conditions of their short laboring lives could be portrayed as inevitable, with no one to blame. Yet political problems ensued from this ill treatment and segregation. For one thing, the European poor had a tendency toward unruliness and rebellion. As Linebaugh and Rediker explain, the poor were

HISTORICAL FORMATION OF RACIAL IDENTITIES   51

vilified in England as "motley urban mobs" and "rural barbarians of the commons," as they fomented some rebellious attacks on the gentry (2000, 329; Hobsbawm 1959). Interestingly, in both the growing transatlantic shipping fleets and the American colonies, these unruly mobs sometimes became multiracial, throwing Europeans together with Africans as well as Asians. The breadth of this collaborative resistance posed an obvious threat to the stability of elite control.

When the system of slave labor began to expand in the plantation-based colonies, the English parliament debated whether it was a good idea to subject the Irish to chattel forms of slavery, in which there would be no possibility, however remote, of buying their freedom. Importantly, the English elite decided against this option, choosing instead to draw a sharp line between what might be done to the Irish and what might be done to other groups, on the grounds of a worrisome domino effect of brutalization (Monahan 2011). The Irish, after all, looked a bit like them. The move to make slavery based on race and to exempt whites from this fate by law occurred over a process of many decades and varied by regions and states in the Americas. But by the early part of the nineteenth century, the system of racially based chattel slavery was instituted nationally in the new United States, rendering the children of the enslaved the property of their parents' owners. From this time forward, there was to be no legal escape from enslavement unless an owner made the choice to free them, as did Thomas Jefferson, but only after his death. The new system recognized status variations among non-whites, based largely on property and citizenship as well as gender, and several non-white groups were subject to enslavement as already noted. But *all whites* were protected from slavery. Eventually more laws were passed making it illegal for Blacks even to employ whites or to purchase firearms, and there was an extension of opportunities for landless whites to gain land through expropriation of Native territory or of the small plots that were previously owned by enslaved people.

This period of transformation instigated the development of what some have named a "Herrenvolk democracy" or "Herrenvolk republicanism." David Roediger (1994) prefers the term *Herrenvolk republicanism* because of the extreme income inequality among whites, which he thinks makes the term *democracy* inapt. Beltrán argues

52 RACE AND RACISM

persuasively, however, that democracy never promised income equality; thus, she uses the term *Herrenvolk democracy*. In either case, as Joel Olson puts it, this is "a polity ruled in the interests of a white citizenry and characterized by simultaneous relations of equality and privilege: equality among whites, who are privileged in relation to those who are not white" (quoted in Beltrán 2020, 13). The equality among whites was thin yet terribly significant: since after the emergence of chattel slavery no whites could be legally enslaved, the unruly or impoverished whites had a motive to be loyal to these new settler states and even to see themselves as in an alliance with those white elites who had ensured their protection from slavery. European-based rankings within whiteness had given way to a uniform identity in settler colonial states.

As Hans Kundnani argues, European regionalism today has a similar equalizing effect on the inhabitants of the European Union, moderating the ranked systems of ethnic and national differences, and creating a sense of unity inside the region (Kundnani 2023). Thus, even though it is extranational, regional European identity remains analogous to nationalism in its exclusionary self-understanding and is therefore able to place refugees and immigrants, who hail often from beyond Europe, as "outsiders" (2023, 19). Kundnani argues further that European identity remains tied to a particular version of a white racial identity because of the historical genealogy that is told about the formation of Europe. The concept of Europe, as a form of shared identity and allegiance, first emerged in a series of wars against Arabs in the early eighth century, primarily in the ongoing epic conflicts portrayed as 'Christianity against Islam' but that, as with the current moment, have a lot more than religious doctrine involved. These were territorial struggles between competing empires. By the end of the seventeenth century, the idea of European identity became closely associated with a white identity credited with the "invention" of science and reason during the period of the Enlightenment. Thus, from its initial origins, on both sides of the Atlantic, whiteness has been identified as having a comparative superiority, as historically Christian, and as the intellectually and morally legitimate global leader.

The historical formation of a European identity today, clearly expressed in the pro-Europeanist position, is an outgrowth of the

HISTORICAL FORMATION OF RACIAL IDENTITIES   53

region's colonial origins, rather than an overcoming of this past, Kundnani argues. Being pro-Europe is portrayed as being anti-Nazi and anti-nationalist and, by implication, committed only to a civic, or nonethnic, form of social identity. But Europe's global leadership is still tied to its long claim of having a civilizational mission, to its unique ability to help rationalize the world and enhance civic solidarity. And this mission persists in creating misrepresentations of Europe's history, especially its intellectual history. The philosophy of liberalism is usually understood as universally available to all, but, as Domenico Losurdo has argued, it was tethered from the beginning to colonial practices and their philosophical rationalization. It is thus historically inaccurate to understand liberalism as the actual pursuit of individual freedom in any inclusive sense (Losurdo 2014; Ghosh 2021). Many argue that the form that the concept of freedom took within liberalism carries this legacy, since it assumes an agent of a certain type and social standing (Rana 2010).

Civilizational projects continue to resonate with the colonial ideologies of the past, without critique. Such projects require the production of constitutive outsiders, including peoples and nations as well as ethnically and religiously defined groups within Europe who can serve as the contrast class for European identity (Sheth 2022). Even if a civilized identity can extend beyond whiteness and beyond Christianity, it is clear who will need to be front and center in order to assure the right outcome, and thus, who will need to remain in the majority in the region.

To return to the history of settler colonialism, white identity emerged with certain privileges to protect property and political rights, including an eventual extension of suffrage, but also, as importantly, in the capacity to engage in extralegal acts of violence, including murder, rape, the theft of land, and the destruction of competitive businesses.[7] Starting in the early part of the nineteenth century, some

---

[7] The term *settler colonialism* describes a variety of forms of colonialism that involve settlements generally created to replace previous communities. Settler colonialism is not unique to the Global North but was practiced by the Japanese in China, Indonesians in Papua New Guinea, the Chinese in Singapore, and elsewhere. The practice can vary widely but, as Patrick Wolfe argued, is helpfully defined as a structure or a process rather than a single, unified event. The moral judgment we make of settlers themselves,

54   RACE AND RACISM

of the now all-white unruly mobs turned their energies and know-how onto the Native groups who were inhabiting arable lands beyond the newly established United States along the eastern seaboard. Life in the colonies was inadequate for the growing population of European immigrants, stimulating what Immerwahr calls "white land hunger" (2019, 37). By contrast, in the late eighteenth century and early nineteenth century, many of the white elites ruling the new nation were satisfied for the country to remain east of the Mississippi River and were content to leave the rest of the continent to the Natives. Forty-six percent of what is now the US was officially designated by Congress to be "Indian Country" or Indian territory, and thus to be a distinct political sphere. But the recognition of this territory was connected to the idea that native Americans then living outside of it, in the East, such as the large Cherokee Nation, would be "removed," or forced west, to ensure enough space—'safe' space—for whites. The policy of "Indian removal" was initially portrayed as compatible with a recognition of Native sovereignty and the goal of amicable relations across the border, and there was even an initiative to recognize delegates from this territory with a seat (a single seat) in the US Congress.

Although elites thought this plan to push Native groups out of the East would solve the problem of "white land hunger," it did not. Non-elite whites began to defy the government treaties and ignore the borders of recognized Indian territorial areas, burning villages, committing massacres, and seizing Native land illegally. Even Supreme Court rulings that tried to protect the Cherokee were ineffective in the face of what Immerwahr calls this "squatter onslaught."

This was an era of class-based struggle between white elites and non-elites over how to create the settler state. As we will see in chapter 3, Thomas Jefferson at one time imagined peaceful coexistence with Native groups who would be 'good neighbors' by his definition.

---

rather than the colonizing governments that sent them, must be nuanced, since some were seeking fortune while most were seeking an available means to survive. It is a mistake, then, to assume a unified account of settler colonialism, either in a descriptive or a normative sense, although it helpfully augments our understanding of the many forms colonialism can take. My interest here is in the experience of settlement for settlers themselves. For some varied views, Wolfe 1999, 2019 and Pederson 2012; Hixson 2013; Dunbar-Ortiz 2021; Khalidi 2020.

HISTORICAL FORMATION OF RACIAL IDENTITIES 55

But the point I want to make here is that the collective agency of white elites was not substantial enough to control all elements of the new nation in formation. It is important to acknowledge that *elites gave in*, realizing that the only way to control the situation and maintain their power over the state was to give in to these landless whites and allow expansion. Elite acquiescence led to many decades of intermittent rioting, in which white mobs pursued organized violence with impunity in many non-white areas, destroying Black-, Mexican-, or Chinese-owned businesses and neighborhoods along with Native towns. They seized land, farms, and commercial areas, wiping out their economic rivals and forcing almost all non-whites into low-paid wage work and domestic service.

For most of the period throughout the nineteenth and early twentieth century, whites had a largely exclusive right to homestead, attain skilled jobs, legally immigrate, attend college, and participate in both state and national politics. Non-whites could sometimes *legally* participate in these practices but were then vulnerable to racist mob violence, the theft of their land and businesses, and forcible displacement, after which no one was punished. The system of criminal justice was skewed toward whites, who alone could serve on juries or be hired into the police. Elites had solved their problem, divided the 'motley' mobs into two broad categories (white and non-white), and secured loyalty from the largest sector of the working class.

This sordid history helps us to understand many incidents that are ongoing in the present day, such as the murder that happened in 2020 of Ahmaud Arbery in Georgia. Three white men pursued Arbery while he was jogging, in what they considered a white neighborhood, and shot and killed him in broad daylight. They assumed they could commit such an act without punishment. One of the lawyers for the defense argued in court that the men who committed the crime "had a duty and responsibility" to protect themselves and their neighborhood, portraying their actions as legitimately motivated by this long-standing historical practice. White on non-white violence, whether enacted by civilians or authorities of the criminal justice system, is still more often assumed to be justifiable, and not subject to punishment.

The historian Jefferson Cowie has recently argued that current movements of resistance against federal government power in the

United States must be understood as continuous with the context of the long history of settler colonialism in North America (Cowie 2022). As we've seen, the struggle of landless whites to obtain Indian land by breaking treaties and engaging in extrajudicial violence pit poor whites against the government. Cowie writes that "the federal defense of Native American rights against white intruders, argued one speculator at the time, struck 'at the root of the tree of Liberty' by subverting the interests of the states and the rights of 'the people'" (Cowie 2022, 11). By thwarting white freedom to dominate, and putting the law above white desires and needs, the conflict turned from an interracial one to an intraracial one.

Whites' demand for Native land was advanced in political processes at the state level as well as in organized raids. These raids engaged in atrocities against Native peoples, but the whites who participated in these actions saw themselves as provoked by a recalcitrant government controlled by those who were happy with the status quo. Much of the same thinking is occurring today to legitimate anti-immigrant violence at the border.

In the eighteenth and nineteenth centuries, many elites in North America benefited from large plantation systems and had no need for an expansion into Western territories. In Alabama, for example, the "hardscrabble subsistence farms and lumber camps contrasted with the opulence of plantation life," as Cowie explains (Cowie 2022, 99). The interests of landowning whites were not aligned with those whites who pined for their own small farms. But the collective violence and organized political activity of non-elite whites created new motivations for rich landowners to support a demand for Indian land, as a way to assuage the white rabble without personal sacrifice of any sort (Cowie 2022, 92). Only with this policy shift could a racially based, cross-class political alliance, however partial, be cemented.

The reasonable demands of landless whites could have been addressed in a way that did not produce racial rivalries, but this would have cut into the profits of elites. The entire economy of the early US was structured by a system of enslavement that drove down the value of wage labor as well. Thus, throughout settler colonial nations, a choice structure was instituted that pitted the needs of landless whites against both indigenous groups and non-white workers in general, who

HISTORICAL FORMATION OF RACIAL IDENTITIES 57

were competing for scarce employment and arable land. The result, Cowie argues, was a conception of white citizens' rights that began to be defined in terms of the right to dominate other groups defined racially: whites had the right to take their land and businesses, expropriate their resources, and commit violence against them. If the value of citizenship afforded to whites had any significance, it had to come with material benefits greater than non-enslavement, and these benefits came at the cost of other non-elites, never elites. Without the right to dominate other groups, some poor whites viewed their citizenship as worthless. Whiteness was portrayed at the time as shackled under such conditions, unfree, enslaved to the federal government, to its taxation demands and its control over commerce and the conditions of labor. Only when their right to dominate others was protected did poor and working-class whites become loyal, patriotic citizens. But their loyalty was and continues to be contingent on relational status, which is today felt by some to be eroding in the face of increasing immigration.

It is important to understand this historical context of white mob violence, because it has sometimes been portrayed as simply reactive to Indian raids against white settlements, as a defensive posture against the attacks by Native peoples, who have been continuously portrayed in popular culture as irrational 'savages.' Such portraits are significantly inaccurate in several ways. It is well documented that intergroup relations between settlers and Natives were often peaceful; treaties were created to manage borders and allow movement under certain conditions, and there was often a productive trade. Land raids were rarely motivated by protection but more often for gain. Most whites could only work in mills or via the widespread practice of tenant farming or sharecropping, and neither provided what we would today call a living wage; both led to premature deaths and families left destitute, into the twentieth century. My (white) mother lived in a sharecropping housing as a child, with newspaper pasted on the walls to keep out the wind, and floorboards so wide she could feed the chickens without going outside. The violence that erupted over land was not created by 'savage' Natives, nor by poor whites whose racist cruelty was born of ignorance. It was created by a system of capitalism that restricted power and profit and undermined democracy at every turn.

58   RACE AND RACISM

The current animosity toward federal power, and the frequently voiced charge that it is illegitimate, is a continuation of past practices and is largely driven by fear of immigrant competition that may drive down wages. Governments at the national level, whether in North America or Europe, are generally the only entities capable of enacting and enforcing policies of immigration, and when these policies are viewed as a threat to livelihoods, a far right social movement is born. As Cowie's work shows, it is a mistake to view such movements as simply rooted in racist ideologies or as embraced by all whites. And it is dangerous to view such conflicts as inevitable.

I want to emphasize that such violent practices and group-based animosities are not the only ingredient in the formation of white racial identity. As I have already related, white immigration in settler colonial societies was a drive to escape from poverty, imprisonment, persecution, and sometimes an early death, which would be their lot if they stayed in the autocratic aristocratic regimes that ruled throughout Europe. Neither survival nor prosperity in the Americas or Australia was guaranteed, and yet the mere chance of a livelihood was enough to motivate permanent emigration. These motives are the same ones that drive most migration today. Together these experiences also informed the developing identity of whiteness and its sense of having competitive relations with other racialized groups, but also its shared misery and precarity.

Most of the white poor who migrated a century ago remain so, or with modest incomes: the United States has the second-highest poverty rate of all OECD countries. We need to look beyond poverty rates, as many economists argue today, to the category of the 'low-income.' Although the percentage of the white population that includes both poor and low-income is lower than the percentages in other groups, still, in real numbers, there have always been more white poor in the United States than any other group. Persons and families who are poor experience food insecurity, cannot afford a two-bedroom apartment in any state, have inadequate health care and education, are more likely to die of drug overdoses, cannot take vacations or send their children to college, and die younger (see the facts on poverty gathered by the Poor People's Campaign at https://www.poorpeoplescampaign.org/resource/factsheets/). For most of the white poor, these deprivations

HISTORICAL FORMATION OF RACIAL IDENTITIES 59

continue what their families have experienced since migration from Europe.

The experiential content of white racial identity in the United States has included a family history of migration generally in the form of an escape, and often involving much hardship, but it also involved an enduring protected political standing that operated as a type of social power, as both Joel Olsen (2004) and Jefferson Cowie have elaborated. The historical memory of hardship lives on as a form of family lore, while the social power to exclude and mistreat non-whites continues within a legal system that either enacts mistreatment in its carceral and police systems or excuses white-on-non-white violence in the private sphere. As Beltrán points out, the most recent violence against Central American refugees mobilizes the tradition of this social power in new ways, in which "the movement of certain subjects [e.g., white European migrants] is understood to be [or have been] the manifestation of liberty, while the movement of others is deemed unruly, excessive and dangerous" (Beltrán 2020, 28). Whiteness is a dynamic historical formation that eventually redefined unruliness as a characteristic of the non-white other (Sheth 2009, 2022).

Violence against asylum seekers is therefore seen, and experienced today, as legitimate and even moral. Whites who engage in informal or formal violence against non-whites at the border do not in general experience themselves as engaging in immoral, unlawful, unruly behavior. As in the Arbery case, violent acts by whites are still portrayed as responsible efforts to protect their own communities and families. This is the central point I want to make: that there is a continuous history of white advantage over other racial groups that has helped shape the formation of white subjectivity. To quote Beltrán again, "Acts of dispossession, slavery, and white supremacy . . . shaped settler relationships to land and labor, as well as creating particular forms of collective identity and shared governance" (2020, 33). This is the historical genealogy of a racial white identity in which a state-backed assumption of rightful entitlement has produced a sensibility such that a loss of *comparative* advantage is experienced as a social death, a dangerous acceleration of vulnerability.

To say this is not to reify or congeal the meanings and experiences of whiteness, or to render it uniform or fixed or politically stable. There

60 RACE AND RACISM

have always been traitors to white supremacy, and as Fanon noted, all of us are "placed in this world, in a situation" not of our choosing (1967b, 230). Like him, I steadfastly believe in the "open door of every consciousness" (1967b, 232). Situations are not closed doors. Today we can clearly see large sectors of white citizenry willing to face police violence to oppose racist states to protect the rights of refugees to migrate, and to oppose colonial genocide wherever it occurs. Yet what we need to understand is that white racial identity, like other racial identities, is not simply the product of policy but of practices, actions, relationships, and experiences that have shaped subjectivity, perception, and judgment across generations in ways that one can discern across the spectrum of white nationalist violence all the way to white liberal paternalism. What unifies large sectors of this spectrum is assumptions of superiority; entitlement to political power, land, and resources (fueling gentrification); skewed definitions of crime; and a collection of interpersonal modes of behavior organized around race. White radicalism has always fought for another way to be.

What will change whiteness will be not just the elimination of categories but changed historical experiences due to the structural dismantling of a system in which social standing is based on race. In the generations to come, as transnational migrations inevitably continue, there will be changes in experience, affect, sensibilities, and a re-forming of intergroup relationships. There will be more intense mixing and, hopefully, more potential to experience a living-alongside rather than lording-over. Whiteness, however, will retain its functional semantic utility, and political importance, as a means to signify, and remember, a different racial history.

2

The Persistent Power of Cultural Racism

Anti-racism has become something of an industry in many parts of North America as well as Europe, generating profits for publishers as well as hefty speaking fees for the recognized experts. In the United States, anti-racist training is ubiquitous, with identity-based affinity groups to follow up the lessons, and every elite university and arts organization, as well as many a corporation, has its own diversity initiatives that are proudly advertised. Predictably, the scope of the profitable sphere of anti-racism is restricted largely to the domain of individual prejudice and achieving diversity in the professional classes. No one worries about diversifying sanitation workers, prison guards, or home health aides. Rather, the project is, as some have suggested, to rebrand privilege without relinquishing its prerogatives (K. Taylor 2016; Currah 2022). And so the structural agenda of anti-racism is circumscribed to institutional improvement, not dismantlement, to inclusion and diversification without substantive challenge to existing processes or profit margins. When portions of the racist public are targeted, it is often the least elite members of society, those very much outside of these elite spaces.

I will argue that the concept of "cultural racism" remains central to understanding racism today although it has unfortunately receded into the background because of the focus on attitudinal racism, the psychology of racism, and the project of diversifying the professional-managerial classes. These topics, while legitimate, can be formulated in such a way that they are unthreatening to current power structures. By contrast, the issue of cultural racism will help us foreground structural issues, global injustices, and the outsized agency of elites by centering the history of colonialism.

Race and Racism. Linda Martín Alcoff, Oxford University Press. © Oxford University Press 2025.
DOI: 10.1093/9780197796948.003.0002

62   RACE AND RACISM

Yet, without question, the concept of cultural racism requires some clarification, which it will be the aim of this chapter to deliver. I will argue that it refers not only to racism in the sphere of culture but to a distinct alibi or legitimating ground that is continuously used to justify the exclusion of immigrants and refugees and the domination of numerous regions in the world. The principal power of the concept lies in its ability to explain discriminatory patterns by which material resources flow around the globe. Why are some countries and regions so persistently poor, while others, often less in need, increase their wealth? What Charles Mills (1997) named the 'racial contract,' and Olúfẹ́mi O. Táíwò (2022) terms the 'global racial empire,' has long required a legitimating explanation, but this has taken different forms.

One of the most important shifts in racist ideologies of the twentieth century involved the shift from biological racism to cultural racism, as Ramón Grosfoguel notes:

> after the Second World War there was an important shift in the global colonial/racial formation. Biological racist discourses about genetically inferior 'Others' fell into a crisis across continental Europe. The Nazi occupations delegitimized biological racist discourses in many continental Western European countries. The decline of biological racist discourses did not imply the end of racism in the core of the capitalist world economy. After the defeat of the Nazi occupations in Western Europe and the 1960's Civil Rights struggles in Great Britain and the United States, global racial discourses shifted from biological racism to cultural racism. (1999, 410)

Here Grosfoguel is following Frantz Fanon, who in his 1956 speech in Paris before the First Congress of Negro Writers and Artists, used the term *cultural racism* to explain the way in which the colonial powers were adapting to the discrediting of biological racism. Fanon explained that cultural racism "no longer [targeted] the individual man but a certain form of existing" (1964, 32). But with the language of culture, the discourse could continue, and the material and political effects of racism could remain in force. And global wealth differentials could be explained without blaming wealthy countries.

Even so, despite the continuities, the switch from biology to culture had important conceptual implications. Biological racism claimed that an individual's ancestry could predict a whole host of attributes and dispositions, but this claim was vulnerable to scientific invalidation in a way that cultural racism apparently was not. It is the latter that has proved to be the more formidable strain of the disease.

Today, as Lawrence Bobo and Camille Charles have shown, explicit commitments to biological racism have declined in the United States to around 10 percent of whites, but there is a continuation of negative stereotyping (Bobo and Charles 2009, cited in Blum 2020). Larry Blum develops a typology of forms of cultural racism, exploring the ways in which it can combine and overlap with biological racism (Blum 2020). And yet he argues, as I will, that it would be wrong to assume that all forms of cultural racism rely on hidden or unconscious commitments to biological causation or that they are simply a concealed form of biological racism. There are diverse ideas in the history of the modern West about the formation of cultures, as I will discuss further on; Blum stresses that there is a "noninherentist culturalism" (Blum 2020, 14), which is not committed to the biological ideas about races (Blum 2020, 6–8). Thus, we should take the data of Bobo and Charles as indicating a real shift, not necessarily, alas, away from racism, but a shift in the formulation of racist ideas and arguments. If we want to counter racism, we need to understand the precise belief systems various forms involve.

For example, in the shift from biology to culture, justifications for racism move from the biological sciences to the social sciences and the humanities in order to characterize and assess diverse ways of life and social systems. Archaeology and anthropology particularly come to the fore. Cultural racism involves misperceptions of people, certainly, but it primarily involves certain misperceptions of *peoples*, that is, ways of being and living, or what Fanon called forms of existing. It is the dress, the religious practice, community values, modes of family formation, and production of goods as well as artisanal production and forms of cultural expression and gender expression, even the types of food that are eaten: all of these now, under the domain of cultural racism, can potentially become signs of 'backwardness' or simply unbridgeable difference. And it is these practices that provide the alibi for exclusion.

64 RACE AND RACISM

If artisanal creations don't meet the Western criteria of art, they can be justifiably excluded from art museums and placed in archaeology museums instead; if land is not privately owned by individuals in a way that Western courts can verify, land claims can be denied, and so on.

The important point is that cultural racism cannot be countered by a reminder of the rights of individuals. It is certainly wrong to preemptively judge what a given individual's beliefs, attributes, and abilities are likely to be on the basis of their connection to a cultural, ethnic, or religious group, but note that this focus on the individual does not necessarily challenge the overall assessment of the group: the individual could be viewed as an outlier. The protection of individuals does not require the respect of their culture or cultural lineage, and many today argue that individuals' rights require the destruction of some cultures.

Many questions, of course, remain. If we say that cultural racism takes aim at cultures rather than individuals, how do we delimit cultures with any clarity or precision? What is distinct about *cultural racism* in relation to other group-based antagonisms? And does the critique of cultural racism disable all critique of cultures? I'll argue here that criticism is a legitimate practice and can even be a sign of respect if done with a dialogical approach, because it reveals that we consider the 'other' to be approachable, rational, and capable of debate. But beyond the way we approach criticism as a respectful communicative practice, we also need to look with care at the *grounds* upon which we criticize a given culture and a given cultural practice. In what follows, I will address these questions, both about the concept of culture as well as the specificity of cultural racism, as well as a further one that is perhaps the most important: What is the most effective antidote to cultural racism?

The category of culture is itself ineluctably vague, and yet, it has a place in our collective commonsense understanding of the world. Fanon expresses the familiar idea that cultures encompass specificities of behavior, practices, and doxa, the patterns of which demarcate 'ways of existing.' Cultures are identified by norms that present individuals with a choice structure that carries associated meanings as well as costs and benefits. Examples of practices that are judged differently in different cultures would include ignoring parental directives when one has reached adulthood, the corporal punishment of children, or starting families at a young age. These examples reveal the need for intersectional analyses, since class makes a notable difference in the dominant norms *within* cultures.

I will put forward an approach to cultural racism as bound to the context of the modern/colonial world system, emerging from this genealogy with specific characteristics. Here, then, is an initial formulation of cultural racism as a distinct form: cultural racism operates from a universal and systematic ordering of global diversity in which some practices are portrayed as transcendent of culture or, in other words, rational and for this reason universally mandated. The habit of characterizing some ideas and practices as 'cultural' and others as modern, enlightened, or rational is characteristic of the modern/colonial world system and sets its approach apart from the more local forms of xenophobia based on preference or personal judgment. Cultural racism does not present its judgments as based on one's own particular way of life but as universal and culturally transcendent (e.g., Dussel 2013; Khader 2019): adults should not have to answer to their parents, children should never be spanked, and teenagers should not have children. These putative universals are actually culturally bound, not simply in how these practices are judged but in their outcomes: for example, whether it is a good idea for teenagers to have children is a function of their community, their family supports, their social system, and their economic condition, not simply their age.

Examples abound of negative judgments of difference: the Ganda people of Uganda complained that the food of foreigners was "tasteless and likely to cause constipation." The Swahili took some foreigners to be superior—such as the Persians, whose calendar they adopted—while they took other groups to be unkind and uncultured (Prashad 2001, 5–6). But we can distinguish between those who dislike the eating of insects and those who view insect-eating as a sign of inferiority.

Interestingly, many groups in ancient and indigenous societies believed that persons from other cultures could assimilate and thus become 'one of them.' This issue of assimil*ability* is often a cornerstone of racism, or a sign of its presence. Of course, there is another issue, of whether any person or group should be forced to assimilate, but we can separate this from the question of whether some individuals or groups are believed incapable of assimilation, since this can be an indicator

66   RACE AND RACISM

of a deterministic racialization. In the United States, for example, certain groups have long been seen as unassimilable, not because they are believed to have no culture but because they are believed to have too much, especially in the case of Asians and the indigenous, whose cultures are portrayed as too old, too substantive, and too continuous, to the point of irrationality (Takaki 1998; Okihiro 1994; Ngai 2021). Hence the incapacity to assimilate is portrayed not as an individual failing but as a group problem rooted in specific cultures.

The ranking system that cultural racism deploys is made more powerful by its veneer of universal rationality and morality. It is on these grounds that states can justify exclusion, displacement, forced assimilation, and sometimes violence. The normative ranking of cultures is inevitably, as Fanon pointed out, "unilaterally decreed," but, in a circular argument, the unilateral nature of the decree is justified by the ranking itself. As Michael Hanchard argues, strategies of political exclusion have long relied on an absolutist form of judgment that decrees the universal criteria by which backwardness and advancement can be identified, yet this allows neutral-presenting judgments of culture to serve as a proxy for judgments of race or color (Hanchard 2018, 14).

Unilaterally decreed judgments will help us define the 'racism' part of the concept of cultural racism. But we still need to ask how to demarcate racism from a simple dislike or, for that matter, a justifiable criticism. Historians are today vigorously debating the genesis and duration of 'racism,' a term that, after all, emerged only in the early twentieth century. Whether the phenomenon predates the modern period is, predictably, dependent on how we define it. Here I will generally follow the approach developed by Francisco Bethencourt in his massive study published in 2013 on the history of racism that I discussed in the last chapter. Bethencourt's definition of racism is that it is "prejudice concerning ethnic descent coupled with discriminatory action" (Bethencourt 2013, 1). This definition is broad enough to cover multiple historical epochs and parts of the world without being restricted to the specific use of the modern concept of race, but its breadth is usefully limited by requiring the element of 'discriminatory action.' Bethencourt wants to focus our attention on practices that are embedded within political and economic projects, such as nationalism or colonialism or economic competition. Thus, his is less a conceptual

PERSISTENT POWER OF CULTURAL RACISM   67

argument than a pragmatic approach that argues in favor of a given definition on the basis of how it directs our attention toward significant types of historical events.

Bethencourt makes four further orienting points I find useful. First, there is a long history of correlating behavior and moral worth with physical characteristics, such as the Greeks and Romans taking the shape and strength of the body to indicate character and intelligence. The ancient world was also rife with theories of environmental determinism, linking climate and geography to the development of the virtues and vices. So, this gives us a way to think about forms of racism that predated the modern concept of race and continue to inform it.

Second, and in relation to this point, Bethencourt thinks it has been a mistake to make the manner of classification the determining criteria. An example of this mistake is the idea that racism could not exist before we had a concept of race as a form of classification. Many philosophers have argued this (including me). By contrast, Bethencourt points out that, historically, racial classification was not necessary for group-directed actions in all cases: groups could be targeted for exclusion and genocidal violence well before the development of biological explanations or any genealogical explanation of a shared identity formation. The wider definition of racism that he puts forward using the category of 'ethnic descent' will allow us to capture practices that are broadly similar.

Third, Bethencourt demonstrates how categorizing done on the basis of natural attributes can overlap with that done on the basis of cultural attributes, a point that is relevant for our understanding of cultural racism. Groups can be naturalistically defined or culturally defined, but one often sees that the formation of culture is taken to be the effect of the natural potential of a people. As Paul Taylor discusses, for example, the rhythm-based, percussion-heavy music of many parts of Africa was taken to be the result of racial characteristics, while the putatively superior melody-based music of Europe was interpreted as the effect of advanced intellectual capacity (2016). In other words, culture is sometimes taken to be *the product* of biological race or of environment, making it difficult to neatly disentangle forms of racism. We can still understand cultural racism as focusing on practices and doxa

68 RACE AND RACISM

and yet realize that these judgments may sometimes incorporate deterministic beliefs about biological races.

And finally, despite finding instances of racism in many different epochs and parts of the world, Bethencourt explicitly rejects the inevitability of racism, or the claim that it is part of human nature. In his extensive historical survey, he finds it to be more situational than innate, arising under certain contextual conditions. There is simply insufficient evidence to conclude that it is universal across human groups, and there is countervailing evidence, as I will discuss further on.

My aim here is to remain consistent with Bethencourt's approach, but we will need to reach beyond his account to develop an understanding of the specific form of *cultural* racism. What makes a criticism of a cultural practice a potential form of racism?

Consider the universalist criteria still commonly used to differentiate cultures, such as the distinction between "traditional vs. historical" cultures put forward in the 1950s by Mircea Eliade, the influential Romanian historian of religion (1961, 1967; Graeber and Wengrow 2021). Eliade defines traditional cultures as those that characterize eternity as cyclical and that engage in rituals of repetition of mythical or sacred events. Individuals are taught to follow in the footsteps of exemplary members of their cultures, not aim to improve or alter their ways of life or their understanding of what makes life meaningful. Eliade characterized historical cultures, by contrast, as those that deny intrinsic value to repetition. Individuals in historical cultures understand themselves as moving through an open or profane space, that is, a secular space without intrinsic meaning, and this allows for greater freedom of innovation. While traditional cultures have the advantage of offering a substantive orientation to human life, avoiding the anxieties associated with modernity, historical cultures make up for this in being open to change and thus capable of progress.

The first dilemma for this characterization of historical cultures is of course how to identify progress if there are no stable continuities by which we can make the necessary comparative judgments. What norms can be used to define what counts as historical progress? But this rather important problem is generally set aside in order not to distract from the hierarchy that the traditional versus historical distinction makes available to us.

Note that the distinction brooks no equality on rational grounds. Reason requires open-endedness, the capacity to launch critiques at every level, but traditional societies as Eliade describes them enshrine repetition, or conformity for its own sake. Those who understand theirs as historical cultures can feel justified in dismantling traditional cultures, as colonizers always do. It is in the best interest of the benighted individuals in those cultures to be dragged into modernity. Such uplift requires deculturation as a prior step to acculturation. By accepting individuals who have been assimilated in this way, societies of the Global North can avoid the charge of racism as it is usually understood. But if we use the lens of cultural racism as I am suggesting here, then we can no longer take the test of racism only to be whether majoritarian groups can accept minority individuals who deculturate.

But the truth is that there are neither traditional nor historical cultures in Eliade's sense. People who attempt to continue traditional ways of life will find the need to adjust to new conditions and unpredicted challenges, thwarting any simple repetition. This requires new interpretations of traditional ideas in order to determine how they apply and what lessons they may still provide. All sacred texts are the subject of varied interpretations, and always there is conflict among the greatest scholars. As many critics of colonialism have argued, colonialism has often thwarted local attempts to modernize institutions as well as intellectual and religious traditions (e.g., Táíwò 2010; Kassab 2009, 2019).

The truth is that all cultures have contestation over the meanings of their shared beliefs and values, and all cultures change. But no culture changes without being affected by the concepts, the ideas, and the practices in their own distinctive past. In other words, none change through processes of pure reason operating in a purely secular space with unbounded innovative possibilities, as Eliade imagined historical cultures. Perhaps we need to understand all cultures as traditional ones, but again, not in his sense of permanent, stale repetitions. What we need, as I argued in chapter 1, is an effective historical consciousness in the sense that Gadamer put forward, in order to understand our own horizons of meaning-making. But the idea of 'historical cultures' blocks the achievement of this. As Michel-Rolf Trouillot warned, "We are never as steeped in history as when we pretend not to be, but if we

70 RACE AND RACISM

stop pretending we may gain in understanding what we lose in false innocence" (Trouillot 1995, xxiii).

The colonial context

Neither Grosfoguel nor Fanon imagine that the form of racism that is focused on culture was new to the post-Nazi period; rather it was in fact central to the long period of European colonialism, starting with the Conquest of the Americas (Mignolo 1995, 2011, 2021). There were, no doubt, precursors even before this, as Bethencourt proposes, but as a systematic approach to ranking different ways of life that was embedded within the emergence of competitive empires and transnational economies, and as a ranking that eventually gained a scientific or rationalist veneer, the form of cultural racism that we are still dealing with today is best understood as endemic to the entire modern era. Fanon is interested in the mid-twentieth-century shift from biology to culture because it emerged just as anti-colonial revolutions were beginning to win formal independence in Africa, Asia, and the Caribbean. Cultural racism helped to thwart the development of collaborative relations with the new nations by labeling them "backward" and in need of tutelage. Critics of extractive capitalism from former colonies could then be dismissed as simply lacking knowledge and economic expertise about such things as financial markets, or assumed to be dupes of the USSR.

For these sorts of reasons, Fanon held that "a colonial country is a racist country" (1964, 40). By this he meant to disentangle racism from either individual dispositions or conscious racist intent and instead focus on the structural organization of exploitation. Thus, he says we must abandon the "habit of considering racism as a mental quirk, as a psychological flaw" (1964, 40). Fanon was clear about the "reciprocal action" between racism and culture but viewed this as contingent rather than universal (1964, 32). He rejected the modernist hierarchy of cultures that makes use of the advanced/backward or traditional/historical categories, but he did not reject normative comparisons. He believed there were cultures with racism and cultures without racism (1964, 32). The so-called advanced cultures of the West overcame what he describes as the "vulgar, primitive over-simple racism" that claimed biological causes, but these then simply gave way to what he describes as "a more refined" racism (1964, 32). Racism, he wrote, "has had to renew itself, to adapt itself, to change its appearance" (1964, 32).

Colonialism used cultural racism to justify its pursuit of "the destruction of cultural values, of ways of life. Language, dress, techniques are devalorized" (Fanon 1964, 33). But the goal, Fanon believed, was exploitation:

> In reality, the nations that undertake a colonial war have no concern for the confrontation of cultures.... The enslavement, in the strictest sense, of the native population is the prime necessity. [But for this to work,] the social panorama is destructured; values are flaunted, crushed, emptied. The lines of force, having crumbled, no longer give direction. (1964, 33)

To destroy a culture is to destroy collective resistance and to create the opportunity for a new system of values and practices to be "imposed" (1964, 34). One of Fanon's main concerns with the way in which colonization was fought on the terrain of culture is that the colonized cultures that attempt to resist don't disappear. Instead, they become mummified, closed, inhibiting individual thinking. The essentialism he saw developing in some forms of cultural nationalism thwarted the needed transformations that might otherwise occur. And this too, Fanon argues, functions for the colonial system: "Thus we witness the setting up of archaic, inert institutions, functioning under the oppressor's supervision and patterned like a caricature of formerly fertile institutions" (1964, 34). This culture then becomes "for the inferiorized [or colonized] an object of passionate attachment" (1964, 41).

Ultimately, for Fanon, disassociating racism from colonialism is a form of misdirection that conceals what we most need to understand. The forms of modern racism we struggle against today have retained their force despite formal decolonization and without biological commitments to racial types, yet they continue to make it possible for richer nations to maintain practices of extraction post-independence, because of the long colonial history of ideas developed to justify a

72 RACE AND RACISM

hierarchy of cultures, sciences, and economic practices. Bringing cultural racism to the fore will help connect present racisms to this long period of the modern/colonial world system and its enrichment of the Global North. Protecting the rights to that enrichment is an ongoing ideological task.

Focusing on the form of racism that is cultural racism will help us keep colonialism and neocolonialism in the frame, indeed, at the very center. And this should help us to see the utter inadequacy of approaches that focus on individual conscious intent or psychological dispositions, or solutions that treat the diversification of corporate leadership as valuable corrective measures. The misperceptions of culture that are promoted by cultural racism will show us quite a different way to think about solutions.

Cultural racism affects the movement of resources as well as peoples, garnering public support for the exclusion of certain immigrants and refugees, legitimating extractivist projects, and enforcing projects of coercive assimilation such as the Native American residential schools used in North America beginning in the nineteenth century that separated children from their families and attempted to destroy languages and yet were portrayed as the humane alternative to genocidal practices, which included offering rewards for the scalps of indigenous men. The aim of coercive assimilation has been, to paraphrase Sartre's account of antisemitism, to 'kill the Indian but save the man' (Sartre 1995). Cultural racism also contributed to the changed attitude toward asylum seekers in Germany after the 2016 New Year's Eve festivities in Cologne, based on demonstrably lowered standards of evidence-gathering and judgment. Investigative journalists only found some months later that the number of men identified as sexual attackers was not around 2,000, as initially reported, but 31 (Redecker 2016; and Brenner and Ohlendorf 2016a, 2016b; my discussion of this case in Alcoff 2018). Yet the characterization of immigrants as likely sexists and rapists legitimated policy changes toward refugees that remain in place [1] today.

---

[1] And this phenomenon of mischaracterizing and blaming immigrants continues, as Esra Özyürek's 2023 book *Subcontractors of Guilt: Holocaust Memory and Muslim Belonging in Postwar Germany* points out. While Muslims are targeted as the main

The discussion that follows will be organized into four topics: the idea of culture as the terrain of political struggle; the internal diversity and variety of cultural racism; how cultural racism can be distinguished from other forms of cultural comparison and normative assessment; and finally, solutions to cultural racism in the form of the theory of transculturation and the possibility of humanism without empire. The solution will not be a happy pluralism (or relativism) but a reunderstanding of culture, as the terrain of power, that can unravel its concealed moves and create the conditions for more open debates.

Culture as the terrain of struggle

To begin our exploration of cultural racism, we must begin with the idea, and practices, of culture itself.

As Edward Said noted in his book *Culture and Imperialism*, "Culture is a sort of theater where various political and ideological causes engage one another" (1993, xiii). The argument of his book is that expressive artistic productions, as well as the work of their interpretation and critique, can be sites of battle over how the past is represented as well as how groups and nations are portrayed and judged. Empires endeavor always to control the narratives that concern their history and activities, and a central feature of colonial narratives involves the ranking of other cultures.

Some wish to protect literature and art and cultural products of all sorts in a kind of gated enclosure, Said says, as if it were possible to create a free space in which expressive art forms could be appreciated on their own, to be seen as the production of a particular individual rather than a particular society. Culture should be judged by universal aesthetic criteria, not by its sociological origins or political effects, on this view. But this too is a tactic of control, an attempt to methodologically invalidate certain lines of critique and in this way protect what Said calls the "pleasures of imperialism." Such pleasures can include the crafting of narratives in which colonizers are rational and heroic

---

antisemites in Germany today, the actual facts are that almost 90 percent of attackers are white and far-right. For a discussion of this book, Mishra (2024).

74   RACE AND RACISM

civilizers when placed in relief against the backdrop of the 'natives.' There can also be forms of imperial pleasure in the display of the spoils, and in the unchallenged right to judge, interpret, and curate without oneself being judged, interpreted, or curated. Said is not imputing intentions to the artists but considering the meaning of artistic works, as well as their influence, distribution, and effects.

In truth, the idea of enclosing culture and protecting it from crass political judgment is just not possible. Unless a great many people are muzzled, there will always be contestation over the merit and the meaning of cultural productions, there will always be resistance to the enshrining of imperial narratives, and there will always be an effort to push against the censure of alternative narratives.

In this book, *Culture and Imperialism*, Said is primarily focused on the high culture of the imperial centers, that is, the culture produced within the metropole for the consumption of its own communities, or at least for educated elites. It is this sense of culture, or high culture, that was defined by Matthew Arnold in the 1860s as simply the "reservoir of the best that has been known and thought" (quoted in Said 1993, xiii). Thus, what today we might call Western high culture had, in Arnold's time, no geographical specificity, no context or qualifiers. The term *culture* signified a universal sphere that operated with putatively universal standards; in this way, its dominion was secured over the mere crafts and myths produced by lower groups. The culture of the imperial centers was the paradigm or the standard-bearer in genre and content. Given that the high culture of the West manifested the paradigm, the only question subject to debate was whether non-Westerners, or even the working classes and women of the imperial centers, could achieve culture, could write in sonnet form or produce symphonies and novels or paintings with sufficient complexity and depth. Thus, the interpreters of culture did debate whether other peoples could achieve culture, but their assumption of universalist standards preempted their exploration of other cultures or how their content, their genres, their forms of expression, and their standards of judgment might differ in substantial ways, generating distinctive aesthetic criteria. And this extended to the definition of art itself, understood as nonfunctional objects, which justified excluding the artifacts of the 'natives,' as well as most medieval art. As Taylor

PERSISTENT POWER OF CULTURAL RACISM   75

explains, the problematics that have garnered aesthetic debate are so diverse as to constitute incongruent conversations: "Where [Western white] philosophers tried to define 'art' and domesticate its ontology, black aestheticians argued that the concept of art was an expression of western parochialism, and that African cultures tended not to lock creative expression away in museums, concert halls, and galleries, separate from the rest of life" (Taylor 2016, 23).

Silvio Torres-Saillant, author of *Caribbean Poetics*, finds himself in agreement with T. S. Eliot, who wrote that we should view "the literature of the world, of the literature of Europe, of the literature of a single country, not as a collection of the writings of individuals, but as 'organic wholes,' as systems in relation to which, and only in relation to which, individual works of literary art, and the works of individual artists, have their significance" (quoted in Torres-Saillant 2013, 11). Torres-Saillant claims Caribbean literature as just such an organic whole, misinterpreted when read outside its context, either in relation to Europe or Latin America. He finds "recurring thematic motifs and stylistic choices" in the Caribbean that require contextual analysis to appreciate and interpret with precision (Torres-Saillant 2013, 11). The principles of literature can differ across contexts, and he affirms the Cuban literary critic Roberto Fernández Retamar's warning about the "pseudo-universality" that would move its categories across boundaries. Aristotle's poetics continues to be taught as if it provides a universal map; Torres-Saillant's book title dislodges this idea and goes on to develop a nuanced account of both commonalities and differences between different poetic domains since ancient times. The West, he allows, has produced a broad cultural form that connects various regions because of its imperial encounters.

Said would surely have agreed with Torres-Saillant and Fernández Retamar that the West's universality is a mirage, but he notes that despite it being portrayed as a universal with no geographical or sociocultural qualifier, the representations of Western high culture have continued to serve as the ground for a very particular Western subjectivity. The works of Austen, of Goethe, of Tennyson and Carlyle and Kipling and so on were presented as demonstrations of the highest cultural achievements of the human race and in this way helped to secure the legitimacy of Western claims to dominion over lesser groups. And

76 RACE AND RACISM

so, Said holds, expressive artistic products, and the interpretations of their meaning and significance made by experts, together created a reservoir for identity formation of a certain sort. Ideas about the cultures to which we are related ground our sense of who we are, since they represent in visual and narrative form a moral life, a manner of reflective subjectivity, a form of intelligence, and in this way a means to both differentiate and rank. Said's claim is that in the contested terrain of culture, it is important to protect positive interpretations not only for the purposes of empire building but simply for collective psychic affirmation. What about the fact that working classes often dislike high culture? What Said calls imperial cultures do not represent the inclinations of a race or ethnicity as a whole but a particular configuration of class, race, nationality, gender, religion, and ethnicity. Still, they set the standard for an idea of aesthetic value that circulated more widely in the society. And more popular or mass cultural productions can carry on the task of psychic affirmation in more palatable forms. Ideas and claims about culture play a central role in self-ascribed identity, intersubjective relations, motivational structures, the breadth and limits of solidarity, and thus to the achievement of hegemony in Gramsci's sense.

As Fanon noted, by ranking groups by their cultural achievements and moral sensibilities, one can appear to avoid the distasteful and less credible biological claims about inherited traits, especially if these achievements are judged by putatively universal standards. Thus, the decline of biological racism by the mid-twentieth century simply shifted racist and racial discourses onto the arena of an already quite well-developed terrain. To be sure, new binary concepts emerged, such as development versus underdevelopment, 'traditional' versus historical, advanced versus backward. Terms like *savage*, *barbarian*, and *primitive* appear less often today, yet the new terms, as David Theo Goldberg has argued, map nicely onto the meanings of the old terms (Goldberg 1993).

So, the decline of biological arguments for racial ranking did *not* in any significant measure reduce racism, given the ready availability of culturalist arguments that had been around since the beginning of the modern/colonial system, as can be seen in the sixteenth-century Valladolid debates between Bartolomé de Las Casas and Juan

PERSISTENT POWER OF CULTURAL RACISM 77

Sepúlveda over the treatment of the indigenous. This debate hinged on the question of whether the indigenous had any culture at all or were simply animal-like, operating from urges, without thought or design. Even though such ideas were regularly contested, they maintained influence, sometimes by slight revisions that took more palatable forms. But we must remember that such philosophical and anthropological debates occurred against the material infrastructure of colonialism and extractivist capitalism. Still today, even in its mildest forms, cultural racism provides a strong alibi to protect the ill-gotten gains of the colonizing powers. The current political divisions within the Global North are generally seen as the struggle between open racists versus humanitarians, but neither side need engage with the issue of colonial history or its legacy in global poverty and war.

At the same time that he helped to develop an approach to the political analysis and critique of cultural productions, Said maintained a complex analysis that could recognize beauty and skill even in such imperial apologists as Kipling and Verdi. What he insists, however, is that while aesthetic analysis that takes into account the real-world contexts is a legitimate aspect of critique, it does not always reveal moral depravity or the hopelessness of building community. The task is always to expand and include more: more narratives of colonialism from those outside the metropoles, more aesthetic forms, but also not to ignore the "overlapping experience" of diverse groups or the "interdependence of cultural terrains in which colonizer and colonized coexisted" (Said 1993, xx). And, he says further that

> what does need to be remembered is that narratives of emancipation and enlightenment in their strongest form were also narratives of *integration* not separation, the stories of people who had been excluded from the main group but who were now fighting for a place in it. And if the old and habitual ideas of the main group were not flexible or generous enough to admit new groups, then these ideas need changing, a far better thing to do than reject the emerging groups. (1993, xxvi)

So, to conclude this section, what is clear is that cultural racism is manifest in both the creation and assessment of high culture as well

78   RACE AND RACISM

as popular culture and that it is an ongoing feature of mass political discourse. I want to affirm Said's approach here, which was always to be very clear about the effects of colonialism but also to remain alive to commonalities. Becoming more attuned to the political dynamics that operate so strongly in the sphere of cultural expression will make us less rather than more likely to become politically reductive in our interpretive work, by giving us a greater understanding and a larger set of conceptual tools.

The diversity of cultural racism

Despite cultural racism's long pedigree, we should avoid imagining it as an undifferentiated or unified ideology. This brings me to the issue of its history and variety. We should heed Stuart Hall's point that both racial identities and racism are local as well as historically specific (Hall 1978). Racism in South America, for example, generally works on the basis of colorism, not lineage or purity as it historically did in the United States, with identity terms such as *morena, pardo, blanquito, prieto*, and many more, which might be distinguished by hair color or skin color and sometimes even eye color. Brazil had the largest trade in enslaved people in the Americas but no laws against interracial marriage as were common in other colonial systems, especially the British and German ones. However, Brazil had an elaborate *casta* system that created official identity categories based on particular kinds of unions, and one's caste determined an individual's legal and political rights and even their level of taxation (Telles 2006). Ranking based on elaborate schemes of colorism worked to encourage mixed relationships as a means to 'whiten' one's family line. And while the quest for racial purity marked racism in many countries, Brazil's apparent embrace of its mixtures was itself used to claim the achievement of a 'racial democracy,' as if colorism was unranked. Thus we need to consider social conventions of practice alongside national policies and recognize that although the concept of white supremacy traverses the world, it can be operationalized quite differently.

Bethencourt's work reveals that types of racism can overlap or combine. However, his work also shows that it would be a mistake to view

PERSISTENT POWER OF CULTURAL RACISM 79

cultural racism as always derived from biological racism. In the sixteenth, seventeenth, and eighteenth centuries, the ranking of cultures was based on geographical and environmental arguments, well before the biological sciences could invent theories of genetic causation. And these arguments remain in play today.

One widespread idea was that hot and arid climates stymied industry and progress, that the indigenous could hunt, fish, and gather the resources they needed without major effort because they lived in areas with such plenty, and hence it was no wonder their scientific and intellectual achievements lagged behind (Graeber and Wengrow 2021). This explanation suggested a "correspondence between moral and physical geography," as Santiago Castro-Gómez argues (2021, 200), or a normative ordering not just of bodies or body types, as conducive to intellectual achievements, but spatial terrains and environments.

Countering environmental determinism requires different sorts of analysis than the later biological theories, which were eventually refuted most decisively through research that disproved the genetic inheritance of behavioral dispositions. But the failure of biological theories led back to the older environmental theories: if the 'fact' of inferiority was not explainable as a result of genetics, then some looked to social circumstances, and this included where people live.

Geographical and environmental arguments for racial ranking made claims about intellectual inferiority, but such claims were groundless. To provide sufficient resources for communities, practices of hunting, fishing, and gathering require an inordinate amount of empirical science, as is well known today. Such societies often require mobility, and so the sophisticated practices of oceanic navigation developed by Micronesian groups informed and advanced the capacities of Western explorers (Harding 2015). Such societies also require knowledge of sustainable practices so that sources will not run dry. Hunting and gathering communities needed to develop knowledge about how to maintain their sources, leaving a river free to be replenished, for example, while moving on to another water source for their food. The necessity of mobility also required maintaining peaceful relationships with other communities: to be a regularized practice, mobility cannot engender war or conflict every time the community needs to shift its

80 RACE AND RACISM

domain, and this requires reflection, cooperation, and political knowledge (Whyte 2013).

Furthermore, lush tropical climates are not simply bounties of food resources that discourage industry, but dangerous environs with numerous hazards and poisonous plants. The tropics present numerous problems of pest control, requiring empirical observation and reasoning. The people of the Choco region in Colombia observed that predatory birds such as falcons could safely feast on venomous snakes but that they typically ate a certain vine before beginning their pursuit. Based on this observation, they developed methods of inoculation by use of what they named 'falcon's vine,' so that they too could operate in areas where such serpents were likely to be found. A Spaniard in the region, Pedro Fermín de Vargas, tested their vaccine on himself in the late 1700s and confirmed its reliability.

The geographical theory of civilizational achievement remains common in current ideations of tropical paradises (even Greece and Italy) that are thought to produce informal, easygoing cultural practices, but as a causal theory of cultural development, it was rejected by most scientists by the twentieth century. Correlations, such as those between environment and achievements, do not establish causality, and in truth, the correlations were so variable that their purported explanatory role was defeasible. But the manner by which cultures were comparatively ranked, and the ways in which the West continues to define knowledge, cultural achievement, and what it means to be civilized, have not been challenged by the demise of the geographical explanation of human difference. We continue to rank, and we continue to assume universal criteria that can identify advanced societies. This is simply to say that normative comparisons continue to be based on manifestly racist ideas and concepts that only a focus on cultural racism can unravel.

Castro-Gómez shows that, in the Americas, the theory of racial and cultural difference that attributed them to environmental causes was not overturned because the actual achievements of peoples in these hot or arid regions gained broad recognition but because these theories threatened white criollo power in the colonies. Fermín de Vargas, for example, wrote that credit for the falcon's vine vaccine "does not go to the people who prepared the antidote but to the falcons" (Castro-Gómez 2021, 167). Despite their observation, experimentation, and testing, the people of Choco were viewed as analogous to the animals thought to happen upon a technique of inoculation (and both judgments, of people and animals, are surely erroneous). White criollos began to oppose the environmental theory of race not because of its racism against local inhabitants but because it began to be applied to them, that is, descendants from Spain who had settled in the new world. Colonizers argued that even white settlers were degenerating in the tropics, becoming lethargic and losing motivation. Note that this was not an argument about the devolutionary effect of reproductive mixing, though those arguments were sometimes made as well, but an argument that the extreme conditions of the geographical region would affect even European settlers, diminishing their industriousness, altering their character, and thus moving them culturally downward. European blood was no match for the effects of tropical paradise.

Such arguments served to legitimate ongoing European offshore rule, of course, which was under serious ideological attack by the late eighteenth century. The Spanish crown gave criollos in the colonies significant privileges to expedite their functionary role, privileges including land and the right to enslave. But their political independence had to remain limited, and the concept of environmental degradation provided support for this. Against the idea that they were degenerating because of the climate, white criollos began to argue that such theories were neglecting the issue of altitude. They pointed to city-states in the mountainous Andean regions and in the highlands of Mexico where impressive cities and cultures had developed. Ironically, they sought to hang onto the coattails of certain indigenous empires that were widely admired, such as the Inca and the Aztec, in order to defeat the claim that their own stock was in an inevitable nosedive due to environmental influences. But such argumentative strategies left the racist criteria used for judging cultures undisturbed. And by emphasizing altitude, they were simply offering a variation on the theme of environmental and geographical causation.

Today, the actual language of racism used against immigrants is largely about cultures, and sometimes religions that act as proxies for cultural difference, rather than genetics or biology. The infamous

82 RACE AND RACISM

conservative commentator Ben Shapiro argues that it is "reason and moral purpose" that made the West "great," not colonial wars. The US President Donald Trump argued against accepting immigrants from what he called "shithole countries," even if they were refugees fleeing wars and violence. Despite the wars of aggression waged by majority-Christian countries, such as the United States over the past fifty years, with hundreds of thousands of civilian lives lost, it is Islam that is portrayed as inherently violent. And so on.

As Uma Narayan has shown (1998), the cultures of other societies are relied on as explanatory devices more so than in the West. In regard to the cross-cultural epidemic of violence against women, and in particular the murder of wives, culturalist explanations are used mainly for the Third World, she argues, while misogynist violence in the First World is attributed to pathological individuals. In her study of the Western press coverage of India in the 1990s, she notes the outsize coverage of dowry murders and sati. Thus gender-based violence was attributed to cultural rituals. In short, India was portrayed as a land where women are killed for cultural reasons. The epidemic of gun violence in a country like the United States does not get a similarly culturalist explanation (at least not within the United States).

Yet in fact, Narayan found that men kill their female intimate partners at about the same rate in both India and the United States; all that changes is the manner of killing, which seems to be governed by what is available. Kitchen murders through immolation are common in countries where a container of oil is stored close to the cooking fire; in too many homes in the United States, a gun is more easily available. We might give some elements of culturalist explanations in both cases, but the fact that it is only given in the Global South indicates the presence of cultural racism. Like murderers of women, we use what is most easily available to portray 'their' backwardness and maintain 'our' superiority.

So, to summarize, cultural racism can encompass theories about biological, environmental, or geographical causes. But none of these are necessary. What unifies the concept of cultural racism is the focus on "ways of existing," to echo Fanon once more, rather than a particular belief about causation. When culture becomes used as a ground to

PERSISTENT POWER OF CULTURAL RACISM   83

legitimate exclusion and ranking, we need to press for further analysis. This raises the question that will be the focus in the next section: How can we distinguish cultural racism from acceptable forms of normative judgment?

Judging cultures

Surely, we need to be able to engage in critique, to compare and judge cultural formations. Yet the critique of cultural forms is a theater of political engagement in a context of economic competition. Ideas about cultures are central to global or transnational relations of all sorts, including military ones. As Said puts it, imperial cultures represent their actions as morally defensible on the grounds that "certain territories and people *require* and beseech domination" (1993, 9). Empires claim to bring innovation, industry, security, and prosperity to the countries they subordinate, but these claims hinge on concepts that are themselves defined differently in different places and require some critical analysis.

The celebrated Peruvian novelist and poet César Vallejo vividly described the colonial restructuring of Peru's economy in the early twentieth century, in a period when the mines were first being created in the Q'eros region of the eastern Andes. Vallejo himself had worked in the mines, and in his novel *Tungsten*, he describes scenes of interaction between workers and local indigenous people around a mine owned by a US corporation. The local natives were the Soras, and some would come to watch, appearing entranced at the process of hammering on an anvil. One man wanted to try out the work. Vallejo writes,

In the end, they gave in and he worked there four days running, getting to the point where he was a real help to the mechanics. On the fifth day, around noon, the Sora abruptly put aside the ingots and took off. "Hey," they called to him, "why are you leaving? Go on with your work." "No," said the Sora, "I don't like it any more." "They're going to pay you. They're going to pay you for your work. Just go on working." "No, I don't want to any more." (Vallejo 1988, 5)

84 RACE AND RACISM

The workmen found this attitude completely unintelligible: working for one's own idiosyncratic purposes, for curiosity or pleasure, to feel helpful, rather than working for a wage or in response to a command. Later the same Sora was seen helping a girl pour water for washing wheat, and he offered to carry a rope down into a mine shaft. Vallejo writes,

> He wanted only to be active, to work, and amuse himself, and nothing more. For the Soras could not keep still. They came, they went, cheerful, breathing hard, their muscles tensed and the veins standing out with exertion, tending flocks, sowing, making mounds for seedlings, hunting wild vicuña and alpaca, or clambering up boulders of cliffs, in an incessant and, one might say, disinterested toil. They had absolutely no sense of utility. (Vallejo 1988, 5–6)

As Garcilaso de la Vega, the son of an Incan woman, explained in his sixteenth-century writings, the Incan civilization that had flourished in this region of the world had three overarching prohibitions: against lying, stealing, and being lazy. The point is not to romanticize such cultures but to understand the depths of differences across various human ways of life, including conceptions of work and of gain.

Ideas about culture also encompass ideas about cultural integrity and geographical borders. Few were surprised that shortly after he invaded Ukraine, Putin began to make claims about the derivative nature of Ukrainian culture and language in relation to the Russian culture, or that he used cultural reasons to deny Ukrainians the right to political sovereignty. As Elif Bautman notes, "the Kremlin now uses Gogol [born in Ukraine] as evidence that Ukraine and Russia share a single culture" (Bautman 2023, 49). In response, Ukraine abruptly shifted its Christmas celebrations to accord with the Gregorian calendar, used in the West, and away from the Julian calendar, used by the Russian Orthodox Church. Ukrainian curator Leonid Maraschak sees the war itself as "a war about cultural identity." Journalist Jason Farago explains Maraschak's claim by saying that "with Russia trying to erase Ukraine's national identity, this country's music, literature, movies, and monuments are not recreations. They are battlefields" (Farago 2022).

Obviously, Russia and Ukraine share important cultural elements and have influenced one another, but the claim useful for Putin's purposes was that Ukraine is the junior partner, the follower, who should therefore accept Russian leadership. In this way, the question of cultural differences and boundaries becomes embroiled in economic and political conflict. This can distort humanistic interpretations of language, literature, and art in general.

Equally important is the way in which Putin has redefined sovereign states, or states whose sovereignty claims merit respect, as only those whose "inner energy" is sufficient to generate common values, beliefs, and history (Paris 2022). The mere existence of a governmental apparatus is insufficient to legitimate the right of nonintervention if the society lacks this 'inner energy.' Right-wing populists argue similarly that immigration weakens nations by diluting commonalities. Speaking in Warsaw and at the United Nations in 2019, Donald Trump invoked the idea of sovereign *societies*, rather than sovereign states, and said that societies can only achieve sovereignty to the extent that citizens are willing to make sacrifices to protect and uphold their culture, faith, and tradition.

The idea that cultures are defined by their shared content and creed has long been part of modern notions of political community: Hobbes, for example, described the state as an expression of an "Artificial man," with a soul expressed by its cultural forms. The artificiality is meant to signal that cohesiveness is a result of collective will, not natural facts. But if states are the means of creating a shared collective identity, this authorizes control over borders based on cultural reasons, as well directing educational curriculum toward this end. If political sovereignty requires cultural cohesiveness, a host of governmental powers will be expanded.

We need to reflect carefully before answering such claims about political sovereignty resting on cultural cohesiveness. For one thing, as with Russia and Ukraine, national cultures are not always distinct; usually there are cross-influences, which is why we often refer to regional, extranational cultural forms such as 'the West' or 'Islamic.' This does not legitimate the bizarre refusals of autonomy such as Putin is making, but it does counsel against implausible claims about the existence of clear and distinct demarcations between languages,

86 RACE AND RACISM

cultures, traditions, religions, forms of artistic expression, and so on. Sovereignty claims do not need to rest on such distinctions, and yet, as the plurinationalists and regional indigenous organizations in South America are demonstrating, political state formations can share power with other political entities both within and outside. Regional political and economic organizations that group Andean peoples across many nation-states have found ways to work with and alongside the traditional nation-states that were founded in colonial times (Escobar 2018; Escobar and Pardo 2007).

Some retreat entirely from the discourse of culture that Putin, Trump, Orban, and others are articulating, putting in its place the idea of a political community bound together only by volitional commitments. The advantage of this decultured definition is clear: societies defined by their chosen institutions rather than their shared culture and history can rebuke ethnic nationalist ideas such as Putin's, in which a group's cultural history is said to set the path for their enduring future. Decultured concepts of politically defined entities coexist more easily with pluralism in the religious and cultural spheres. But there are three significant disadvantages to this familiar classical liberal approach.

The first is its descriptive implausibility. Has any political community, whether national or subnational, created its institutions and mechanisms of governance through choice, without being affected by a specific historical and economic experience and place in relation to others? Has any political community truly risen above its various cultural influences rather than being formed in ways that manifest the legacy of these influences? Western-style secular liberalism emerged from Protestant cultures in which individual autonomy was prized and religious belief was a choice. Ignoring this genealogy leads to neutral characterizations of Western ideas, as if they are simply 'rational' or grounded in metaphysical absolutes. Secularism actually takes distinct forms in different cultures (Bilgrami 2016).

Second, the ability for all to share in the government of their political community is curtailed today by citizenship requirements that advantage those who claim a legacy of attachment, not necessarily to land but to states. Those on the fringes are most likely to have racialized

PERSISTENT POWER OF CULTURAL RACISM 87

identities. Thus a decultured approach that focuses on citizenship papers retains unfair racial advantages.

The third problem with decultured approaches to political community is that they can become, and in fact be motivated by, a form of avoidance. If what holds societies together is formal, volitional, and intellectual, and not shared forms of life or historical experience, then we need not engage with the fascist worldview. We can dismiss ethnic nationalists as irrational or insufficiently modern, which is to covertly make use of, and thus reenforce, the ranking systems rooted in colonialism, such as the traditional/historical distinction that Eliade elaborated. Most importantly, avoidance means that we have no counterarguments to the claim that the ethno-racial diversification that results from immigration will diminish our sense of relational commitments, our willingness to sacrifice for others in our communities, or the strength of our political institutions. This connects, I believe, to the tendency to assume that if a country accepts immigrants, it can only be on humanitarian grounds, which is an act of volitional charity, or on economic grounds, which is simple self-interest. It allows us to avoid engaging in critical reflection on our own culture and even to feel justified in demanding assimilation, although this is an inevitable failure (Kim 2015).

It also allows us to avoid the task of working through our different histories and different ways of being in order to form communal bonds. In the following chapter, we will see the long tradition of skepticism Western liberal societies have manifested toward such a project, starting with Thomas Jefferson's call to return the enslaved to Africa. He believed there was no possibility of a functional democracy that could include the formerly enslaved together with their enslavers.

Cultures and nations are of course not natural kinds but social constructions, both in a formative sense and in an interpretive sense. Their content and boundaries are always subject to motivated interpretation. But cultural content is itself the product of dynamic historical movements that are defined and demarcated, often by over-determined, motivated interpretations. As those from the former Yugoslavia know, after the civil war that broke apart the nation, literary, musical, and other genres associated with Serbian or Croatian identities could be

88   RACE AND RACISM

honed, promoted, funded, and shaped into instruments used to establish the pedigree of distinct ethnic identities, overlooking all the historical research that reveals pan-ethnic or cross-ethnic similarities.[2]

The interpretation and categorization of expressive arts seems always to be tasked with nation building. This has generated skepticism
toward any and all claims about cultural distinctiveness and about the
concept of culture itself. But as Said showed through his case study of
Orientalism, everything one can say about cultural traditions is not
equally false. Interpretative rubrics always have some variability: they
are best understood as frameworks for directing our attention rather
than representations of an absolute. Recent scholarship is directing our
attention to facts that have been in some cases willfully mislaid, about
the entwined nature of many languages, religions, agricultural practices,
forms of technology, metaphysical beliefs, and ways of making art. Thus,
as I will argue shortly, the idea that "inner energy" requires homogeneous
belief systems is false in a way that no interpretive inventions can overcome. Confluence is everywhere, but true homogeneity is hard to find.

In fact, the line of argument that would make of culture a unified
substance is not only a mistake but also a danger. And this raises the
question, what does the word *culture* even mean?

How to define 'culture'

Sociologists of the concept of culture have been exploring for some
time how best to define the concept without underplaying the diversification of the public sphere. The debate between Raymond Williams
and Paul Gilroy is instructive in this regard. Williams wanted to avoid
portraying culture as a reservoir or repository of unified content and
to maintain Herder's idea that there is a plurality of cultures. Against
Matthew Arnold, who imagined a singularity to human culture,
Raymond Williams defined cultures as plural and, also against Arnold,
as broad and ordinary rather than exclusive to the high arts. Williams
understood cultures holistically as organized systems of practices,

---

[2] See https://www.wilsoncenter.org/publication/216-language-identity-and-balkan-
politics-struggle-for-identity-the-former-yugoslavia.

PERSISTENT POWER OF CULTURAL RACISM   89

meanings, and values that are "essentially involved in *all* forms of social activity," irreducible to economic causes and beyond the control of the state (1981, 13).

But most helpfully for our purposes, Williams argues that a culture is best understood as a "realized signifying system" (1981, 209). In other words, culture is not a way of life that is simply followed or adhered to but a process of meaning-making in which shared historical experiences—living through the blitzkrieg, the migration of the Windrush generation, or Thatcherism—become part of one's hermeneutic horizon, influencing both creation and interpretation. Culture, he said, since it comes from the concept of cultivation, is a "noun of process" (1981, 10). Signifying systems are not producers of coherent uniformity, yet there are connecting patterns that can be discerned in language, in intellectual ideas, and ideas about values, and not only in the traditional arts.

Williams stressed that the Weberian attempt to distinguish spheres of society in the modern era (distinctions that Weber and others used to establish cultures as more or less modern or advanced, depending on how well they honored such distinctions) never obtain in reality. For Williams, the organized system of practices, meanings, and values that Weber puts in the category of "culture" is not separable from those that operate in the spheres of economics, politics, or spirituality. The extensive critiques of neoliberal economic ideas, to give recent examples, show the entwinement of spheres, in which facets of our specific cultural histories render certain economic arguments, such as arguments that value individual choice, to sound like simple common sense, conferring a familiar feel to new proposals and thus increasing the likelihood of their acceptance.

Williams's approach is concordant with the concept of the coloniality of power developed by Anibal Quijano (1999, 2008) and other decolonial theorists. This is the idea that post-independence, or post-formal colonialism, global relations remain infused by colonial meaning-making, or signifying systems, that maintain the ranking of racialized groups. But Paul Gilroy, among others, sharply criticized Williams for continuing to render culture overly coherent. This makes it easier, Gilroy argued, to conflate national with cultural identity, which gives rise to the sort of exclusivist nationalism the fascists

90 RACE AND RACISM

today, as in the past, dream of achieving. If national identities are cultural identities, then newcomers must be culturally assimilated, and some will be justifiably excluded or permanently marginalized. Gilroy worries further that, in fact, both conservative *and* socialist treatments of culture can evince "an absolutist definition of culture tied to a resolute defense of the idea of the national community" (1993, 30). The assumption that substantive cultural identities ground national identities, providing the 'inner energy' Putin considers necessary for sovereignty claims, will have the effect of centering some citizens, sidelining others, and justifying immigration restrictions.

Gilroy is also concerned that tying cultures to nations produces unproductive forms of resistance in the beleaguered minority communities, such as cultural nationalism and what we used to call narrow nationalism. Such forms of resistance create all sorts of problems, he argues, from general pressures to conform, rather than question, and from policies that restrict adoption along racial lines. Gilroy, like Said, Fanon, and Amilcar Cabral (2016) as well as more recent theorists such as Beltrán (2010), is as concerned with the ideas about culture in the resistance movements as he is with the ideas about culture in the conservative mainstream.

I share Gilroy's worries but will argue that the solution will not be found in separating cultures from political entities. We should focus on rejecting the idea of culture as a uniform or unified way of life, and also the idea that unity is necessary for national legitimacy or resilience. I will suggest that we can modify Williams's idea of cultures as sources of signification in a way that will help to demarcate cultural racism from other sorts of cultural judgments. Before turning to my alternative, I need to address how Williams's approach to culture can answer the question of the specificity of cultural racism as a form of normative judgment.

In the face of the persistence of cultural racism, there are hard tasks for those from supremacist cultures, who must begin to critique and examine the very basic epistemologies that govern normative judgment in our era. But there are also hard tasks for those whose cultures are misidentified, misinterpreted, and derided.

Cultural racism should not be understood as a marginal view with limited influence. In truth, cultural racism imbues the Western discourses in every domain, from art to philosophy to medicine, and particularly affects discussions of global security and global trade. Therefore, we should not limit the concept of culture to a focus on expressive cultural productions. Rather, we should go back to Said's earlier Foucauldian-inspired analysis in *Orientalism* (1979), which focuses on enunciative modalities, the delimitation of objects, and an overall way to approach knowledge. This is closer to Williams's concept of cultures as a distinct process of signification, rather than its substantive result. In other words, the content of concern here in regard to culture is the manner of producing meanings, rather than a settled and closed set of meanings that needs critique. In this way, Williams's approach can be linked to a dynamic and open hermeneutic horizon that plays a role in the task of interpretation and judgment from a place that contains substantive content from the past. New significations are never ex nihilo, never objective or neutral by the standard definitions. The process of judgment is itself embedded within discursive formations with particularist elements. The point is to make these as visible as possible and thus part of the discussion and debate.

The idea of a 'cultural imaginary' can be useful here. This is not simply a repository of meanings but an operational apparatus in a Foucauldian sense. Foucault uses the idea of an apparatus (or *dispositif*) as a larger and looser amalgam that would include laws, institutions, and bureaucracies but also has effects on the formation of identities and subjectivities. Castro-Gómez then uses this concept to explore the apparatus of whiteness operative in post-Conquest societies, which were organized with the aim of ensuring a livable life for white settlers (Castro-Gómez 2021, 43). The emerging 'sciences of Man' that developed within colonial spaces, with their taxonomies of populations, creation of specific market rules, and specific forms of governmentality, gain intelligibility when we see them as connected by this apparatus of whiteness.

Castro-Gómez argues that this apparatus was concealed by what he calls the hubris of the zero point: the assumption of a disinterested, objective, sovereign gaze that actually disabled the motivation for self-reflection and the development of dialogical models of knowing. Coming into a foreign space, with unfamiliar forms of life, colonizers

92 RACE AND RACISM

took the stance of judge, expert, interpreter, and arbiter of all conflict. Colonizers and settlers like Fermín de Vargas could judge and categorize and classify without engaging with local counterpoint. De Sousa Santos (2018) argues that the colonial context helps to explain why resistance to *external* critique became instantiated in the scientific method, which is only subject to internal or immanent critique based on recognized expertise and shared methods of knowing. The hubris of the zero point, then, is this idea of perspectiveless, disembodied knowing in which knowers need not engage with epistemologies diverse from their own.

In this way, I suggest, Castro-Gómez's approach can augment Williams's to show that the idea of 'culture' relevant to the concept of 'cultural racism' is a signifying system that incorporates the *habitus* of groups from which new knowledges and new possibilities of action are produced. If some groups have a *habitus* developing from a position of social dominance, able to choose between treating the Other with cruelty, disregard, or a magnanimous charity that will signal their own virtue, that habitual dominance is not itself dislodged whether one chooses disregard or charity. What is truly unsettling to such a signifying system and corresponding form of subjectivity is when the right to make unchallenged decisions comes to an end. This is what decolonization and looming demographic changes seem to threaten.

Culture as an apparatus, then, denotes practices and a *habitus*, not conscious intentions. The sovereign gaze of the zero point enacts racism at the epistemological level by preempting the scope of dialogue.

Decolonial theorists such as Quijano and Mignolo use the term "the colonial matrix of power" to explore persistent colonial frameworks that generate, govern, and link economies, labor, families, political institutions, authority, and knowledge, with resultant effects on subjectivity (Quijano 1999, 2008; Mignolo 2021). Quijano in particular helped to bring social identities to the fore here within an overarching theory of modern colonialism, showing that in the colonies, lineage, visibility, and socially recognized categories such as religion, gender, race, and ethnicity structured labor markets and political systems as well as epistemic positions. He argued that coloniality brought "a new way of legitimating the already old ideas and practices of relations of

PERSISTENT POWER OF CULTURAL RACISM 93

superiority and inferiority" and that, in particular, "race became the fundamental criterion for the distribution of the world population into ranks, places, and roles in the new society's structure of power" (2008, 183). The colonial imaginary also influences and organizes the interpretation of cultural productions.

This helps us see the difference it makes to take colonialism as the key to understanding racism. Colonial systems operate with a signifying system that organizes, justifies, and consolidates racial perception and judgment, with effects on patterns of empathy and what is taken to be reasonable or common sense. Within the colonial matrix of power, biological racism emerged and bloomed for a time, but also other theories of the cause of human differences, such as environmental and evolutionary approaches that ranked groups on a single temporal map of progress. Some groups were portrayed as too inferior to develop on their own and thus requiring, as John Stuart Mill believed, instruction from more culturally advanced societies such as his own. Anthony Bogues describes Mill's view in this way: "the duty of English society and imperial polity was not to restore slavery but to develop forms of *tutelage*, which could eventually lead the black population into civilization" (Bogues 2005, 221). This project of tutelage toward uplift allowed Mill to critique the most onerous forms of racist violence, as occurred after the Morant Bay Rebellion in Jamaica, and yet continue to support ongoing British rule in the colonies. Colonialism could then cloak its extractions with the language of civilizational development.

Mill's paternalism is a clear enactment of the position of the zero point, which conferred final arbitration only on the most advanced, to enlighten the inferior races. The Millian approach is the dominant ideation in the liberal, nonfascist West today: a multiracial multiculturalism that believes many peoples from underdeveloped societies can advance if they have access to Western education, cosmopolitan experiences, and assimilation to advanced cultures, thus making it possible to diversify corporate boards and institutional leadership. This is not decolonization.

The dominant colonial imaginary and its associated apparatus can accommodate structured refugee admissions, affirmative action, the forgiveness of some loans to the world banking system, and other

94 RACE AND RACISM

reforms. It can also survive the demise of biological racism and address ongoing implicit bias and the remaining vestiges of attitudinal racism with diversity training and focus groups. But what the colonial matrix of power cannot make sense of is the push against westernization, or the decolonial critique of cognitive racism and Western epistemologies in general (Mignolo 2021, esp. 85–98, 314–348). As Sabelo Ndlovu-Gatsheni explains, the decolonial turn "cannot be fully comprehended without an understanding of the 'colonial turn'" (Ndlovu-Gatsheni 2018, 73). Resisting Western cultural and political dominance is continuously misrepresented as a resistance to rationality, humanism, modernity, science, even morality, because all of these have been defined in terms of universal neutrality through the hubris of the zero degree. Ndlovu-Gatsheni argues that the aspiration for de-westernization is so mystifying to the West because it presents a challenge at the epistemic level of the West's signifying system simply by rejecting the assumed universal stance of unilateral judgment and demanding dialogic engagement on equal grounds. And thus, de-westernization feels like chaos and a violent anarchy, a wholesale attack on reason and moral order, so unintelligible is it to the mainstream.

Cultural racism, then, is most importantly a mode of judgment created over our long colonial history. It is built into scientific practices that claim hegemony in vaccine production on epistemic grounds, and the exclusive right to nuclear weapons. It is not just a misperception of other cultures but a misperception of our own cultures. Cultural racism should be understood as a general way of seeing and knowing that is central to nationalism and ethnic self-formation, but in my concluding section, I will argue, it need not be.

Counterpossibilities

In this final section, I will explore a partial antidote to cultural racism in the concept of transculturation from Fernando Ortiz. Ortiz's work provides us with a departure point from the West's ruling fantasies of cultural superiority, and the hubris of the zero point. But beyond this, his work also helps to address the concerns of Gilroy, Fanon, and Cabral about the ways in which some forms of resistance to cultural

PERSISTENT POWER OF CULTURAL RACISM   95

racism operate with the same ideals of cultural homogeneity and exclusivity. In Ortiz's work, the border zones of conflict are reunderstood as internal rather than exterior, and cultures are characterized as open and hybrid formations.

Ortiz was a Cuban anthropologist writing in the first half of the twentieth century whose early work manifested aspects of a colonial mentality and racism. In 1906, for example, he published a book that characterized Afro-Cuban religions as forms of sorcery that were culturally backward. He initially viewed Cuban culture as inferior to 'more evolved' European societies. Like the celebrated Uruguayan essayist José Enrique Rodó, Ortiz thought that imbibing European intellectual culture was the cure for Latin America's cultural malaise and political quandaries. Such views are not surprising in the early twentieth century: Ortiz had his academic training in Spain.

As Fernando Coronil (2019) argues, the ferment of new anthropological and social theory during the first few decades of the twentieth century convinced Ortiz to change his views. One of his main influences was the historian Ramiro Guerra y Sánchez, who gave a markedly different account of the root causes of corruption, poverty, and political authoritarianism in Cuba: Guerra located the source of the problem not in Cuba's non-European practices but in its insertion in a global sugar industry, with its plantation economies, its history of slavery, and its need for a large number of unskilled laborers and a workforce that could be hired seasonally. The problem was not Cuba's culture but Cuba's dependent economy that kept the population uneducated and desperate. The global sugar industry had no need for thriving democracies and in fact, had motivations to thwart emerging democratic, anti-colonial movements. As the historian Robin Blackburn explains, "By the latter half of the seventeenth century, the English and French planters had demonstrated that owning a sugar plantation was more gainful than working a silver mine, but only so long as there was a coercive structure with enough slaves to plant and harvest the crop and arduously process it" (2024, 3). He goes on to recount the continuity of these coercive structures that were used in plantations both before and well after the end of legal slavery, including brutal punishments, curtailed freedom of movement, and political control.

96   RACE AND RACISM

Also, a number of social theorists began to replace the idea of culture as a singular universal, as Matthew Arnold had imagined, with the idea of multiple cultures. Theorists such as Franz Boas began to resist the idea that cultures could be ranked by a simple uniform rubric, arguing instead that anthropologists should embrace cultural relativism. But Ortiz was primarily influenced by the work of Oswald Spengler, whose writings were translated into Spanish and widely read, including by a number of Latin American intellectuals (Spengler 2018). Spengler was a German philosopher of history and a nationalist, but his metahistorical approach recognized that plural forms of culture contributed to world history. His work helped to abate the idea that European practices could be taken as universal, making it possible to analyze specific cultural forms, such as Afro-Cuban music, without a judgment based on a comparison to European forms. These new theories of plural cultures gave rise to a newly decentered global imaginary. Spengler in particular inaugurated the idea that cultures are like organisms, with periods of growth and periods of decline, and that the West was not a culmination of universal rationality but a specific cultural form that would itself eventually decline like all the others.

So, it is in his masterwork, *Cuban Counterpoint*, published in 1947, which is a treatise on the competing cultures of tobacco and sugar production, that Ortiz invents the new concept of transculturation that I want to make use of here. With this concept, Ortiz intended to provide an alternative to the concepts of assimilation and acculturation, which are imagined as operating "in a unidirectional process" involving an evolutionary uplift (Coronil 2019, 85). Much of our current thinking about migration continues to operate with these concepts, albeit implicitly, so that the question is framed as whether a particular group *can* assimilate to a modernity defined as a form of cultural advancement. Will they be motivated to adopt the ways of the dominant culture, or will they be recalcitrant and oppositional to acculturation?

By contrast, the concept of transculturation, as Ortiz develops it, portrays a process of reciprocity that affects all who come into contact. Whether we resist or not, close cohabitations have an effect on us. Importantly, transculturation is neither a one-way nor a two-way assimilation: *it is the creation of something new.* I find it very useful for our current challenges that Ortiz acknowledges that transculturation involves loss and may therefore instill fear as well. No less than the ground of one's prior identity is subject to loss here, along with its 'signifying system' for producing meaning. However, his is not a replacement theory, since what emerges in the place of the lost cultural formation is a creative adaptation that involves both collective and individual agency. It is not one culture replaced by another but a transformation that involves agency, with often invigorating effects, and indeed, the central feature of Ortiz's account is the multiple influences that reconstitute all sides.

Cultural border walls are, after all, imaginary projections intended to protect existing forms of domination, just as stone and concrete border walls promise. Yet neither ever succeeds. Even if laws are put in place to ensure that only one language may be spoken, linguists find elements of the outlawed language cropping up in the dominant language, such as Irish and African influences in UK and US English. Dominant religions enforced on all, such as Catholicism was throughout the Americas, experienced major transculturations, as historians of religion have shown. We largely have the indigenous of the Americas to thank for the prominence of the Virgin Mary, for example, whose exaltation was controversial in Europe, where some Mary-worshippers were executed as heretics and their temples burned to the ground. But many indigenous groups in the Americas had female goddesses, and the images created of the Virgin Mary in the Americas—beginning with the most famous, the Virgin of Guadalupe—resembled these earlier figures in stance and dress. The first recorded apparition of the Virgin in the West, in 1531, appeared at a temple built for the Nahua goddess Tonantzin, which had been destroyed by the Spaniards. Thus, indigenous groups could continue to honor and travel to this familiar site while ostensibly performing Catholicism. But it is surely wrong to see this as simply an insincere ruse: the concept of transculturation offers a way to see this as a creative act that retains elements of prior cultural forms while also altering them.

As Coronil's interpretation of Ortiz makes clear, the concept of transculturation has a de-essentializing effect on how we define and approach cultures (Coronil 2019, 86–89).

98 RACE AND RACISM

Using the idiom of fetishized renderings of Cuban culture, he presents a counter-fetishistic interpretation that challenges essentialized understandings of Cuban history. In this respect, his work resonates with Walter Benjamin's treatment of fetishism. Unlike other members of the Frankfurt School, who were primarily concerned with demystifying the fetish in the service of reality, Benjamin sought to apprehend how the fetish commands the imagination, at once revealing and appreciating the power of mystification. By treating tobacco and sugar not as things but as social actors, Ortiz in effect brings them back to the social world that creates them—re-socializes them, as it were—and in so doing illuminates the society that has given rise to them. (Coronil 2019, 87)

Countering essentialism ushers in a relational ontology in which the decentered nature of cultural forms is revealed, undermining hard distinctions and binary oppositions and revealing the limits of their descriptive adequacy. Binaries, after all, are rarely fixed or stable. In truth, even oppositions between the center and periphery of colonial empires are unstable and partial: Catholicism became reimagined and "indigenized" in a way that was available to all and, as importantly, and more successfully, imposed on all.

Given the inevitability of cultural dynamism and reciprocity, the geopolitics of transnational economies in the modern, post-Conquest era activated new forms of sociality even while they operated within colonialism and imperialism. It is not quite correct to name all of these transmutations of cultural forms as theft or appropriation, as if agency only existed on one side. And some of the most fertile transculturations occurred across marginalized communities to produce forms like bebop and Latin jazz. Genealogies of various cultural forms are today being revised, such as the genre of 'country music' in the United States that has been characterized as originally white even though its instruments, such as the banjo, and its musical styles (e.g., of picking rather than strumming) were brought by Africans to the new world and creatively transformed (Taylor 2016). The emergence of new forms of expressive culture impacted relations between marginalized communities, in particular, poor rural whites and former slaves, both of whom contributed to developing forms of folk and country music as

PERSISTENT POWER OF CULTURAL RACISM 99

well as the artisanal crafts found in bed quilts, carved wood furniture, and garden decorations. On Ortiz's view, neither dominant nor subordinate groups can effectively patrol their borders of influence.

New histories of modern science and modern political theory are retelling the story of European modernity as a process of transculturation precisely in Ortiz's sense (for example, Graeber and Wengrow 2021; Hämäläinen 2022; Dodds Pennock 2023). The encounter with Native peoples and cultures, with their different value systems and forms of life, animated the imaginations of Montesquieu, Rousseau, Condorcet, and Kant, sparking debates about previously unquestioned ideas in the elite circles of European societies. Indigenous peoples found the European practice of subordination to the aristocracy inexplicable. As the Jesuit missionary Le Jeune wrote in 1642, from the perspective of the community of the Innu (Montagnais-Naskapi), "the French were little better than slaves" (Graeber and Wengrow, 41). Native peoples could not understand the European practice of performing obsequiousness to others whose only claim was landownership, but they also asked other questions, such as why communities with abundance did nothing for those starving, ill, and unhoused in their midst. The indigenous brought different practices of political organization and open debate. In the widely circulated "Royal Commentaries of the Incas," written in the late 1500s by El Inca Garcilaso de la Vega, elaborate details are given of Incan social life that portray recognized rights to social support and the ability to resist unfair labor demands. Tribute, or taxation, was imposed on nearly all, but these were used for public works such as irrigation and could be resisted or deferred on a variety of grounds. Such traditions supported the opposition to colonizer demands. The Incan Emperor Atahualpa engaged in a lengthy reasoned critique of the Spaniards' demands for silver:

> you give no reason for paying the tribute, and I have certainly no obligation whatever to pay it. If there were any right or reason for paying tribute, it seems to me that it should go to the God you say created everyone [and not King Charles] who was never lord of these regions and has never set eyes on them. (Garcilaso de la Vega 2006, 104)

100 RACE AND RACISM

The Spaniards had no answer to this argument except violence.

Yet this "American indigenous critique," as Graeber and Wengrow call it, enlivened the imagination of many Europeans, such as Rousseau, and led to new antiauthoritarian directions in European political theory. Recent intellectual histories show that even subordinated groups are very much a part of the intellectual and political story of modernity (e.g., Puchner 2023; Barreiro 1992). Yet, the myths of modernity, as Dussel calls them, have misrepresented our histories to make it appear that the European Enlightenment was, like God, self-caused, that philosophy began in Greece, and that rationality and ideas of autonomy were most fully developed in the West.

Ortiz developed his concept of transculturation very self-consciously from the perspective of the colonized area of the world, to push against received ideas, including those he previously held. He understood Cuba to have experienced one of the most profound cultural transculturations in recorded history. And it was an experience of transculturation that emerged from transatlantic colonialism in the modern era. Ortiz writes:

> There was no more important human factor in the evolution of Cuba than these continuous, radical, contrasting geographic transmigrations, economic and social, of the first settlers [from Europe], the perennially transitory nature of their objectives, and their unstable life in the land where they were living, in perpetual disharmony with the society from which they drew their living. Men, economies, cultures, ambitions were all foreigners here, provisional, changing, "birds of passage" over the country at its cost against its wishes, and without its approval. (Ortiz [1947] 1995, 101)

Ortiz also developed the concept of transculturation not with the central example of aesthetic expression or religious practice or other domains generally associated with the word *culture* but through an analysis of the colonial agribusinesses in Cuba based on tobacco and sugar production. Thus, he places cultural forms in the context of economies to demonstrate the elaboration of forms of life that could accord with the particular way these products were produced in this colonial space. As he explains:

PERSISTENT POWER OF CULTURAL RACISM   101

Tobacco requires delicate care, sugar can look after itself; the one requires continual attention, the other involves seasonal work; intensive versus extensive cultivation; steady work on the part of the few, intermittent jobs for many; the immigration of whites on the one hand, the slave trade on the other; liberty and slavery; skilled and unskilled labor; hands versus arms; men versus machines; delicacy versus brute force. The cultivation of tobacco brought about the small holding; that of sugar brought about the great land grants. . . . The native against the foreigner. National sovereignty against colonial status. The proud cigar band as against the lowly sack. ([1947] 1995, 6–7)

Ortiz is not the only one to give us concepts of cultural reciprocity, but I think his is of particular interest precisely because of this detailed contextualism that highlights the influence of the economic context and formation of labor practices.

Despite the power imbalances in the Cuban colonial context, the result was not an acculturation in a single direction but major transformation of all participants, or what Coronil calls the "intermeshed transmigration of people" (Coronil 2019, 86). Ortiz describes Cuban history as "an intense, unbroken process of transculturation of human groups, all in a state of transition" (Coronil 2019, 86), and suggests that this is not just the story of Cuba but of the whole of the Americas. He traces the effects of the transculturation in economic practices as well as topics more commonly written about such as the forms of music, dance, and humor and the shared sensibilities manifest in every cultural form caused by disruption and diaspora. The rumba has no origin story that can establish a pure lineage or singular geographical source; the antiphonal and percussive elements of Cuban music today is a creative response to the joy that sometimes accompanied contact. There are few signs of nostalgia or a quest to repeat or return to the past. The temporal attitude is on the present, and the aesthetic practice is on an unfettered assemblage.

Europe has a different history than the Americas. But since the time when it became self-consciously Europe, self-identified as Europe, it too should be understood as the product of a transculturation wrought by imperial conquest and subsequent migrations, mobile borders,

102   RACE AND RACISM

multiple empires, some of which were centered outside of today's Europe. There were also transformations wrought by the contact between majority and minority cultural communities within Europe, with peoples such as the Roma, the Sinti, and Jewish groups. As Benedict Anderson says, "It is easy to forget that minorities came into existence in tandem with majorities," that is, that they were there from the beginning (Anderson 1998, 318). State formations create and define both majorities and minorities and regulate their relationships, but they cannot police their influence.

Perhaps the most pernicious myth of all has been the persistent portrayal of an idyllic homogeneous past, as if there was a time prior to group-related differences, in which trust and understanding were easier, even automatic. The truth is that the British Isles have had Black people at least since Roman times, that Scandinavia had an internal ethnic diversity as well as one caused by Viking conquests elsewhere, that Mediterranean communities traded and developed commonalities across every shore, and that religions cohabited throughout these regions and influenced one another. The connections between Africa and Europe are particularly strong and began at least with the third century, as Olivette Otele's award-winning book demonstrates (Otele 2020). The truth is that the historical eras that fascists want to reclaim as pure and isolated from others never existed. Europe has been transculturated since its inception, and it is not only now that it is being affected by immigrant populations. Transculturation replaces the replacement theory with a more accurate account of what has happened and what is likely to continue. But the concept itself comes out of the experience of the "New World," more thoroughly and deeply altered than anywhere else.

For a long time, Latin American intellectuals bridled under the European assessment that ours was a debased hybridity, as if the mix of peoples and cultures quashed the chance of creating an 'internal spirit,' with the result that no coherent life-form emerged to contribute, in Hegelian fashion, to the development of the 'world spirit.' Against such ideas, influential thinkers such as Martí and Vasconcelos found ways to valorize the creative potential of *mestizahe* and even to portray the mix as itself superior to moribund ideals of cultural stasis. These ideas of *mestizahe* were often put to the service of projects of postcolonial

PERSISTENT POWER OF CULTURAL RACISM 103

nation-state formation and are today receiving needed critique as harboring in some cases anti-Black and anti-indigenous racisms of their own. If the national identity is predicated on the superiority of the mestizo, this leaves unchallenged the old ideas about the cultural backwardness of continuous, or so-called traditional, communities.

But Ortiz does not make use of the concept of transculturation to aid in the sanctification of *mestizahe* but to offer a more descriptively accurate account of mutual transformations and creative agency enhanced by the experience of contact. Here is a different source of 'inner energy' than homogeneity, and here, there is no zero point. The practice of normatively ranking cultures assumes distinctions that colonialism has thoroughly destroyed. Cultural racism today is a vestige of empire's attempt to maintain its hold over the historical narrative and the myth of the integrity of boundaries. So, I will conclude with some thoughts on the role of cultural racism in national formations, as a way of understanding the sources of its influence and also to postulate where we might go from here.

Conclusion

The concept of transculturation helps to undermine the narrative of Western supremacy that has been reproducing cultural racism in every generation since the Conquest of the Americas. It is not a sufficient solution, yet it forces a reassessment of the nostalgia for a fictional homogeneous past, and it helps us decolonize what we think we know about the emergence of Western culture in general. If we continue to use familiar geographical-historical categories like "the West," they will need to be able to accommodate the truth of their complex genealogies (Lucy Allais 2016 on this point).

White nationalism is today a transnational phenomenon whose basic premise is that a racially and ethnically defined homogeneous community of citizenry is the only means for a stable, successful state. This premise finds resonance in many non-white parts of the globe, such as India, in which a kind of ethno-essentialism grounds national identity and the right to exclude. But we should be clear that ethnic essentialisms of this sort are enabled by cultural racism: others are

104   RACE AND RACISM

thought to be justifiably excluded not simply because they may be newer to the nation but because they have a culture that is inadequate in some significant way, and it is believed that mono-culturalism is the only feasible political option for a nation to flourish. Transculturation shows the lie of these claims.

We should also be clear that noxious forms of nationalism that seek to exclude refugees and immigrants need not be 'whites only.' Nationalism can be formulated in such a way that it is ethnically and racially inclusive. There is a new form of multiracial Christian nationalism in the United States, Brazil, and across Europe today in which acceptance of the creed provides entry into some levels of power-sharing. Multiculturalism and even multiracialism are not guaranteed antidotes to colonial thinking. Not all groups are considered capable of inclusion, and the most notably excluded are indigenous groups whose economies and ways of life threaten capitalist extractive projects as well as predatory real estate practices. But instead of working through these differences with the aim of peaceful and just cohabitation, cultural racism allows states to deny that there are other values, other ways of life, that have a right to survive and flourish.

So, how do we move forward?

In this chapter, I have argued that claims about cultures are a critical site of political contestation, not a diversion from material or economic issues. This is because culture is entwined with ways of life, including ways of making a living, and not merely doxa or ideology. I have argued there is no need to take off our critical hats to avoid cultural racism. What we need to avoid are absolutist criteria that serve as unilaterally defined litmus tests, and the continued use of colonialist binaries such as "advanced versus backward" or "traditional versus historical" that animate global ranking and serve to legitimate imperial projects.

Attending to cultural racism will link present-day forms of racism to transnational histories of colonization, which have given us deficient concepts and misleading binaries, mobilizing fear and creating a subterfuge for explaining global poverty. But I have also argued that the solution to cultural racism cannot be a refusal to engage with the concept of culture, however messy it is, nor can we succeed with the strategy of avoiding cultural issues to focus on volitional political

PERSISTENT POWER OF CULTURAL RACISM 105

commitments. In order to counter ethnic nationalism, we need to engage with the epistemic concepts, historical myths, and procedures of judgment that produced cultural racism over the colonial period. In this way, we can counter cultural racism's claims with a better descriptive account of how cultures in the modern era came about and what this portends for future migrations across the world.

The concept of transculturation opposes the liberal strategy of defending immigration on the grounds that 'don't worry; our country won't change.' Change, as well as some loss, is inevitable, but as Ortiz shows, there are always new creations and adaptaticns that can be quite wonderful. Some demographers have attempted to show that immigrants are not to be feared, because they will assimilate to the dominant ways of life in their new locations (e.g., Le_ie et al. 2012). And good empirical work has shown that, for example, the intensity of religious practice is reduced in a generation or two after immigration, and that intermarriages further affect the socialization of children to accept mainstream practices in their new societies. But those arguments only track a one-way assimilation and leave unchallenged the desire for an implicitly white "French culture," for example, to remain intact. This is a defensive move intended to counter white nationalism, but we need a stronger argument, a point I will take up in the following chapter.

Some recent political theorists, many from the Caribbean, are developing a new approach to the idea of *creolité* as a way to re_magine political communities, both in the past and in the future. One of their claims is that the creolization of colonial cultures effected a 'modernism from below,' meaning that there were changes and productive innovations without permanent coordinates (esp. Gordon 2014; Sealey 2020). In this process, as with transculturation, there is simply no untouchable base, no "foundation principles [that] remain outside the bounds of negotiation" (Gordon 2014, 167; Kompridis 2006; Nascimento and Lutz-Bachmann 2018). Jane Anna Gordon gives numerous examples from linguistics and symbolic life to demonstrate that creolization denotes mixture but not a resolution of difference or a simple end to conflict, because all elements are not in fact lost or replaced. Rather, the concept of *creolité* is meant to provide an anti-essentialist approach to culture that acknowledges, like Ortiz, the agency of the

106   RACE AND RACISM

oppressed and, like Hall, the multiaxial nature of the structural forces that exert causation (class, and race, and gender, and so on). From this more descriptively accurate starting point, we see that any approach to the future must be pragmatic rather than foundationalist. We must let go of the hubris of the zero point; to escape hubris, we need dialogic procedures that allow everyone to be at the table.

As Édouard Glissant (1989, 1997) showed, multiple temporalities and signifying systems can cohabit a space, but they will rub up against one another, causing friction. Processes of transculturation are clearly efforts at making productive use of friction to create a new formations, such as a Virgin of Guadalupe who can be worshipped while retaining some continuous elements with Tonantzin. Glissant was concerned with the difficult application of these ideas to national identities and nation-states, but he suggests that we can learn from the Caribbean, where nations are self-consciously transcultural. Nations *are* expressions of cultures, as Spengler thought, but with a fundamental structural contingency because of the ongoing phenomena of transculturation. Thus, nations are expressions of multiple cultures in constant transformation. In her recent book, *Creolizing the Nation*, Kris Sealey argues that "the political effect of alternative creolizing imaginaries is in the rupturing of existing structures, in the ways those imaginaries contest the directionality and telos of existing power" (2020, 173). Her point is to reunderstand nations as having a directionality, a movement guided by substantive imaginaries, and that these are dynamic and regularly contested rather than being the emanation of a foundational idea, as Hegel and Spengler both believed.

Without minimizing conflict, Said pointed out in his final book, *Humanism and Democratic Criticism*, that "far more than they fight, cultures coexist and interact fruitfully with each other" (2004, xvi). Said reminds us that the post-structuralist critique of humanism developed in the United States partly out of revulsion with the war in Vietnam and its humanistic defenders with their civilizing language, and because conservatives were wielding the concept of humanism in order to maintain the untouchability of the Western canon of 'great books,' then under assault by student radicals. But, as he recounts, antihumanism then became infallible doctrine and was used, ironically, to

PERSISTENT POWER OF CULTURAL RACISM   107

represent the Western academy as more theoretically and politically advanced than any other.

Said suggests we return to Vico for our understanding of humanism not as doctrine but as practice, a making relation to knowledge. What unites human groups is their universal "capacity to make knowledge, as opposed to absorbing it passively, reactively, dully" (2004, 11). He wisely put forward that one can be "critical of humanism in the name of humanism and that, schooled in its abuses by the experience of Eurocentrism and empire, one could fashion a different kind of humanism" (2004, 10–11).

His is, I suggest, a humanism without empire: a rejection of ranked types in favor of the claim that all human groups engage in meaning-making, or in other words, culture. This was also the basic idea of Las Casas's defense of the Indians in his mid-sixteenth-century debate with Juan Gines Sepúlveda: the Aztec should not be classified as barbarians, or animalistic, Las Casas argued, because they had reasons for their actions. Thus, from the very beginning of modernity, up to its present day, there have been contesting alternatives to cultural racisms, alternatives we very much need to resuscitate in these dark times.

3

The Crisis of White Identity

Shortly after World War II, Albert Camus traveled to Brazil, Uruguay, Argentina, and Chile on a South American speaking tour. The trip was arranged to promote his recent publications of *La Peste* and *L'Étranger*, two books that were celebrated, then and now, as a compelling rumination on the value of human existence despite the absence of God, the inevitability of death, and the absurdity of the quest to discover the meaning of one's life. Both novels fashioned plots with meaningless deaths, and in *L'Étranger*, a meaningless murder.

Camus took the opportunity that the tour to South America afforded him to hear local music and observe Santeria rituals in person. He also insisted on visiting villages rather than only cities, and he recorded his thoughts about these experiences in a fascinating set of travel diaries. The trip was quite taxing for Camus, given his ill health and the truly absurd scheduling that his publishers had arranged. But these difficulties were compounded by Camus's growing sense that in comparison to these regions of the world, by the middle of the twentieth century, Europe and Europeans were floundering and their inflated sense of self-importance should be checked. While flying over the Brazilian rainforest, Camus wrote:

> The faster the plane flies, the less importance France, Spain, and Italy hold. They were nations, are provinces, and tomorrow, will be the world's villages. The future is not on our side, and there's nothing we can do about this irresistible trend. (Camus 2023, 85)

We should recall that Camus was a French Algerian from a working-class family. Despite his European lineage, he felt a familiarity and connection with the non-Europeans in Algeria. He came to defend the Algerian struggle for independence from France, expressing hope that the end of colonialism might allow more truly egalitarian relationships

Race and Racism. Linda Martín Alcoff, Oxford University Press. © Oxford University Press 2025.
DOI: 10.1093/9780197796948.003.0003

CRISIS OF WHITE IDENTITY 109

and temper Europe's "mechanistic foolishness" (2023, 85). Yet he also expresses a fear of what this future would bring, using phrases that invoke a colonizer's perspective:

> Brazil, with its thin framework of modernity laid over this immense continent teeming with natural and primitive forces, makes me think of a building slowly chewed, bite by bite, by invisible termites. One day the building will collapse, and a small and teeming people, Black, red and yellow, will spread out over the surface of the continent, masked and brandishing spears, ready for the victory dance. (Camus 2023, 98)

Here Camus seems to be experiencing not a generalized existential anxiety but a very particular apprehension toward a world he sees just on the horizon, in which non-white people will be dominant not just in numbers, as they have always been, but in power. Following soon after the above passage, he writes, "I wish to die" (Camus 2023, 103).

The nature of the crisis

In this chapter, I want to address and analyze what I am calling the crisis of white identity, a crisis that is manifest across all white-majoritarian countries, fueling the rise of the far right, and well-expressed decades ago by Camus. This crisis has been simmering for a long time. I will explore shortly what is meant by whiteness in the current moment and argue that it is not possible to define and diagnose this crisis without the category of whiteness, even though this term throws together a widely diverse collection of peoples with widely divergent political views and experiences. Yet the sensation of a crisis that Camus describes is characterized by a fact that all might see and feel today: that whiteness, or European lineage, is *losing ground.*

The mid-twentieth century was a period of immense anti-colonial ferment, in which the desire for sovereignty swept throughout the formerly colonized areas of the globe. This movement was sparked by the sense that the European claims to have rightful, legitimate control of these regions were ideological mystifications intending to cover over

110   RACE AND RACISM

massive theft. Today there is a sense not only that Europeans (and Westerners in general) are still widely distrusted and unwanted in their former colonies but that the former colonial subjects of Europe and the West are now invading the lands of their former colonizers and demanding the legal right to do so. Increased numbers of non-whites are migrating and cohabiting the spaces that were previously, and comfortably, majority-white, including towns, schools, and workplaces, even governments. Migration is hardly new, of course, but the sense of lost power and declining influence flows from a sense that societies in the global north are being forced, however slowly, to change, to give way, to share their space and their resources, and to revise their own self-understandings.

It is notable that this loss of dominance, or really, the right to dominate, is *experienced* as a crisis. Camus describes it as an impending primitive force that will collapse buildings and replace civilization with spears, although one could also easily imagine, as Camus himself does at times, that the demise of European colonialism could produce an outcome of greater peace. After all, Western powers have regularly thwarted democratic movements around the world, refusing to allow any tinge of socialism to flourish, instead assisting military dictatorships and genocidal regimes with financial and military support as well as political cover. And then the West acts surprised by the mayhem, and blowback, and dictatorships that ensue. But the idea that limiting the global power of the West is a better solution than ongoing coercive mechanisms engineered unilaterally from rich outsiders is rarely entertained. There is a reason for this.

The reasoning behind Camus's more dire predictions is not, I argue, reducible to false consciousness. Camus says, "the future is not on *our* side," and it is clear this is indeed true, though perhaps not in the way he perceived. It's not just about global population distributions, or young cultures versus old ones, but about the change in perspective that is rewriting the script of modernity and diminishing Western claims to superiority over all other parts of the globe. Clearly, there is more at stake here than an alteration in how we narrate modern history. The wealth that has accumulated in white majoritarian nations is largely ill-gotten, and the military power these nations have wielded against nations in the Global South is, on the whole, illegitimate. The

CRISIS OF WHITE IDENTITY 111

Emperor's fine garments have been torn off, rendering apparent the injustice of global material distributions. The historian Jason Sokol encapsulates this sensibility in the title of his book on white Southern reactions to the Civil Rights Movement: "There goes my everything" (Sokol 2007).

Western control over global finance capital cannot continue forever and has been challenged for some time by China as well as several new economic trading blocs. It is thus not irrational to expect a change in circumstances due to the declining enrichment that has been regularly coming from the Global South, whether in the form of resource extraction, consumer markets, or the lower wages that keep consumer goods in the West so affordable, or the ever-available cheap migrant labor willing to do the most dangerous and unpleasant jobs within nations of the Global North. It is also not illogical to expect blowback or demands for reparations, which are already being voiced. The subsequent sense of a lost world and fears of an uncertain future span the divide between white-majority settler nations and "old Europe." This can also support an intra-white cohesion despite many political differences, although generational rifts among whites on global politics are growing.

What I am calling the crisis of white identity involves two parts: a narrative crisis and a legitimation crisis. The narrative crisis has been brought about by challenges to the official group history of European peoples whether at home or settled abroad. The legitimation crisis follows soon on the heels of the narrative crisis: if the richer nations of the world committed as many atrocities as the corrective histories recount, why do they continue to assume a right to an outsized degree of global wealth and power?

Certainly, many today in the global north recognize the weaknesses of Europe's global leadership; the carnage Europeans have been responsible for throughout the twentieth century and into the present can hardly be hidden in today's world. But, as Churchill said of democracy, there seems to be a widely held belief that European supremacy may well be flawed but still beats the alternative. Ongoing political chaos and mayhem in many parts of the Global South is viewed as proof of this dictum. Hence, the end of Western world dominance is taken to spell impending world chaos.

112 RACE AND RACISM

We need some political therapy.

The dominant narratives of European and white history have long promoted their cultural superiority and sidelined their injustices, as I discussed in the previous chapter. And it is these narratives that have served to legitimate not only particular settler colonial nation-states but the global arrangements of economic power.

As the distinguished historian E. J. Hobsbawm argued, Europe's fairy story about its formation naturalized European nation-states and borders, as if the genealogy of these nations evolved innocently based on sharing a language, a territory, a history, and a singular religion (Hobsbawm 1990). In truth, language use was policed and manipulated, territories were seized in war, and histories were always entwined. The portrayal of European nations as natural kinds neatly sidestepped the fact that they came about through historical crimes such as the Inquisition, religious wars, ethnic cleansing, racial ranking, numerous internal colonizations and genocides, the attempt to destroy languages, and the coercive control over global trade routes and migration. Modern nationalism used religious and ethnic identifications to craft an ostensible unity that could cover over class as well as other divisions, consolidating support for imperial agendas cloaked as national defense.

However, disposing with the naturalist pretensions is today experienced as a cultural attack, and cuts across the divide between settler and nonsettler white-majority nations, since both benefited from slavery and pursued colonial projects. Denaturalizing the ethno-racial makeup of white-majority nations reveals these to be the product of choices and policies—laws against intermarriage, and integrated schools—and thus, willful exclusions rather than happenstance (e.g., Blackhawk 2023; Grandin 2019; Burrough et al. 2022; French 2021; Hixson 2013). The denaturalized narrative raises questions about borders and current demographics. Calling out Western colonialism has also led to new coalitions and new conceptions of what global justice could look like. See, for example, Quynh N. Pham and Robbie Shilliam's (2016) discussion of the important Bandung Conference that united Asian and African anti-colonial thinkers in 1955 to articulate a shared agenda for global justice. New coalitions for economic and political cooperation are today mushrooming beyond the

CRISIS OF WHITE IDENTITY   113

control of the United Nations Security Council. As Camus rightly said, nothing can be done about this irresistible trend.

If white-majority nations, and their economies, are not the product of luck, industry, and natural forces, it can begin to feel as if all those that share a white racial designation are morally suspect, or guilty until proven innocent of racist dispositions and an unjust income. And the comforting assumption that one will remain in the majority group of one's town, or one's nation, is declining. And with this, the assumed dominance in the political sphere is also disappearing, causing whites to fear for their children's future. Jared Taylor, a thought leader for the far right, explains that his desire for segregation is simply based on a preference for homogeneity (J. Taylor 1998) But tellingly, he also argues that only separatism can guarantee white survival. The spaces—both figurative and literal—that whites assumed would always be theirs are experienced today as being invaded. And it is a fact that good jobs with benefits, pensions, and affordable housing, as well as quality education through the university level, have all become scarce. Many governments today no longer prioritize the flourishing of white families over others, such as more recent immigrants, with preferential policies. Thus, the perception of threat has a basis in reality and includes economic and political as well as cultural and psychological elements.

We should not overplay the demographic shifts alone as a sufficient cause of this mood of apprehension. The problem is better understood as a social one. Even while political power remains largely in (some) white hands, recent population changes have produced "shifting patterns of political strength, of social contact, and of symbolic representation that have real implications for the meaning of whiteness," as Monica McDermott argues (2020, 111). The usual forms of life that have long existed in white-majority societies are changing, and the public sphere is increasingly diverse not simply by identity but by point of view. Even liberal whites fear the perceptions and judgments of others, and though this is not entirely new, the others whose judgments they fear are today in closer proximity and less intimidated. Thus, the far right's warning resonates: that only a white-dominated country is a safe country for whites. Another version of this is the claim is that only a white-dominated country will ensure white people's rights to

114 RACE AND RACISM

self-determination, to freedom of speech, and to self-protection. So it is not simply a matter of a demographic transformation but a changing interpretive frame by which groups, and group histories, are understood as in conflict and in competition.

In the United States, the economic security of whites has been deteriorating for several decades: white people are dying at younger ages, and drug addiction has increased sharply (Metzl 2019; McGhee 2021). Some respond to a general social deterioration by moving to what they hope will be a more white-friendly neighborhood, city, or state, while others will simply vote in a way that seeks to undo the changes they fear. In Europe, the economic well-being of whites has not fallen as dramatically as in the United States, but significant increases in the cost of housing and a diminished public infrastructure are widely bemoaned, as is the fear of an oncoming "Islamization." Far-right racial nativism and Christian nationalism are growing with alarming rapidity in many countries known for their social liberalism, such as Sweden, the Netherlands, Greece, France, Italy, and even, again, in Germany. Sweden, once hailed as the most equitable country in the world, is today pulling back on its social democracy where immigrants are concerned, but this comes after decades of neoliberal privatization and tax cuts. Border and immigration policies are being tightened in all white-majority countries, and those who try to assist migrants with humanitarian aid, even water, are sometimes prosecuted. The Great Replacement theory, to be discussed shortly, and the concept of "Fortress Europe" have gained wide influence as ways to understand both the threat and its solution.

Yet we need to understand this crisis as epochal rather than merely current. The long era of colonialism, slavery, imperial interventions, and selective government protections for the well-being of white populations is all being increasingly exposed by historians and criticized regularly in the public culture with newly circulating concepts like 'intergenerational wealth transfers' and 'settler colonialism.' This has upended the long period after WWII in which it was mainly Germany that had to be called to account, when the catastrophic regime of German Nazism could provide a contrast that made other nations in the Global North look relatively innocent. As the fuller story of slavery and colonialism and genocide against both the local indigenous and in other continents comes into wider public view, there is no more innocence to be had (e.g., Blitzer 2024; Frank 2018; Luiselli 2017).

Thus, I want to stress that the crisis of white identity is not a manufactured crisis, a product of white-nationalist conspiracy theories, or a pathological delusion in the form of what Hegel called false consciousness, created out of an incorrect understanding of one's situation. The crisis is real to the extent that business as usual cannot continue. We certainly need to contest the interpretive frames that view increasing diversification of peoples and points of view as inevitably undermining the possibility of functional governments. And I agree with those, such as Derrick Darby, who call for a united front for economic justice, and for building coalition across ethnic and racial divides as well as differences in citizenship status (Darby 2023). Yet white nationalist and Christian nationalist movements in many parts of the world are today creating rather large roadblocks against such efforts. Nationalist movements, and the fears they mobilize, need to be addressed directly and forthrightly. Building economic justice cannot sidestep a consideration of what racism and colonialism have done to create the world of today, such as the mythic narratives of modernity, and the indefensible justifications of Western global dominance.

In this historical moment, what is fueling the far-right movements is an actual identity crisis around the category of whiteness. No white-majority settler nation can claim a virtuous past in which their territory was legally or morally obtained. No European nation can claim that their current share of the world's wealth and resources has been achieved virtuously. These facts must unsettle the presumed right of these nations to control their borders and reject all who want to enter, especially those from regions that have been the subject of this historical mistreatment. Yet allowing *these* groups to enter creates fear that the political divisions already apparent in the public sphere, based on the disparate historical memories of different groups, will be exacerbated, as Thomas Jefferson himself predicted more than two centuries ago. Jefferson believed slavery to be clearly unjust and yet feared that freeing those who had been enslaved and then incorporating them into the new nation would threaten its self-preservation (Roosevelt 2022, 237). He expressed these sentiments in private, fearful of their

116 RACE AND RACISM

effect. Yet to his chagrin, his views quickly became public. Even in the eighteenth century, communication could not be centrally controlled.

In today's less centralized and more diversified public sphere, an attempt to control the narrative is even more difficult. Those who experience white identity and the legitimacy of white-majority nations as under ideological assault are correctly perceiving, I argue, their social condition.

An identity crisis

By using the concept of an identity crisis, I mean to signify that the current crisis of white identity is of a similar sort that besets other groups, typically young people, but also migrants and displaced persons. As the onset of adulthood looms, many young people experience a phenomenon that has come to be called an identity crisis. This involves apprehensions about their future and a reassessment of the influential others in their lives. Similarly, migration, as Stuart Hall explains it, creates an identity crisis by upending our social maps through which we understand the world and our place within it, until "suddenly everything looks different" (Hall and Schwarz 2017, 173).

Though I was quite young, I well remember my own period of migration, in which my sister and I abruptly lost a language and a loving family. In our new Anglo surroundings, our origins from Latin America suddenly became a source of unease, as if we were oddities, and our looks took on new meanings. Hall is right that immigrants must develop new tools for navigating their social spaces, given how we are seen in our new location.

Immigrants have long known the disorienting effect of transformed social identities; whites en masse are now learning it.

The affective condition of identity crises can be acutely uncomfortable. Psychologists portray identity crises as manifesting a self-directed uncertainty with concomitant feelings of anxiety and instability. The *Diagnostic and Statistical Manual* describes those with identity disturbances as having a "markedly and persistently unstable self-image or sense of self." Thus, the term *crisis* is used quite purposely to describe a scenario that cannot be managed or withstood for long (*DSM-5* xxx, 664).

CRISIS OF WHITE IDENTITY 117

The philosopher Charles Taylor has argued that it was modernity itself that engendered the possibility of identity crises, by engendering the possibility of individual self-creaticn. What he calls premodern societies did not conceptualize individuals as forging their own identities: only modernity created the conditions for breaking away from family governance and legacy professions, as well as departures from home into new spaces in which one's prior social standing was transformed. Modernity created the possibility of self-creation, but this is also a burden. Yet Taylor's hermeneutic approach understands that self-creation in modern societies is never pursued ex nihilo but enabled by an accessible stock of circulating possibilities and meanings. The persistent denunciat.ons of this existing stock of possibilities for white identity has generated a new crisis of self-formation.

Taylor defines an identity crisis as an "acute form of disorientation, which people often express in terms of not knowing who they are, but which can also be seen as a radical uncertainty of where they stand." What he calls our "inescapable frameworks," or the familiar narratives about who we are, constitute the meaning-laden horizons in which we discern how we ought to live. Thus, he argues that we should understand our identities as horizons "within which I am capable of taking a stand" (C. Taylor 1989, 27). When horizons shift, the ability to discern the proper action can disintegrate.

Taylor and Alasdair MacIntyre have argued that the narratives that human beings create about our pasts are necessary not only to understand who we have been but what our future portends, since our future can only be predicted, or even guessed at, on the basis of our past. As Taylor puts it, "In order to have a sense of who we are, we have to have a notion of how we have become, and of where we are going" (C. Taylor 1989, 47).

Thus, major disruptions in our accepted group histcries cannot but have disorienting effects, producing a malaise of doubt and apprehension. Taylor points out that the narratives we need to fashion our identities are not found objects, as if built out of the indisputable facts of history. Narratives that orient identities certainly make use of factual claims, or purported factual claims. But the key to both individual and collective narratives is that they provide an orienting map by *curating* the facts and *interpreting* their meaning and significance.

118 RACE AND RACISM

In this way, we create an understanding of our passage through time. Those interpretations of our histories that provide an orientation and direction for future choices reveal our values, that is, our collective *moral* selves.

Bernard Williams (1995) wrote that the stories that orient us are those that *we choose to take up*: this is what gives them their force and influence. Acknowledging this means also, however, that we can come to reject or doubt the stories we have lived by, that we can change our choices of emphasis and even reorient the narrative around a different center.

What is especially valuable about this tradition of thought about human personhood—as found in Taylor, MacIntyre, and Williams—is that it complicates the usual easy distinctions between reason and ir- rationality. Making interpretations of the meaning of one's life and of one's identity, and making decisions about what one ought to do based on a thick context of historical experience and cultural embeddedness, is not irrational on the face of it, though liberalism sometimes portrays anything but atomistic individualism just so. But our interpretations of our past are simply what MacIntyre calls the "antecedent conditions" that inform the norms and procedures we collectively devise to orient, and judge, our actions (MacIntyre [1971] 1978, 191–210; MacIntyre 1984). These conditions include the accompanying emotions that bubble up in a particular event, the painful memories from the past that suddenly appear in the present, but also the positive memories of specific family members we wish to emulate. Overcoming our histories is not achievable by an act of will. And this is part of what is always brought to bear on the way we make interpretations and judgments in the present as well as plans for the future.

Thus, it is not our embeddedness within history and culture that dooms us to irrationality; rather, on MacIntyre's view, irrationality is defined as the willful acceptance of important inconsistencies be- tween the diverse things one believes. Denialism of the new and more widely available historical explanations of the founding of modernity within the crucible of colonialism is a form of such irrationality. But eschewing denialism is not going to be sufficient. The crisis of white- ness concerns how to make an intelligible, plausible, and affirming group narrative that orients people toward a desirable future without

CRISIS OF WHITE IDENTITY 119

denying what we now know to be true. And this may of course redefine the 'we' itself, and who it includes.

The anxiety and instability that identity crises of all sorts engender can be assuaged by developing a new way to conceptualize one's identity, *if* we can find a way that renders it both coherent and livable. Just like teenagers, we need to find ways to integrate newly apparent aspects of family history in constructive ways. Uncovering painful truths can motivate making different choices and taking different actions, such as deciding to change the way we interact with our children or our spouses, for example, to accord with our moral values.

But the effort at a new integration of one's life narrative must address in some plausible way our relationships to others, to places, or whatever else may have brought on the crisis. Young people having identity crises may need to reassess their relations to specific members of their families, especially those involving difficult relationships, while migrants and displaced persons must consider new relations not only to people but to locations, communities, countries, and sometimes religions. Migrants cannot solve their social navigational problems by pretending that everything is the same as before.

Fundamentally, identity crises can only be assuaged by creating new narratives that render our lives coherent and livable once again.

The familiar experience of relational dislocation is relatively new to many whites, at least those beyond their teenage years. For white people, the value and meaning of national and ethno-racial positionality has remained largely stable in a world that is, for others, swirling with change. Throughout the last century, the West largely maintained its self-understanding as the global leader in science, technology, innovation, the arts, and political progress. Europeans and European Americans were still singled out as carrying this positive lineage. The blip of Nazism was restricted to a narrowly defined grouping, while other massive atrocities and genocides were relatively invisible or unremarked. But this basic orientation is now under threat, and this has diminished the expectations for a congenial and comfortable cohabitation with others at work, at school, even in one's own neighborhood. Whites can no longer rely on being in charge or being associated with enlightened, advanced societies. They are now associated with the massive toll of modern/colonial violence and the

120 RACE AND RACISM

displacement and destruction of cultures. The expected ease of social interactions is now replaced with tense apprehension, which may lead to a caustic disregard. Hence, a more fully adequate *social* integration of diverse groups is not the automatic result of a diversification of the public sphere: some can insulate themselves from different points of view, carefully curating their media consumption and conversational topics.

A real solution to any identity crisis, however, will not be successful by denialism, avoidance, and segregation from uncomfortable interactions. Rather, what is needed is reflection and the creation of altered narratives. Although identity crises involve and even require individual action, or what philosophers call agency, there are also ways in which individual agency is dependent on the ideas, concepts, and historical facts that are accessible in one's social context. Young people of mixed religions and races are aided when narratives are made available to them that cast their complex identities in a positive light rather than as inevitably tragic or unworkable. Young people can also be affected by prevailing ideas about divorce or about the effects of growing up in a single-parent household. Migrants and displaced persons are hindered by forms of exclusionary nativism and nationalism and aided by ideas of multiculturalism. It is not hyperbole to say, then, that the solution to the crisis of white identity will require a collective response. As Ariel Dorfman wrote on the fiftieth anniversary of the 1973 coup in Chile, today, "we need to find a way to forge a shared understanding of our past so we can start creating a shared vision . . . for the many tomorrows that await us" (Dorfman 2023).

Global memories

The crisis of white identity cannot be rightly understood if we imagine it to be a national crisis, or a set of discrete national crises that are besetting only certain nations. Although there needs to be specific local analyses of both the prompts of the crises and possible solutions, this is a global crisis sparked by the exposure of colonial myths and the steady ideological resistance of the dominated. While the era of settler colonialism continues, today's colonial practices to control the flows of

CRISIS OF WHITE IDENTITY 121

resources often manifest through more covert ways that allow an interpretive sleight of hand. This, too, is yielding to exposure.

Ariel Dorfman narrowly escaped torture and murder when a military coup took place in his home country of Chile. This was the infamous coup orchestrated with the help of the Central Intelligence Agency of the United States, a coup that deposed the democratically elected socialist President, Salvador Allende, on September 11, 1973, signaling to anyone across the hemisphere, and indeed, the world, that the United States would not tolerate a socialist government even if it came about peacefully through an electoral process. Covert operations in Chile actually began in September 1970, two months before Allende was even inaugurated. The Allende government, as Peter Winn and other historians have shown, was the result of an impressive degree of participatory democracy enacted especially by masses of workers, who continued their participation in policy implementations during his short, three-year presidency (Winn 1986). General Augusto Pinochet, who replaced Allende in the 1973 coup, without elections, ruled Chile for the next seventeen years. His government tortured tens of thousands, imprisoned upwards of eighty thousand, and executed more than three thousand people, some by throwing them out of planes into the sea. Chileans who were critical of Pinochet were effectively terrorized into self-censorship, undermining any semblance of a democratic public sphere. Chile's dictatorship forced one million Chileans into exile, most of whom had to leave their belongings and loved ones behind. They became immigrants.

I myself know something about military dictatorships, since my family in Panama lived under one for more than two decades. Soon after ours began in 1968, my father was summarily fired from his university position, and the family had to learn to live under autocratic rule, carefully negotiating interrogations, police stops, and colonels who would sometimes show up in the kitchen, seeking female prey. In relation to Chile and the whole of Latin America, but particularly in relation to Central America (which is still conceived of as the United States' "backyard"), the actions taken by the most powerful nation in the hemisphere were notoriously undemocratic and inhumane, assisting brutal regimes and undermining many social movements that attempted to make economic changes in favor of the poor.

122 RACE AND RACISM

Dictatorships were judged by how compliant they were to US interests, no matter their actions at home.

What gives the United States the right?

In the Western hemisphere, Latin America has long been spoofed in Hollywood movies as a place where coups d'état are routine, replete with comedic dictators and generals who pass as buffoons. I always felt discomfort when smiling singers like Carmen Miranda, who wore fruit on her head, came on our television where I grew up in Florida, representing the desirable but silly exotics south of the border, presented as obviously incapable of directing their own affairs. Richard Dreyfuss put on brownface to play a South American dictator in the 1988 comedy *Moon over Parador*, in which both guerilla fighters and state-sponsored violence were played for laughs. Woody Allen's first movie, *Bananas*, also used brownface to portray the heroic schlemiel Fielding Mellish, attempting to pass himself off as a revolutionary guerilla in a small Latin American nation. He fooled them so well that he became president of the country. Such images provide a pleasing contrast for nations that are believed to be governed by the rule of law, no matter that it has been those very nations that have recognized, funded, and sometimes fomented dictatorships around the world.

Such cultural representations of backward regions of the world are symptoms, not causes. But one can see the invisible hand of imperial craftwork here, to produce an image of European-based whiteness as altogether distinct from the rest of the globe. There is no question that Chile, Brazil, Argentina, Panama, the Dominican Republic, and the other countries that suffered under dictatorships had, and have, their own share of evil homegrown oligarchs. The very practice of political murder by throwing "undesirables" into the sea has a long history in the internecine battles within Chile and other nations in South America (Allende 2003, 42). Yet as Frederic Jameson wrote in his review of Gárcia Márquez, "despite Colombia's eternal civil war, the enemy is always the U.S." (Jameson 2024).

And so the question that has tormented me for decades is to wonder, would progressive, socialist movements have been successful without the CIA? Would my father have been able to continue teaching courses on the French Revolution at the University of Panama? Would the

CRISIS OF WHITE IDENTITY 123

activists who were murdered or scattered have been able to create lasting democratic institutions?

I hate counterfactuals.

As a staff member serving Allende's presidency, Dorfman was one of those who survived by escaping into an unhappy, unwanted exile. Today he calls for the creation of "shared understandings" of Chile's history, but he fully understands the challenge that such horrific historic events pose to this effort in his home country. In the statement quoted above, Dorfman is speaking to Chileans, all Chileans. But, given the transnational support for Pinochet's coup and subsequent dictatorship, Dorfman's call requires a transnational response. It requires that the crimes of colonial and imperial nations be made visible and called to account. This is what fuels both crises of white identity, the narrative crisis and the legitimation crisis.

Chile can serve our exploration in this chapter in another way as well. Chileans today share openly and publicly the trauma of their past and continue to argue over its cause, its legacy, and most importantly, the means by which they might avoid its repetition. Many in Latin America constrain their hopes by a pessimistic realism about the possibility of achieving a robust political sovereignty in the shadow of the imperial colossus to the north. Many know from cruel experience that democratic desires must be tailored to accommodate US foreign policy priorities. The flows of needed corporate capital depend on assessments of 'risk,' the risk of nationalizing key material resources as Allende was doing with the copper mines before he was deposed. Yet some hold out hope for a future different from the past.

This transnational sensibility—this internationalism, as it used to be called—is one we need to cultivate to understand the interdependence between political crises as well as consumption patterns and ways of life in far-flung locations. The migrant crisis is often portrayed as an invasion of foreigners, when the truth is that those who come often have motivations that can be traced back to transnational relationships (Gonzalez 2011; Luiselli 2017). These can include covert operations such as Chile experienced, as well as extractive capitalism and global financial systems that exploit and impoverish, not to mention climate catastrophes.

124 RACE AND RACISM

I would qualify all of this, however, in the following way. Certainly, a transnational consciousness is needed to supplement a narrowly national consciousness, to understand local economies as well as local politics, but it cannot replace or wipe away the need for a nation-based reckoning as well. Governments in every part of Latin America committed social crimes in the post-independence era after winning a long a bloody war against Spain in the early 1800s. These crimes encompass colonial displacements and the massacres of indigenous groups and their continuing racist treatment and segregation. And there is land theft still occurring today. But the difference experienced by most of the Global South remains: while their nation-states are guilty of local crimes, they have enjoyed only limited sovereignty in a global order governed by the interests of others (Grandin 2019).

The United States is another matter, as are all of the nations of the Global North with colonial histories. The white-majority countries of the world need memory museums that can encompass transnational atrocities, extractions, territorial appropriations, and covert operations that sabotaged democratic movements, none of which have yet ended.

How can the world, or any nation-state in the Global North, achieve a shared understanding of the "planet-sized system" of colonialism and slavery, as Olúfẹ́mi O. Táíwò puts it, that created today's wealth disparities? How can a set of common interests be forged given this history? This planet-sized system put into place a complex set of processes that still, today, governs the transnational flows of resources moving around the world. Backward-looking reparations, to redress historical wrongs, is not enough; it may even be the wrong solution if it exacerbates transnational injustice by keeping a lock on local resources for internal wrongs. The point is to look at how our current global and national economies were constructed and to find a way to construct a new world.

This is a tall order, but it is already being forged in the creation of new trading blocs in the Global South. Yet the crisis of white identity that is driving far-right extremism as well as anti-China rhetoric on both sides of the Atlantic needs to be understood as a reactive response to emergent economic competitors as well as the truth-telling about

CRISIS OF WHITE IDENTITY 125

this colonial history, a history that indicts nation-states and calls into question the legitimacy of border control. Too many mythic narratives have been used to legitimate the political claims to power and sovereignty of rich nations. As these crumble under the weight of historical scholarship, governments try to divert their populations' attention, marginalize the humanities, control school curriculum, invent new enemies, and invest in new security technology. Such strategies cannot defeat forever the world's decolonized majority.

Decolonizing whiteness

These topics used to be largely relegated to the left fringe. Well-researched facts and figures were published in pamphlets, sometimes using nothing more than a mimeograph machine, and sold (or given away) on the "literature tables" I and my comrades staffed on our college campuses starting in the 1960s, often side by side with army recruitment tables and sailing clubs. The well-developed political histories and the economic and social analyses we hawked were considered cultish and were rarely part of the mainstream academic debates in history or philosophy or any of the social sciences. But today, leading historians and political scientists are engaging in myth busting. Their scholarly research is now getting reviewed in major publications, winning prizes, and inspiring new screenplays. The word is getting out.

This mainstreaming of what was heretofore passed off as a "far-left" critique is creating a crisis, a reactive set of social movements attempting to shut out the new information and thus delay and disable the project of memorializing the crimes of the past. Such reactions also are attempting to disable the project of finding a new way forward. Predictably, the order of the day is "containment": to minimize the necessary historical revisions. As Dirk Moses (2007) has argued, the strategy pursued by the German government to denazify the nation is motivated by a set of contradictory goals. Germany has supported the creation of a 'memory culture' that tells the truth about the Nazi Holocaust, but it has also wanted to secure and relegitimate Germany's capacity to be a leader on the international stage as well as within the

126 RACE AND RACISM

European region. As he shows, many historians have shown how the official narrative of the Holocaust had to be carefully tapered to excise its connection to earlier colonial projects and practices. Calling out its Nazi past can serve the effort to maintain German regional and national power as one of the largest nations in the European Union and one of the richest in the world, by presenting today's Germany as a morally responsible, civic-minded global player whose demonic genocidal mania is a thing of the past, a blip or a diversion. There are some truly excellent Holocaust memorials in many parts of Germany, but this foreshortened agenda has not been able to stem the tide of support growing for the far right within Germany itself. Anti-migrant policies are disentangled from Nazism, as if today's ethnic and religious exclusions, and fears, are rational and justifiable in contrast to those of times past.

But what gives Germany the right? What gives it the right to the exclusive control of a national wealth that reaches back to the genocide of the Herero in Namibia and the colonization of Togo, Cameroon, and other countries?

The memory culture developed in the United States is often similarly limited. Only after the Black Lives Matter protests gained steam in 2020 did a sitting US president use the term "white supremacy" to describe the country's national history. Yet these rhetorical turns, however useful, can also operate in the form of confessions about wrongs in the distant past, which confer absolution on the present and redirect our attention away from current empire building and imperial attitudes.

Which is all to say that acknowledging past wrongs can be done in a way that thwarts rather than assists real solutions to the narrative problem of Western nation-states. Facing the unvarnished record of past policies, practices, and ideologies needs a forward-looking agenda aiming to make effective structural changes rather than simply apologies for the past. The question is not simply what happened, who participated, and who benefited, but how did past events shape today's world and its current migrations? Too often, past injustices are chalked up to regrettable but understandable side effects of modernization in a way that portrays the present world as legitimate.

CRISIS OF WHITE IDENTITY   127

As the new histories mount up, however, the ongoing effects of colonial systems are no longer invisible. For both Dorfman and Táíwò, both of whom have a lineage that places them squarely with the targets of colonialism and imperialism, the project now is to learn from the past so that peoples who *were* at odds might craft a shared understanding on at least some of the central features of national and global history and from this, articulate a common set of interests toward reconstruction. For those who believe such a quest to be impossibly utopian and thus hopeless before it is begun, I would point them to the ideology of the European Renaissance and Enlightenment, the master narrative of the modern period that has credited Europe, and European settlers, with the invention of science and democracy, even reason itself. That narrative explained and often justified both global and national policies, such as the seizure of indigenous lands and the invention of *latifundias, gamonales,* and homestead laws, the organization of enclosures and labor reduced to waged work, and the regulation of migrations and borders. Marx called this transformative period, with some admiration, an unleashing of the productive forces of capital.

At the dawn of the modern/colonial order, the world was given a structural reordering that was planned and defended with numerous philosophical ideas and theories. Philosophy, dare I say, has power. But the ideas that legitimated the modern world are in a long overdue crisis (Fanon 1963; Eze 1997). It is these ideas that need replacement. Not all Enlightenment ideas should be shelved, of course, and today, throughout the humanities, there is lively debate over how to reassess and reinterpret, over what can be maintained and what cannot, no doubt fueling the right's desire to fire us all.

In what follows, I will take on just one small part of this project of crafting new narratives, the part that concerns white identity. This is no small part, since white people were and still are represented as the primary agents of modernization, the builders of cities and factories, whether workers, miners, soldiers, or scientists, engineers, philosophers, and legislators. New understandings of modernity cannot help but dislodge the historical narratives that have undergirded whiteness (Frankenberg 1997).

128   RACE AND RACISM

It is critical to understand whiteness within a decolonial framework such as I have tried to lay out, that is, a framework that encompasses more than any given national historical formation, with its specific ethno-racial identity. National histories are simply too narrow. Only a decolonial frame will shed light on the way to achieve a "shared understanding" of the past that can lead to a "shared vision" of the future, as Dorfman calls for.

To summarize what I have been arguing up to this point, we must understand the crises of white identity as neither artificially manufactured by malevolent forces nor based on a mistaken identity formation, such as a false idea about biological race. Rather, it is rooted in what I have called a narrative crisis and a legitimation crisis. Together these crises have shaken the collective understanding of modern Western history to its core, producing a truly existential crisis about what it means to be white. What does it mean to be connected to these histories of colonialism and slavery, to have benefited from them, to have a citizenship status and economic security today that were constituted in relation to these histories of modern empire? The narrative crisis—concerning how we tell the story of modern history—if it is told with any amount of honesty, will necessarily create a legitimation crisis for every wealthy nation-state, most of which are now made up of white majorities.

A decolonial approach will give us a more honest and thorough understanding of the crisis. And it will show, I will argue, that overcoming the far-right extremist threats of fascism, of the sort that beset Chile as well as Germany, cannot be successful by reinstating the kind of liberal democratic regimes that brag about their political superiority, their deep respect for democracy, while seeking to protect at all costs the hegemony of the current global economic order.

White reaction to the existential threats that target white identity recognize, correctly and presciently, that the current radical reconstructions of national historical narratives call for more sweeping structural change at both the political and the economic level. On these points, we might actually be able to begin a productive conversation from which to craft a shared vision for a different and more just future. This vision, however, will have to *produce* common interests, rather than assume they are already there. And it will have to forgo the desire for a return to the past.

The centrality of whiteness

Let us now step back from the past and into the present and consider the epidemic of mass shootings. On May 14, 2022, in the beleaguered, deindustrialized city of Buffalo, New York, thirteen people were randomly shot while doing their Saturday grocery shopping. Ten Black people were killed, ranging in age from thirty-two to eighty-six. As he rampaged through the Tops Friendly Markets grocery store, the murderer, eighteen-year-old Payton Gendron, apologized to the white people he had shot, explaining that he had shot *them* accidentally, making clear that this was not actually a random shooting. Gendron drove several hours to Buffalo from another part of the state after spending months preparing the attack by researching potential target areas and purchasing body armor and other tactical gear along with a military-style AR15 semiautomatic rifle. He chose this particular low-priced grocery store in Buffalo because it was in a largely Black neighborhood. During the attack, Gendron live streamed the murders from his phone.

We could tell this story in multiple ways, focusing on the murderer's youth, his gender, his rural upbringing, his religion, or his obsessive use of social media. We might also consider his ability to access semiautomatic weapons despite an earlier display of antisocial behavior in high school that had triggered a psychiatric evaluation. But the one aspect that cannot reasonably be set aside from the story is Gendron's self-identification as white. This fact is relevant to some of the other aspects of the story, such as his ability to purchase a semiautomatic rifle despite his troubles with authorities. But Gendron himself foregrounded his race in the 180-page manifesto that he posted online shortly before the murders, expressing his desire to reestablish the United States as a white Christian nation.

In this manifesto, Gendron expressed his hatred of Jews, Mexicans, and Asian Americans as well as African Americans, making reference to familiar stereotypes about these groups in the long racist history of the public sphere in many Western societies. And, like the murderer of random Mexicans who were shopping in El Paso, Texas, and the murderer of worshipping Muslims in Christ Church, New Zealand, Gendron referred to the 'Great Replacement Theory.' Thus, he put his

130　RACE AND RACISM

actions within a transnational framework that imagines a global threat against himself and those he considers part of his community.

To be sure, if we focus on the problem of similar sorts of mass murder in the United States in recent years, we will find that both the murderers and the murdered are racially diverse. But there are patterns. The victims have included Jews worshipping in a synagogue in Pittsburgh, queer youth in a Florida nightclub, Asian American women working in a massage parlor, African Americans in church, as well as Central Americans and Mexican Americans who live in Texas. But the murdered have also included white children in an elementary school and white women in several college areas. And it is also the case that mass murderers and serial killers are not uniformly white, as used to be the case, though all the murders of people of color that I just listed were by white men.

So although there are in truth many stories to tell here, almost all involving social identities of one sort or another, a significant portion of the complex story of mass murder in the United States involves non-white victims and white male perpetrators. And though the regulation of gun sales does make a difference, the phenomena is transatlantic, as we can see from Anders Behring Breivik's 2011 attack on Norwegian liberal youth and the 2020 racist shootings in Frankfurt.

The epidemic of such murders justifies my claim that white identity is experienced as the target of a persistent and widespread cultural, economic, psychological, and political threat. The usual forms of life that have long existed in white-majority societies are being forcibly changed in such a way that feels frightening and even catastrophic. Educational institutions at every level are incorporating the new historical scholarship, including diverse group histories, and thus calling into question national myths in a way that feels unpatriotic. And the very public focus on attitudinal and structural racism is felt to be accusatory, producing a minefield for whites in their immediate social and personal interactions. Certainly, few will purchase an automatic weapon, but more than a few are moving to what they hope will be a more white-friendly town, province, state, or city. Both conservative and progressive populations are migrating internally to areas with compatible politics. The result is a heightened culture clash.

CRISIS OF WHITE IDENTITY 131

Some theorists and activists argue that we can best address the crisis of whiteness by eliminating the category through exposing the speciousness of biological race. As if. Although I addressed the general issue of racial concepts in chapter 1, in the following section I will address whiteness in particular.

The meaning of whiteness

I have emphasized that the operable meaning of all racial terms, including *whiteness*, has a strong element that is local. Who is included in the category will change in relation to both location and time period, along with the physical signs used to determine boundary conditions, and the connotations enlivened by the term (Haney-López 2006; Allende 2003, 34). In the United States, North Africans are officially designated white, though often not treated as white, while in the Dominican Republic, many people self-identify as white although this can end abruptly when they leave the island (Candelaria 2007). Some groups, such as Mexican Americans, were officially designated white at some points during the history of the United States, but without enjoying any of the associated privileges (Gómez 2007). The belief that Jews are white is still contested by some white Christian nationalists. Whiteness has been legally defined in terms of biological lineage in North America, but by appearance—and especially skin color—in Brazil and other parts of Latin America (Telles 2006). In Europe whiteness is said to extend to the Middle East as well as North Africa, though Muslim identity can itself operate as an essentializing racial term.

Given all these complications, it may seem as if the general concept of whiteness is hopelessly contradictory and inexact, with little relation to our street-level experiences of judgment, perception, and attitude, and thus impossible to define with any precision.

Although our concepts are variously interpreted and applied depending on the local context, the modern/colonial world not only propagated ideas about global ranking but institutionalized its beliefs about the racial status of people, through policies controlling labor markets, political participation, and the right of mobility. Individual membership varied by local conditions but the category itself retained

132   RACE AND RACISM

its power, and as the historian Jefferson Cowie (2022) has shown, this included its right to dominate others. The modern/colonial world rendered Christian whiteness quite distinct from other ethno-racial categories of identity, posing particular problems when we try to fashion a pluricultural and democratic social amalgamation. Those who had a claim to whiteness had such a special status that some believe whiteness without such associations and government protections will become a liability. Whiteness can then become a target.

Some argue that we should let the category of whiteness go the way of the dinosaurs. The 'race traitor' position advanced by Noel Ignatiev and John Garvey (1996) holds that we can opt out of racial privileges by our anti-racist actions and, in this way, opt out of the liability of whiteness. Barbara Applebaum (2010) also argues that whiteness is something we do, not something we are. It emerges from an environment of distributed possibilities rather than from anything truly internal. If whiteness is constituted by its external conditions, and if it requires our participation, can we move away from having a white identity?

I would be as happy as the next person to cease and desist using the category, but as I argued in a previous book, the question is how to stop 'doing whiteness' when we have limited individual agency (Alcoff 2015). And we need to ask whether the refusal to self-identify really means that the identity is no longer in play. There is a structural scaffolding of white advantage that affects our everyday interactions in airports, at job interviews, in schools, during encounters with police, even on social dating apps, whether we want it or not. Beyond any intentionality, whiteness is part of how the social world works. And whiteness has a particularly long history of effectively concealing its power and influence while controlling outcomes in its favor: in her 1992 book, Toni Morrison called this "playing in the dark." This closeted feature of whiteness is the primary motivation behind critical race theory: to bring the functional and structural character of whiteness into the light of day, with its formative effect on juridical and historical interpretations as well as social interactions and the formation of subjectivity. Sunshine is the best cure.

Race is only a single feature of anyone's identity, but the constitutive nature of intersectionality means that it interacts with all aspects

CRISIS OF WHITE IDENTITY   133

of our socially recognized identities to alter their meanings and their effects. Our racial identity interacts with ethnicity, gender, class, sexuality, and nationality in the social imaginary of expected norms of behavior, likely skills, likely dispositions. We imagine white working-class men who live in rural areas differently than we imagine white female professionals living in cities. The way we are perceived by others, and the way we anticipate being perceived, affect our development, our trust in ourselves, our confidence, our aversion to risk, our sense of optimism, our baseline knowledge, and what we take for granted. Thus, our *perceived* race, with its context-based advantages or disadvantages, produce elements of our subjectivity, and remains a critical feature to include in our self-understanding.

It is notable that *Blackness* became the term of choice of the Black Lives Matter movement that united over fifty organizations to coordinate anti-racist social organizing against police violence. The term *Black* is distinct in meaning from the term *African American* and signifies a grouping of people that are all potential targets of hatred, fear, and violence because of their visible features, no matter their nationality or lineage. And this movement has viewed Blackness not as only a form of victimization but as a political subjectivity with epistemic salience. This is why it is considered critical for Black people to be in charge of the movement, to be speaking, writing, documenting, filming, developing strategies and organizational forms, and setting out acceptable tactics. So 'Blackness' is understood as having an objective reality, but also as a form of subjectivity with associated epistemic content and orientation as well as affect. Affect constantly comes up in reference to representations of racism and suffering: What affect will be enlivened by a given tactic, and for whom? These questions also indicate the intersections of race with elements of subjectivity in the sphere of emotional responses.

We need to recognize how deeply racialization works in constituting selves and at the same time recognize its complex contextual variability and its dynamic character.

So, given that, at least for a time, we must continue to talk about white identity, how do we go about it? Too often, when we talk about whiteness, we talk past one another, referring to different things. So, it can be helpful to unpack the concept, to slow down and to process

134   RACE AND RACISM

the discomfort and fear this topic can enliven, for both white and non-white alike. Let me offer a schema for doing so, dividing whiteness into three parts: the empirical, the imaginary, and the subjective.[1]

Empirical whiteness is what we are talking about when we are talking about wages and wealth, housing and health care, voting patterns, and also history. With the help of social scientists, statisticians, and demographers, we can now map whiteness, measure it, locate it, and date it. We can establish median real estate values in white-majority neighborhoods and compare those to other neighborhoods. We can find its fertility rate and its mortality rate, its employment patterns, and its rate of incarceration and compare these to other groups. Empirical whiteness is a measurable object in the world.

In some countries in Europe, such as France, such empirical metrics are hard to obtain since the state has made it difficult to collect such data. Yet clever demographers find a way: besides surnames that can be used to identify North Africans, for example, the presence of sickle cell anemia in a given neighborhood has been used as a proxy for Black identity. I have been told they discovered this method from clever racists who wanted to be able to make rough predictions about where non-white people lived.

It would be easier if the state collected the data and demographers would not have to mimic the tactics of the far right, but the worry of the French state is that racial concepts will appear more real, and more stable, if they are used in official documents. This is a well-motivated worry, but the policy of refusing to collect race-based statistics has not led to less racism or to changes in the ideation of who the 'true' or paradigmatic Frenchmen are.

This brings us to the second dimension of whiteness: its meaning in the cultural or collective imaginary and thus its power as an ideology. Beyond the empirical facts about whiteness, there is an imaginary of whiteness that comes in both explicit and implicit forms, from unapologetically explicit ideologies of white supremacy to interpretive frameworks that subtly place white sensibilities, and white lives, at the center. As Danielle Allen has shown, even in the *New York Times*,

---

[1] Some of the following section riffs off the analysis I develop in (Alcoff 2015).

CRISIS OF WHITE IDENTITY 135

unemployment statistics in the double digits are not given crisis priority until they affect whites (Allen 2004, 39–49).

Imaginary whiteness renders the paradigmatic Frenchman, or human being, or worker, white, while all others are inflected with an added conditional. This can make whiteness the controlling term even when it remains invisible. An assumed default position for whiteness also makes the work of dialogue and negotiation more difficult, not simply because interlocutors have different perspectives or opinions but because some can see the background assumptions more clearly than others. The imaginary needs to be made visible so that it can become subject to analysis.

The content associated with whiteness in the cultural imaginary has certainly shifted over generations, and yet some important content generally remains in place, such as credit for science and technological innovation or rational statecraft.

The result of these persistent empirical realities and powerful imaginaries is to produce a form of subjectivity that is marked by whiteness, and this is the third part of my schemata. There is an increasingly common way of speaking, sometimes in good humor, sometimes not, about white ways of being in the world, such as assumptions of entitlement or cluelessness about certain topics. Many comedians have made their careers in this way, not all of them non-white. But for some decades now, there have been a significant number of empirical studies that have measured aspects of white subjectivity (Richeson and Trawaltar 2008; Gallagher 1994). Initially this was done by social psychologists, such as Claude Steele (2010), the former director of the Center for Advanced Study in the Behavioral Sciences at Stanford. Steele and his colleagues conducted experiments over several decades that revealed a distinct content to white subjectivity—not universal to all whites but still statistically significant. This content includes different ways of interacting with non-whites (verbally and nonverbally) and problematic perceptual assessments, such as significantly overestimating how many non-white people are in a room (Gallagher 1994). When forced to interact for significant periods of time with nonwhite strangers, whites have been shown to exhibit cognitive deterioration, such as a reduced ability to perform simple math tests, indicating that the cross-racial interaction has been cognitively taxing

136 RACE AND RACISM

(Richeson and Trawalter 2008). Whites tend not to hold eye-contact with non-white people, to stand further away, to be tense and self-conscious, and to assume (perhaps quite rightfully) that conversations will be uncomfortable. As phenomenologist Shannon Sullivan (2005) argues, there are clear patterns of hostility exhibited by whites toward non-whites. There are also patterns of behavior that indicate enlarged assumptions of entitlement: to space, to resources, to attention, and to protection.

Thus, whiteness is real. It can be measured. It serves as a predictor. It is not simply a false idea. Yet it is demonstrably capable of change. Opinion polls across the Global North show marked differences from a generation ago in white attitudes and beliefs about the persistent prevalence of racism in society, including in key institutions such as schools and prisons. Polls also show marked changes in attitudes toward interracial marriage and integrated schools. But, as we know, progress is neither inevitable nor stable.

We need to keep in mind these three related but distinct elements—the empirical, the imaginary, and the effect on subjectivity—without conflating them. We should not be concerned only with the imaginary of whiteness, as some anti-racist works seems to be. I believe we also need to bring actual white people into the picture, into spaces of dialogue, to share their lived experience and subjectivity (for exemplary models of this, Norris 2024; Haney-López 2019; Allen 2004). So that's the point of separating out the three elements: the empirical (historical, economic), the ideology-laden imaginary of whiteness, and the subject formation. Often in the humanities, we are solely focused at the level of the imaginary of whiteness and the ideology of white supremacy; the social sciences focus more on the empirical, and some of this work reveals aspects of the subject formation of whiteness. While these three aspects have connections, we need an overall account that can distinguish them.

The experience of living in a society as a white person spans extreme poverty and disregard from the state as well as an excessive representation among the rich and powerful. Whites are liberal city snobs, members of rural militias, gay and trans, women and children. Straight white men can be low-wage workers, mistreated prisoners, and economic conscripts in imperial wars. White women can exert

CRISIS OF WHITE IDENTITY 137

military power as well as power over financial markets, even while most are underpaid and subject to sexism. These differences of experience within the category yield extreme conflicts of interest over economic and social issues. The much-discussed political polarization in many white-majority nations is mainly a division among whites, often over social democratic policies and immigration. In other words, the most significant social conflicts tearing our societies apart are white-against-white. White nationalists often vent their greatest anger at the apostates in their midst.

It is wishful thinking to believe that the political divide runs parallel to class or that we can set race aside as we develop a class-based agenda for change. Both labor and livelihoods are heavily organized by racial identities, as empirical studies continue to reveal. The most significant indicator of electoral tendencies is not class by itself but whether one lives in a rural area, whether one is male, whether one belongs to a labor union, and whether one has gone to college. These criteria, I'd suggest, track experiences of interaction more than they do class. Urban life makes it difficult to live cloistered in racially homogenous spaces; integrated schools, public transportation, and workplaces are more familiar to white workers in cities, and union membership creates, at least some of the time, real (and rare) opportunities for participating in collective decision-making that involves people from diverse backgrounds. Class is without doubt a critical element in the political disaffection and fears that drive conservative nationalism, but its role is complex, and we must guard against the tendency, or the desire, to locate racism among the poor and the uneducated, thus outside of elite institutions and outside of power.

White wage workers are no longer a protected category; their economic situation is declining nearly everywhere. In the United States, mortality and drug abuse are getting worse instead of better, and there were disproportionate numbers of white deaths in the US military incursions into Iraq and Afghanistan, quite different from Vietnam. We might imagine both economic and cultural reasons for this. The white grouping who continues to have the greatest advantages are elites of the professional-managerial classes (Liu 2021). These classes are protected from losing the values of their retirement savings, protected from military service, protected from having to send their children

138   RACE AND RACISM

to more highly integrated and challenged schools, and also protected from having to live in poorer and more polluted areas of towns and cities. This class divide generates different interests and motivations. What is perhaps most significant about the diminished livelihoods of white workers is the experience, since the 1970s and the rise of global trade, of change, of declining opportunities, of lowered expectations. This creates the potential for stronger multi-racial alignments. But these need to address up front the causes and conditions of decline, and pose the question—do we want a return to the past, an agenda that protects white workers first, or a new agenda that aligns interests in new ways? As the policy analyst Heather McGhee argues persuasively, racism adversely affects everyone.[2]

Avoiding the topic of race, and whiteness in particular, is especially foolish given the influence of the Replacement Theory, so let us turn to that next.

The Great Replacement Theory

The Replacement Theory may feel too obviously wrong, too easily discredited, to merit theoretical analysis. However, I suggest that it is key to making sense of the crisis of white identity. The Replacement Theory is a claim not just about the replacement of nationalities, or ethnicities, but of racialized groupings, or groups designated by a racial concept even if only by subtle inference, such as the phrase its advocates often use: 'indigenous European.'

The crisis across North America and Europe today is fueled by language offered by the Great Replacement Theory, generally credited to another French writer named Camus—Renaud Camus, no relation to Albert—who wrote widely influential books that developed the concept (R. Camus 2018). Camus's principal claim is that replacement is a planned event, that there is a conspiracy to displace the numbers and influence of white Christian populations in order to diminish their group-based political power. The agency behind the conspiracy is

---

[2] For some of the best road maps for creating a new agenda that unapologetically includes white interests, Haney López 2019; McGhee 2021; Barber 2016.

CRISIS OF WHITE IDENTITY   139

sometimes portrayed as a cabal of global elites, sometimes as Jews, but as we know, these categories are almost coterminous for antisemitic-leaning audiences.

In the midst of our current global conflicts and climate crises, which are spurring migration especially from poorer, war-torn areas of the world, the influence of this concept of replacement is growing across many Western countries (Beltrán 2020; Chavez 2008). It has been referenced by numerous politicians in Europe running for office, including those considered centrists, and is touted publicly by some influential journalists. Proponents include Éric Zemmour of France, Tucker Carlson in the United States, Hermann Patrick Kelly in Ireland, Paul Golding in the UK, Giorgia Meloni in Italy, Lauren Cherie Southern in Canada, Davor Domazet-Lošo in Croatia, and, of course, Viktor Orbán in Hungary. Opinion polls throughout the US and Europe show significant support among the general population, with about one third of respondents expressing the belief that the demographic changes taking place along ethnic, racial, and religious lines are part of a plot. Despite the absurdity of the conspiratorial aspect of the thesis, the actual demographic shifts and immigration patterns, as well as the persistent decline in white births, are taken to provide putative support. However people understand the cause, many feel the changes and perceive them as an invasion of their safe spaces.

The idea is circulated without censure on so many varied online platforms that journalists are beginning to call the Replacement Theory part of the new mainstream. The conservative commentator Tucker Carlson, long a central figure on the conservative US network Fox News, began using this theory explicitly in the fall of 2021 to supplement his long-standing tirade against US immigration policies. Carlson explained to his viewers that "in political terms this policy is called the 'great replacement,' the replacement of legacy Americans with more obedient people from faraway countries." He said this change in "the racial mix of the country" is a "suicidal" path for the nation.

Replacement is hardly a new concern; it has certainly been a recurrent worry in the United States since the influx of southern Europeans and the Irish began in the late 1800s. These migrants were also referred to as vermin, as likely to be anarchists, as too ignorant for democracy

140 RACE AND RACISM

and thus simply incapable of assimilation to an Anglo-dominated social system (Ngai 2004, 2021; Brodkin 1998). After many decades, most southern Europeans were accepted as white, and thus legitimate members of the nation, probably in no small part because their numbers in many cities constituted significant political factions that could cement powerful coalitions.

In 1924, however, the United States turned the tide on immigration by passing sweeping measures that set quotas using the category of 'national origins.' The most restrictive quotas were set not only on applicants from Asia, Africa, and Latin America but from southern and eastern Europe as well, some of whom were viewed by social conventions at the time as non-white, such as, particularly, Italians and Jews.

Restricted immigration policies were not pursued as a behind-the-scenes conspiracy but openly defended on the grounds that the particular mix of ethnic and religious groups that dominated the United States at the time—Christian and northern European—would be replaced if migration patterns were allowed to continue unabated. The newcomers had large families, it was said, and would out-reproduce the rest, rendering the 'founders' of the nation a beleaguered minority. The Eastern Orthodox and Greek Orthodox Christians were also anathema to both many Roman Catholics and Protestants.

As the political theorist Cristina Beltrán points out, the fear of replacement assumes a model of democracy defined by scarcity and a zero-sum logic. No sharing of power or common interests seems to be imaginable to either Camus or his followers. The fear invoked is clearly more than a fear of mere numbers but of reprisal, of colonial memories, of payback.

The conspiracy aspect of Camus's claim is supported by US conservatives who predict that the expected voting tendencies of non-white immigrants will forever alter electoral outcomes, providing a motive for the Democratic Party elites to support liberal immigration policies. Camus's book offers a more European focus that is primarily concerned with Muslim immigrants, which is of course a multiethnic and multiracial group identified only by their religion. Yet white nationalists tend to identify Muslims by their geographical or national lineage, which makes them inevitably Muslim whether

CRISIS OF WHITE IDENTITY   141

secular or observant. Here, Muslim identity operates very much as a racial designation, providing deterministic predictions of behavior that spans the entire group (Sheth 2009; Khalidi 2010). In the United States, the adherents of the replacement theory are certainly concerned with Muslims but also with non-whites in general, particularly those from Africa, Latin America, and Asia. Thus, for its adherents, the Replacement Theory takes ethnicity, race, and religion to be determinative of behaviors and beliefs.

In both North America and Europe, what primarily determines who will be in the vilified contrast class is Christian whiteness itself: everyone outside this group is a potential threat. Camus's theory is only the latest articulation of a general theory of "white genocide" that often portrays Jewish global elites as in alliance with non-Christian non-whites, and as the actual brains behind the operation. This is a replay of claims made during the Civil Rights Movement in the 1950s and 1960s, that the struggle to end segregation was being orchestrated by Jews, in which Black people were simply frontline soldiers following orders. One will look in vain for either empirical evidence or logical consistency in white genocide theories. These take numerous forms, but what unites them is a concern with the declining political power of whites, who are themselves conceptualized as if they constitute a united political bloc.

As this concept has taken root, sometimes the term *white* is itself replaced by *indigenous European* or *legacy American*, perhaps to offset the charge of racism and identify the injured group by its culture, nationality, or geographical longevity. Some of the more mainstream conservative groups in the US try to portray their concerns as 'simply' nationalist rather than racist: open white nationalists have been barred from attending CPAC (Conservative Political Action Committee) conferences. But there is a unified theme across these differences, that the group who should rightfully govern is today facing an existential threat. And this threat is portrayed as destabilizing our nations' economic health and political stability. It is important to note, then, that this is not just a concern about the distribution of scarce goods, though that concern is also voiced. This is a concern that the modern political regimes that are portrayed as having been legitimately constituted by democratic measures will be toppled.

142 RACE AND RACISM

The Replacement Theory undoubtedly connects with the sense of precarity some whites feel as their lives and livelihoods change for the worse. And it provides a narrative that offers both a causal explanation and a solution that obscures the colonial past and shields current economic power brokers, whether nationally or internationally. Camus, for example, calls non-whites who reside in Europe "colonizers" and "occupiers," making it clear that they are not where they belong, and suggesting their intention to dominate whites, who are portrayed as victims of colonialism, not perpetrators of it. He assumes that belonging in these lands is restricted, like a country club.

We should not be too quick to dismiss such concerns as nothing but old-fashioned racism and antisemitism. I suggest we interpret this set of influential ideas symptomatically, less for their explicit factual claims than for the values and ideals and worries they reveal. One of the charges conservatives often make against liberals is that they dismiss the desire for 'belonging.' This is not simply about having a right to live in a given place but about being part of a community that shares one's beliefs and values. Thus, liberals are said to offer nothing to replace the lost sense of belonging many are experiencing today. Yet conservatives generally sidestep the debate we need to have over the assumption that racial, ethnic, and religious homogeneity are required for such a sense of belonging to materialize.

Although white birth rates are down on both sides of the Atlantic, the fact is that white people are in no danger of extinction. It is true that the new immigrant populations are changing every national demographic, and whites will make up an increasingly small percentage of their home countries. But in the United States, whites will soon lose their majority status no matter what happens with immigration, since the majority of babies are already non-white. This may also occur in Europe in another half-century or so and may be driving the demands for deportation. But changing demographics is not an inherent existential threat. A reduced percentage is not elimination, nor does it entail becoming powerless. And further, political divisions among whites are not likely to disappear; a united white bloc is not likely to materialize.

The replacement theory is also an important influence in several current political conflicts that may appear to be distinct from immigration policies or racial demographics, such as gun sales, abortion rights, and education. Guns are promoted by manufacturers as "protection," as if in newly diversified neighborhoods, everyone will need an automatic rifle with a standard magazine capacity of thirty rounds that can be fired in less than half a minute. The legalization of abortion has long been debated in the context of social demographics and concerns over declining white birth rates. At a rally for Donald Trump in 2022, US Representative Mary Miller made a public statement that the US Supreme Court decision to limit abortion rights was a historic "victory for white life." She later said this was a slip of the tongue. But the government in Hungary also praised the new restrictions on abortion in the US and elsewhere, citing the Great Replacement Theory. The ongoing battles over school curriculum concerning both regional and global histories reflect the intense need to maintain control over the narrative of national formation.

Demographic changes no doubt have a powerful symbolic meaning for whites in particular, since whites as a group will lose their claim to legitimately dominate the public sphere or maintain a majority in governing bodies, courts, and other institutions that run our societies. All whites, I should stress, are not bothered by this, but the changing demographics will create a different sensibility about who can serve as the norm or the default, and the concept of 'minority' will come to have a different set of referents. Some whites are uncomfortable being in the minority because of the fear of reprisal or prejudice. White-majority nations have had long histories of structural racism that perpetrated an everyday violence against non-whites both inside nations as well as in transnational wars and economic relations. There is a legitimate fear that the diminution of white majorities will fundamentally alter the West, causing it to lose its standing in the world and damaging the economic prospects of white constituencies. It makes sense to predict change and new challenges; it does not make sense to predict an inevitable political and economic catastrophe for whites.

In what follows, I will suggest there is another concern as well that fuels our collective pessimism about the future. It can seem nonsensical to assume that a transformation in ethno-racial and religious demographics will have such drastic, and automatic, effects on our

144   RACE AND RACISM

national political and economic conditions, but this is based in long-standing ideas about the relationship between democratic forms of government and the ability of particular groups to act effectively as rational citizens. The very possibility of functioning democracies has been linked to specific narrative histories to explain why demographic shifts will spell political disaster. The explanations I will explore also explain why only whites have rightful belonging and why others can be legitimately excluded or kept in a minor role.

Thus, Camus's Great Replacement Theory has been fueled by older narratives, as we'll see, that offer a semblance of rational reasoning to justify exclusive white entitlements to land and to power. In this way, entitlements are tied to lineage, to longevity in a location, to what Carlson calls 'legacy.' White identity, then, whether in North America or in Europe, provides the grounds of legitimate political and economic entitlement. The crisis of white identity destabilizes the historical narratives that play this political role.

But before we turn to the narratives at work here, let me offer a symptomatic reading of the Replacement Theory, so that we can more fully understand its wide popular appeal. I suggest that this appeal involves five elements that make it particularly powerful for its intended audiences.

1) The Replacement Theory is a call to return to a prior era, *a quest to 'go back.'* Nostalgia is continuously evoked, for a previous moment in time when societies had less violence, when neighbors were friendly, when we did not have to lock our doors at night, and when young men could have a reasonable expectation of a job with a pension. Such nostalgia can be critiqued on the grounds of historical accuracy, and this is important to do, but I'd suggest we also consider some of the potentially usable and constructive elements that are expressed in this romantic conception of the past: a desire for being part of a community, for achieving economic stability for one's self and one's family, for a reasonable trust in the various institutions that affect one's life and livelihood, and for peace. Such desires are not in themselves illegitimate, and constitute issues we can build on. The following three elements are less defensible.

CRISIS OF WHITE IDENTITY 145

2) For societies built historically through settler colonialism, such as in the Americas, Australia, and New Zealand, the determination to thwart replacement also signals the project of *consolidating and defending the settlements*. The histories of all settler societies are replete with wars of aggression against local indigenous populations and neighbors. For example, the United States gained half of its current territory in the Mexican-American War, in which, after 1848, fully half of Mexico was annexed to the United States. The Mexican populations who lived in these regions were promised full citizenship and the ability to maintain their property rights; instead, most found their property confiscated so that their only way to survive was by becoming low-wage laborers working on land they previously owned. Clearly, the settlements that the Replacement Theory wants to protect have a racial component, with laws and policies designed to favor *designated* settlers rather than all who share the space, or even all of those who worked in agriculture and industry to bolster the settlements. The effort to consolidate the settlements is meant to apply only to the original way the settlements were crafted: with special protections and benefits for whites. These protections and benefits are what is being replaced, but new protections and benefits could be crafted in such a way that there is justice for all.

3) Based on historical practice, the Replacement Theory takes for granted the existence of *an identity-based power* and accepts this as a legitimate feature of political institutions. The concern about replacement does not make sense if one is using a concept of the abstract individual as the basic unit of political rights. When power is rooted in a specific identity group, it makes sense to predict a loss of their special privileges when they lose majority status. We can point out that such protections have been woefully inadequate for the white working-class majority at least since the 1970s, but for whites as a whole, there has remained a comparative advantage over others in relation to rates of incarceration as well as wages, bank loans, and housing values. The white poor are persistently mistreated by police, wrongfully sent to prison, and subject to other social injustices, but not to the

146 RACE AND RACISM

same degree, and a fear of the further loss of status when one is already near the economic bottom might certainly feel potentially catastrophic. Sociologists Michael Omi and Howard Winant developed the concept of "racial projects" to explain the phenomenon in which a political agenda is organized racially: "A racial project is simultaneously an interpretation, representation, or explanation of racial dynamics, and an effort to reorganize and redistribute resources along particular racial lines" (Omi and Winant 1994, 58). Racial projects take race and racial identities as the organizing principle for policies and laws that govern access to a variety of public goods. Adherents of the Replacement Theory impute immigration to be a racial project itself, a conspiracy of elites to replace one racial project with another. White Christian nationalism is, then, portrayed simply as a response.

4) The Replacement Theory offers an *explicit identity politics* meant to contest the identity politics they believe is at play among liberals and the left. White groups organizing around their racial identity are simply responding to non-white groups who have done the same, agitating for policies that will advance their group interests. Hence, it is white identity power, more than white populations themselves, that is seen as in danger of replacement, as Cristina Beltrán argues. What is actually being displaced are not white people but the "power and status of whiteness" (Beltrán 2020, 9). Thus, proponents of the Replacement Theory put forward a white identity politics not as a form of race hatred but as a rational response to group conflict over a scarcity of goods.

5) My fifth point is a caveat or *qualification*. If the Replacement Theory references identity-based rights to land and political power, the way in which these group identities are defined is subject to some variation and multiracial inclusion. In the United States, "settlers" or "legacy Americans" can be defined in relation to longevity, contributions to building the country, and patriotism in regards to the cause of protecting the settlement. The targeting of Muslims in Europe can also invite a multicultural opposition with some racial and religious pluralism that would

CRISIS OF WHITE IDENTITY 147

include Christians, Jews, and secular Europeans. The discourse of replacement has been wielded in such a way that some non-whites can feel a 'belonging,' and vote in support of the far right, as well as participate in far-right political actions. We should be wary of overly simplistic formulations of what is wrong with the Replacement Theory that miss its variations.

These points show how the Replacement Theory encapsulates and addresses the unease of the current moment experienced by many people. But it also offers a solution with a justification: reclaim and protect the settlements and the origin stories, in the name of community and economic stability. Characterize the beneficiaries as those who are deserving in some way, not simply in terms of race. This is a strategy to overcome both the narrative crisis and the legitimation crisis: state legitimation can be defined once again in terms of the state's protections for a deserving and innocent group.

Early accounts of the political relevance of identity

So, let me return to the question I posed earlier: Why is group identity of any sort taken by some to be *legitimately* relevant to claims of political power and territorial rights? This is, after all, what the Replacement Theory contends, that certain nation-states are *rightfully* in the control of a particular group defined in particular ways. Although what we today call ethno-nationalism is considered by many to be irrational and racist, others consider the desire to maintain the power of a particular group defined in terms of their history justifiable. Why?

To explore this question, in what follows, I will consider two different lines of argument that help explain the logic of ethno-nationalism. Both of these continue to be relevant today in many political cultures. The two sets of arguments were developed respectively by Hector St. John de Crèvecoeur and by Thomas Jefferson, both writing in the eighteenth century during the period of the first attempt to create Western democracies in the new settler nations as well as in Europe. Neither Crèvecoeur nor Jefferson are the sort of political

148   RACE AND RACISM

theorist we generally rely upon to think through issues of sovereignty or group rights to territory, but their writings were very influential in their day, and they will help us understand the ideas that remain circulating in spheres of discourse that motivate the far right as well as many liberals. The first argument, by Crèvecoeur, applies mainly to settler societies such as in the Americas and Australia, but the second argument, by Jefferson, applies to all nations that were formerly engaged in and enriched by enslavement or colonization.

Both Crèvecoeur and Jefferson are addressing the feasibility of democracy, a topic very much debated in the period of the late 1700s when they are writing. They each argued that democracy's feasibility is conditional and the conditions of its success have to do with ethnic and racial identities, as well as, for Crèvecoeur, the particular nature of one's motivations for migration. All migrants are not going to be capable of participating in the new nation.

Importantly, both Crèvecoeur and Jefferson are developing their thinking about democracy during the period of democracy's emergence across the domain that is now called the "West." The United States was the nation that most influenced subsequent ideas about democratic formation then circulating in Europe, even though it should have shared that stage with Haiti as well as with many indigenous groups throughout the Americas that had long-standing forms of participatory democracy in their societies. As is now more widely known, these indigenous forms directly influenced North American theorists such as Jefferson (e.g., Barreiro 1992; Trouillot 1995).

The particular forms of democracy that emerged in the West during the late eighteenth century and early nineteenth century are identified by numerous political theorists today as Herrenvolk democracies. As we saw in chapter 1, Joel Olson argues that this term more accurately describes how the franchise was carefully restricted and, in fact, never intended to be universally inclusive. Such an approach to democracy was thus much closer to the form developed in ancient Greece and has little in common with the ideas of universal suffrage that we have today. Outside of the circles of political theory, public cultures in the West continue to wield the term *democracy* as if there is only one form, but it would be a useful corrective to begin to recognize the variety of actual forms and to open up debates over which form we want (e.g.,

CRISIS OF WHITE IDENTITY   149

C. B. Macpherson's classic 1966 work on the varied forms of real world democracy).

The creation of the United States required an intellectual as well as a political revolution. Proponents had to contest the ideas that legitimated monarchies and aristocracies and the colonial presumptions of the British Empire. Importantly, defenders of revolution who wished to inspire support had to address the issue of feasibility. This question played an important role in the particular ideas of 'self-government' that emerged victorious in these debates. Feasibility arguments narrowed the provenance to certain groups by virtue of their social status and identity, who alone were fit to self-govern (Foner 1999). Property owners had a strong motive to care for and steward the land, it was thought; indeed, participating in the political stewardship over the nation was an extension of their political stewardship over their own farms, households, workers, plantations, and factories. Ideas of universal suffrage or of women's suffrage were rarely entertained. As many historians argue today, the Founding Fathers of the United States, who are credited with creating the first Western democracy, never in fact imagined that it would extend suffrage to all (esp. Foner 1999, 2019; Roosevelt 2022).

The exclusions to suffrage that were written into US laws based on gender, race, and property took more than a century to overcome. Today, there are debates over the exclusion of noncitizens, since this significantly disempowers millions who work and live under the US government. And there is a constant need for vigilance to protect existing voting rights from forms of sabotage. Two hundred years after the revolution, the United States still does not have secure suffrage even for all citizens.

Before one jumps to the conclusion that, in times past, no one could conceive of an inclusive democracy, it is important to note that during the same historical period in which Jefferson and Crèvecoeur were writing, there were in fact many substantively egalitarian movements in both Europe and the Americas that contested elite rule and fashioned authentically inclusive democratic and participatory modes of political organization and even governments (Hobsbawm 1959; Linebaugh and Rediker 2000; Maher 2022). These include, in England, the Diggers, the Levelers, and the Ranters and, throughout

150 RACE AND RACISM

New England, communal religious communities such as the Shakers, the Quakers, and the Oneida Community, the latter of which called themselves "Bible Communists" (Robinson 1970). Many such groups supported universal participation, including women, and they also understood that economic power imbalances would have to be addressed if democratic institutions were to function as intended.

There were also numerous social arrangements among indigenous groups such as the Haudenosaunee (otherwise known as the Iroquois) that were more truly democratic by comparison to either white settlements in the Americas or to European states. As John Mohawk recounted, "it takes a lot of courage" to hold a leadership position in the Iroquois tradition, whether as a chief or a clan mother, because they "really have to withstand a great deal of criticism and an awful lot of pressure from the people" (Mohawk 1992, 20). Mohawk explains that the gifts the Indians gave to the settlers was much more than the celebration of Thanksgiving, and included

> a tradition of meeting and democracy, of free speech, and free thinking, of tolerance for each other's differences of religion, of all those things which got attached to the Bill of Rights. All those things that we say are truly American were born on *this* soil generations before Columbus ever sailed. (Mohawk 1992, 25; emphasis in original)

Today the Grand Council of the Haudenosaunee, in which representatives of the six nations of the constitution have continuously met for a thousand years to resolve disputes and achieve peace, is recognized as the oldest representative democracy in the world. The federated nature of the Haudenosaunee tribes influenced both Jefferson and Benjamin Franklin's formulation of a federal government that would share power with local and state governments. Franklin published a series of Indian treaties and attended ceremonies and treaty councils, and listened as Scarouady, an Oneida chief, gave a speech in 1753 explaining the Iroquois Great Law (Grinde 1992, 52–53). Jefferson was in continual contact with Native peoples from the time he was a child, and heard discussions on issues of dispute and negotiation, as he wrote in a letter to John Adams.

CRISIS OF WHITE IDENTITY   151

Yet during the era of settler colonialism, these examples did not gain a wide influence among those tasked with crafting new constitutions. The settlers chose carefully which ideas and practices of democracy to accept from the traditions they encountered. The Haudenosaunee's inclusion of women in their political system was ignored, as was the horizontalism instituted by the Shakers and Quakers. Instead, colonial elites argued for a limited democratic rule in which a subgroup of cohabitants of the land, based on their ethno-racial and gender identity, their property, and their status as citizens, would be the only ones privileged to select their representatives through voting. Even the class of white males was restricted since only "free" or nonindentured whites could be enfranchised. Such requirements were key elements believed necessary for a feasible form of self-government, and the reasoning used at the time to defend the exclusions conforms closely to elements of white nativism espoused today.

Hector St. John de Crèvecoeur

The first line of argument comes from a farmer, Hector St. John de Crèvecoeur, who, in the midst of the revolutionary war against British rule, published a book entitled *Letters from an American Farmer* that became a bestseller ([1782] 1981). This war required an ideological battle alongside a military one, to justify armed opposition to overcome divine monarchy and the exalted rights of the aristocracy. Crèvecoeur's writing no doubt struck a chord with the European colonists on these points. Crèvecoeur, who came to be known as 'the farmer of feelings,' describes life at the frontier from the perspective of a recent immigrant from Europe who finds a new world of great beauty and potential for communal harmony even with the stress of living precariously next to unpredictable neighboring groups. And he emphasized that migration to this new world demanded an ability to adapt and learn rather than simply repeat the traditions from home.

The book is written in epistolary form as a collection of twelve letters in which Crèvecoeur shares his observations of frontier life. He includes such topics as the unfamiliar wildlife and the specific agricultural challenges posed by the American terrain. But he also engages in

152 RACE AND RACISM

some acute social analysis about how the experience of settling new lands affected the political subjectivity of the immigrants.

Crèvecoeur suggests that the experience of migration from Europe created a particular orientation toward the new possibilities of group self-creation, in which prior traditions of interaction might be dislodged and new social relations fashioned. The letter entitled "What Is an American?" defines this new identity and became an early document of multiculturalism at least in the form of a multiethnic white European American identity. This was later referred to as a melting pot, in which diverse European nationalities first began to fashion a shared identity through their practices of cohabitation and regular intermarrying, and eventually came to define themselves simply as Americans. But this was understood to pertain only to European immigrants, meaning, in effect, white immigrants.

Crèvecoeur answered the question of feasibility thusly: democracy *is* possible for this *particular* group of people under these *particular* conditions.

Crèvecoeur described the "American people" as those who had immigrated voluntarily from Europe, even if the voluntary nature of this migration contained some elements of economic and political coercion. He argued that this group shared an attitude substantive enough to put them in a unique condition to launch the democratic experiment with some promise of success. The most important thing they shared was the fact that they were looking for refuge from the "variety of miseries and wants" inflicted by their countries of origin ([1782] 1981, 66). This gave them a motivation to dispense with those prior allegiances that had inflicted such miseries and wants. As a result, they were open to the creation of new ways of life and new forms of relationality, and quickly began to invent new forms of identity and social interaction. He describes their outlook as follows:

> We are nothing but what we derive from the air we breathe, the climate we inhabit, the government we obey, the system of religion we profess, and the nature of our employment. ([1782] 1981, 68)

In this way, he imagined that the innate human capacity for self-creation, both as individuals and as a collective, could develop in the

CRISIS OF WHITE IDENTITY   153

New World without hindrance by the demand to follow the orders of social rank or prior forms of social organization. The motives that drove them to depart from Europe also drove them to disconnect from those nations and their cultural customs, even including their religions, languages, and ethnic groups in the "old" country.

Such an immigrant, Crèvecoeur surmises, "must greatly rejoice that he lived at a time to see this fair country discovered and settled; he must necessarily feel a share of national pride, when he views the chain of settlements which embellishes these extended shores' ([1782] 1981, 66) Crèvecoeur felt such national pride to be both natural and justifiable, as he exclaims, "There never was a people, situated as they are, who, with so ungrateful a soil, have done more in so short a time" (68). This resonates with John Locke's labor theory of value, which provided a useful support for Marx's theory of the source of all value, but also for settler societies, since the idea that those who mix their toil with the land have the right of it, by that action and that action alone. With such a view, one might believe that if the practice of "settling" produces agricultural communities, their territorial claims outrank those of groups seen as hunter-gatherers who have not "improved" the land. In this context, Crèvecoeur's comparative claim is striking, that "there *never* was a people . . . who have done more in so short a time." How can he know this? And why must it be a comparative claim?

Crèvecoeur suggests, plausibly, that national pride is the natural effect of the difficult labor of settlement. This creates ties of loyalty and concern among the settlers, concern for each other as well as for the proper stewardship of the land. But this creates the idea that those who engage in *this* labor are the land's rightful stewards, thus legitimating exclusions on democratic participation. The labor of the prior peoples on the land is then discounted, sometimes because their stewardship prioritized the sustainability of forests and animal life, a labor unrecognized as such by the colonists and conflicting with the creation of new settlements. Nonetheless, Crèvecoeur's arguments that link political rights to the labor of settlement remain influential even today. Minority groups in the US, including African Americans, Asian Americans, and Latinos, often make claims about *their* longevity, as well as their collective labor in the development of infrastructure, railroads and agriculture, as a basis for political rights. Sometimes

154   RACE AND RACISM

indigenous groups as well as non-white groups make claims based on military service, showcasing their loyalty to the nation and their commitment to defending the settlements. If such forms of argument are challenged, some experience this as a betrayal, especially given that they have no secure place, nation, or country to which they can reasonably be expected to return.

Crèvecoeur, of course, is only writing about European settlers, and crafting a notion of their political subjectivity and relationship to the newly emerging state, always emphasizing their desire to be free from their "wants and miseries" in Europe. It is this group of migrants who he believes can forge a new political collectivity on democratic grounds without being circumscribed by old systems that enact obedience and conformity, not to mention an obligatory performance of obsequiousness.

Thus was set out the basic creed of American exceptionalism still with us today and regularly extolled by liberal political leaders. Americans (meaning European Americans) are an exceptional people precisely *because* they have freely immigrated and chosen to leave "old Europe" behind, with its irrational distinctions of rank that control social interaction and stymie creativity. Voluntary migration is a willful choice of self-renewal. "We are nothing but," Crèvecoeur says, signaling a presentist approach that foregrounds volitional commitments as well as volitional labor. The key is that particularist ethnic and cultural histories no longer have the ability to determine current attachments. All that counts is what *we* choose to do here, whom *we* choose to obey, and what ideas *we* choose to profess.

And it is quite true that most European migrants to the Americas had been starved and driven out of their countries, with no alternative to penury or persecution except migration. Given this perspective, as Crèvecoeur describes with some phenomenological insight, the new immigrant is predisposed toward democracy, since the moment

on a new continent: a modern society offers itself to his contemplation, different from what he had hitherto seen. It is not composed, as in Europe, of great lords who possess everything, and of a herd of people who have nothing. Here are no aristocratical families, no courts, no kings, no bishops, no ecclesiastical dominion, no invisible

CRISIS OF WHITE IDENTITY   155

power giving to a few a very visible one, no great manufacturers employing thousands, no great refinements of luxury. The rich and the poor are not so far removed from each other as they are in Europe. (67)

This is the enduring myth of American class mobility, the infrastructure of the "American Dream," in which anyone can achieve economic prosperity by their own efforts alone, a myth that has at times been taken up by diverse groups of immigrants beyond those who come from Europe. Strong class distinctions certainly existed during the time of Crèvecoeur's writing, and yet the revolution promised to dispense with the practice of landed entitlements handed out by English monarchs, replacing such systems with land grabs and land entitlements legitimated on the basis of need and labor, as was later instituted with the homesteading system. Thus, the new state promised economic democracy, and delivered on this promise, but it was enacted throughout the nineteenth century in a way that largely enshrined racial and gender exclusions and the profligate disregard for the very people who had welcomed the settlers and shared their knowledge.

Crèvecoeur is quite right that many early European immigrants changed their manner of social interaction. From the very beginning, white immigrants began to intermarry across ethnic and national lines and felt no inclination to hyphenate their new identities or name themselves "English-American" or "French-American." They were happy with a replacement term that would allow them to signify an entirely new identity, as the term "American" provided, without honorific titles such as 'Count' or 'Baron.' They hoped for a new social world where they might achieve a new standing with more social equality.

Hence, there is certainly a logic to Crèvecoeur's claims, despite the partial nature of his description of the formation of the settler society. He helps us see an aspect of the group experience that founds white identity even today, in which many Europeans as well as those who have European lineage feel very grateful for the opportunities for survival provided to their forebears by their governments. Opportunities such as homesteading continue to benefit families in the present. Patriotism is, after all, an expression of gratitude, an acknowledgment

156 RACE AND RACISM

that the nation has functioned positively for their families, even if it required significant sacrifice, such as military service, and almost always involved difficult labor.

The overcoming of arbitrary and unjust ranking systems that Crèvecoeur describes, however, did not in fact range equally across differences of property: the elites who led the new nation continued to pull rank with each other by the conventions of old Europe and hounded anyone who, like Alexander Hamilton, was a recent immigrant with a modest family lineage. The mass of European Americans, however, were no doubt happy to leave such manners of judgment behind. As the still-popular saying goes, it is not where you come from but what you do. In Lin-Manuel Miranda's rendition, Hamilton rebuffs his detractors by connecting his modest past to his new nation, singing, "I'm just like my country, young, scrappy, and hungry." He turns what some might see as weaknesses into strengths, and as the basis of his right to citizenship.

Thus, Crèvecoeur provides a description of a key aspect of the white imaginary in the United States as well as other settler nations, the mythic signing of the social contract that united the new immigrants into a cohesive entity based on the shared experience of migration as a form of escape and salvation, however difficult it in fact was, and the shared motivation to create a nation of a new type without irrational ranks and orders that would be an obstacle to their survival and flourishing in a new land. Being white was a key element, not out of racism—simply, or only, or even necessarily—but out of the particularity of the shared experiences and aspirations of most of the European immigrants. By the 1800s, the poorest indentured Irish laborer could achieve freedom of employment after paying off their debt for the transport, usually within seven years. And homestead laws encouraged landless European immigrants to acquire property, allowing them to petition for up to 160 acres once they could demonstrate that they had "improved" the land by clearing it, building structures, and growing crops.

The democratic state thus became the vehicle used to ensure that white men of all classes had access to political and economic advantages in creating new lives for themselves. This certainly gave them a stake in the system, an interest in its good governance. However, all whites did

CRISIS OF WHITE IDENTITY   157

not survive or thrive under these systems, and many have remained consigned to landless poverty up to the present generation, as I can attest is the case with some of my own family, who came penniless from Ireland. More prosperous whites castigated these poor whites as being of low character, blaming their poverty on their cultural disposition to laziness, drunkenness, and ignorance, sometimes with specific ethnic overtones. The much-debated question is why whiteness remained so often a critically important and defining characteristic even for those who were so regularly mistreated by authorities, cheated out of wages, subject to occupational hazards at work, and snubbed by the local gentry. Prisons are disproportionately non-white, but their inmates are a multiracial conglomerate of the poor.

The southern journalist W. J. Cash, one of few whites to cover lynching in the 1930s, developed a sociological explanation with psychological overtones for the phenomena of racial solidarity among whites. As a journalist, he could travel the region, interviewing the bystanders as well as participants in racial violence. In 1941 he published a book based on these interviews entitled *The Mind of the South* that continues to be useful for its analysis and insights. Most importantly, his account sought to explain the strength of a racial identification that crossed significant divisions of class.

Cash found that poorer whites enjoyed the social connection that was sometimes offered them by the property-owning gentry and professional classes, however minimal it might be. For example, they might get invited to a backyard barbecue in the context of an election campaign, or a holiday celebration held for the hoi polloi. Despite the fact that these were unequal, narrowly proscribed, and often transactional relationships, such experiences softened the class distinctions and gave poor whites a sense of acceptance. Cash likened it to a relation with an older brother: one would never expect to attain equality but could gain some material advantages as well as the psychological benefit of familiarity, proximity, and recognition (Cash 1941; J. Morrison 1967; Alcoff 2021b).

The gentry had the money, the land, and the cultural capital; poorer whites were economically dependent and a bit starstruck. But their racial commonality created an alliance, a sense of being kinfolk even in a lesser status. Cash suggests that they are happy "for the very gesture of

158 RACE AND RACISM

notice." Of course, such a superficial acknowledgment as being invited to a backyard barbecue is something that demagogues can feign for their own purposes, handing it out with little cost. But their patronage sometimes carried real benefits for landless whites, in the form of sanctioning land theft from the indigenous, from Mexican Americans, and also from the Black farms and businesses that began to emerge after the Civil War.

It is clear that the significant racial distinctions between white Europeans and other groups codified in government policies and laws worked effectively to create a sense of shared identity. These *produced* a set of common interests—both material and ideational—that spanned class divisions. Most non-whites were separated from their home communities, kidnapped into slavery or coerced into peonage, and then abandoned in a society that sanctioned racist violence. Both Africans and the indigenous were enslaved, and this experience provided a different perspective on the new nation than the one Crèvecoeur describes for the European migrants. In some cases, Africans were enslaved by Africans and then sold to Europeans, but many were enslaved by peoples of other groups and still maintained a felt connection to their original communities, religions, languages, and cultures, so distinct from what they found in the Americas. Neither they nor the indigenous could be described as happy to make themselves anew (French 2021; Diaz 2020; Dunbar-Ortiz 2021; Simpson 2014).

Crèvecoeur's answer to the question he poses, of what it means to be Americans, is to describe an outlook, an attitude, a motivation. The outlook is hopeful about the future, optimistic about their new country, and motivated to let the memories of their past fade away. If this is what it means to be an American, then non-whites do not quite fit the mold. In most cases, they did not join willfully, and so it makes no sense for non-Europeans to set aside their prior history, to focus only on the present and make common cause with those who have favored status over them. The effects of their original oppressive conditions are ongoing, unlike the famines and persecutions of old Europe.

As a result, non-whites have never had quite the same emotional relationship to the forming of the United States, never seeing it as the unadulterated salvation white immigrants could, never feeling the

CRISIS OF WHITE IDENTITY   159

same patriotism or loving loyalty to the same extent or in quite the same unvarnished way. As the former slave Frederick Douglass put it, referencing the day the country celebrates its founding, "What is the Fourth of July to *me*?"

Such national histories create a problem for the demand that all citizens express an undying, unambiguous, and fervent patriotism. This is in effect a demand to honor governments that instigated irreparable harm, that tore families and communities apart, assassinated local leaders, and did all of this in the name of the nation. Some of these past events have been acknowledged and apologized for, but many have not. These large historical experiences produce distinct group-related patterns of memory and affect.

My own home country, Panama, was bombed in 1989 by the United States in an operation that was misnamed Operation Just Cause. The ostensible motive was to end a cruel dictatorship that many Panamanians had suffered from, including my family. My father, Miguel Angel Martín, was a young professor fresh from earning his PhD, happily teaching at the University of Panama, when the first dictator, Omar Torrijos, usurped power in 1968. Not being one to self-censor, my father was summarily fired and had to scramble for odd jobs for many years before he was allowed to return to his position. Many Panamanians wanted the dictatorship to end, and there was a vigorous movement through the 1980s in which people bravely marched in the streets demanding elections. The US government did not collaborate in a meaningful way with these groups, or uplift their demands, or use diplomacy to support this internal democratic movement.

The real motivations behind the 1989 military invasion had little to do with democracy, as has been outlined in numerous reports (e.g., Independent Commission of Inquiry 1991; Dinges 1991). The United States gave financial and political support to many dictatorial regimes in Latin America throughout the twentieth century, including barbarous dictatorships in Brazil, Chile, Argentina, Guatemala, Paraguay, Uruguay, Nicaragua, Bolivia, and the Dominican Republic. Anticommunist dictators were preferred over elected socialists. The US had continuously worked with the Panamanian dictatorship since its beginning in 1968, until Noriega, who succeeded Torrijos, began to

160 RACE AND RACISM

sell arms to the communists in Nicaragua, and it became clear that he would not be reliably loyal to the US agenda in the region. So, on the pretext of security for the Panama Canal, the US sent 24,000 troops with high-tech weaponry, AH-64 Apache attack helicopters, and tanks in the middle of the night, and over the next few weeks, as Noriega hid, the army bombed poor areas such as El Chorrillo, murdering thousands, demolishing homes, treating Panamanian lives as so much dispensable, collateral damage. Noriega was eventually trapped and extradited to the US to face trial, and a new government was installed in a ceremony held in a US army base outside Panama City. In the report prepared by the Independent Commission of Inquiry on the invasion, a leading military figure stated that one of the principal purposes of the invasion was to test the military's newly developed weapons under conditions of live fire, in preparation for the first Gulf War. That war was indeed launched one year later.

So, when I look at the US flag, or hear "The Star-Spangled Banner," which is a war song that pays tribute to military operations against the British in the war of 1812, I cannot but feel ambivalent. I grew up in the United States after immigrating here as a young child. I have a strong attachment to the country, but I cannot simply forget the plight of my family and friends *there*, who have been living under the coercive economic and military power of their imperial neighbor to the north. Unwavering, unvarnished loyalty is not an option, and I stopped standing for the national anthem at the age of seventeen.

Many immigrant groups feel a strong loyalty to the United States since their families were allied with it in Southeast Asia, Central America, the Caribbean, Iraq, Afghanistan, or elsewhere. Some of these newer immigrants come to the US with a similar outlook as the early Europeans: ready to invent themselves anew and grateful to be here. The novelist and cultural critic Viet Thanh Nguyen, however, writes of the paradox of needing both to forget and to remember the past in order to make sense of his life as a refugee (Nguyen 2023). He writes often of ghosts and of his early fascination with hauntings, understanding this as an effect of the survivor guilt that waits ceaselessly on the corners of our consciousness. I suspect many migrants today experience their new countries with the ambivalence Nguyen describes, including elements of appreciation as well as anger, and at bottom, a

CRISIS OF WHITE IDENTITY   161

deep-seated distrust toward the public pronouncements about global justice that the leaders continuously make.

In some ways, Crèvecoeur's is an epistemic argument. The feasibility of democracy hinges on the possibility of democratic deliberation over the *common* good, but this requires participation from individuals, and groups, who are motivated to think beyond their own narrow interests or their own particular historical grievances. One needs to be able to consider in an open-minded way proposed policies and actions that might positively affect the whole even if they also disadvantage the few, and these policies include forms of taxation or regulations on commerce or changes in immigration law. And the capacity to consider such a broader set of interests that go beyond the individual or group is one that Crèvecoeur links to specific histories of *European* immigration in a way that will exclude others. It is because European immigrants desire to break their ties with former nations that they are oriented toward *presentism*, to make themselves anew as "nothing but" a people living here and now, to prioritize their current social relations and set their past ones aside.

Crèvecoeur imagines European immigrants in the eighteenth century as having no significant ties—no affective ties—to their former nations.

So, this is the first line of argument: that a specific form of group identity—white, European—renders democracy feasible, and thus justified the revolution. For Crèvecoeur, the risky experiment in democratic self-governance is possible for *this* group of settlers *because* they have happily relinquished prior ties, even ties of sentiment, that might sway their thinking or complicate their loyalty. But others who may share the territory are not included here, others whose reasoning may involve grievances here, or who retain loyalty to their places of origin prior to migration. Some may be excluded simply because they have not had the experience that the first settlers had, of empowered self-transformation. A democracy that includes such people, as we'll see Jefferson arguing, is simply not possible.

Unfortunately, such reasoning has powerfully influenced the political culture of the United States up until the present day, as I argue in a previous book, *Visible Identities: Race, Gender and the Self* (2006). Both liberals and conservatives have argued against the politics of

162 RACE AND RACISM

grievance and the organization of political blocs by ethnic or racial identity, often on the grounds that this replaces processes of open-ended rational deliberation with positional bargaining between interest groups, in which none consider the common good. This concern has some legitimacy, but the demand that immigrants and people of color forget our histories and disavow our ties is unrealistic, and it is also unrealistic to imagine that these memories will not inform our views about both foreign and domestic policy. The truth is, many such memories can be usefully mobilized to unveil lies and craft better policies, if we are allowed to voice them in the public sphere.

Thomas Jefferson

Thomas Jefferson, third president of the United States, played an important role in the actual crafting of its democratic institutions and ideas. Although he was a wealthy landowner and enslaver, Jefferson took a radical position against British colonial rule. He warned against the powers of the rich, of the church, of the 'dogmas of schoolmen' and 'men on horseback,' all of which could undermine the quest for a feasible system of self-rule after the British were forced out. As early as 1781, he expressed in writing his hope for the abolition of slavery. The contradictions in his political thought have been examined and debated for many decades; here I will focus on a single text and a single idea, that of the impossibility, in Jefferson's view, that the United States could become a successful and functional multiracial democracy. As we'll see, the reasons he gives will, unlike Crèvecoeur's, apply beyond settler states to all those former colonizing nations that have immigrants from their old colonies knocking at their doors.

Jefferson was not a farmer in the way that Crèvecoeur was: it was those he enslaved and their overseers who did most of the actual farming on his extensive property in Monticello. He thus had direct acquaintance with the slave system, and many moral concerns about it, including its effects on the character of young white children, who were inculcated from an early age into practices of moral disdain and cruelty. Yet a measure of cruelty persisted in Jefferson's own practices. During the Revolutionary War, some of the enslaved who had escaped

CRISIS OF WHITE IDENTITY   163

chose to fight on the side of the British, since the latter promised to give them their freedom after the war. When some of these formerly enslaved soldiers were captured by the revolutionaries, Jefferson chose to return them to their owners, after first selecting one to give to his wife. Of the six hundred people whom he enslaved, Jefferson freed only five in his lifetime.

What is odd about Jefferson is that, despite his participation in the slave system, he described it as an abomination and appeared to sincerely believe that there should be a process of gradual emancipation. In fact, he wrote that abolition was inevitable, and it was this belief that motivated his support for the purchase of the large Louisiana territory as a means, he hoped, to slow the process. This territory, once purchased, was divided into fifteen new states reaching from the Mississippi River to the Rocky Mountains and the northern border with Canada. Prior to its incorporation into the United States, there were free Blacks residing in New Orleans and elsewhere, and Jefferson feared that if they remained free, and able to vote, they might well augment the speed with which slave revolts would threaten the economic system of the new nation.

Thus, importantly, Jefferson's view that abolition was inevitable was never based on the idea that whites would see their way to what he believed was the moral truth, but based on his belief that Black revolt was an ever-present possibility that needed to be managed for the larger goals of maintaining national stability and cohesion and a gradual approach toward ending slavery. When the Louisiana Purchase was made, all of its residents were initially disenfranchised, and a large US military presence was dispatched to control this "colony" full of former British subjects (Immerwahr 2019, 30–32). Its administration would require careful statecraft to ward off the threat of revolt from the formerly free Blacks who were now newly enslaved. Thus, Jefferson's critique of slavery never overcame his determination to maintain the power of the landed gentry, both north and south.

Jefferson is not the first person in the world who preferred to push the morally correct action into the future, leaving its enactment to his heirs. What is useful for my purposes is the reasoning he gives on this matter during the period when he is helping to fashion a new democratic state. This will be instructive for us in understanding the

164   RACE AND RACISM

current crises around whiteness, and it offers a contrasting argument to Crèvecoeur's about the grounds of national legitimation and national formation.

In 1780, in the midst of the Revolutionary War, Jefferson began work on his *Notes on the State of Virginia*, a text he wrote in response to a series of questions posed by a French diplomat, François Barbé-Marbois (Jefferson [1785] 1999). The list of twenty-two questions Marbois posed were intended to help the French understand the condition of the colonies that together had formed the revolutionary Constitutional Congress, intending to create a newly autonomous government, a Congress that was asking for French support. Marbois's questions asked for a wide variety of information—ethnographic, political, historical, and geographical—and it seems clear that Jefferson's own interest in taking up this assignment so assiduously, a task that he indeed worked on for many years, was motivated by his desire to explain and defend the nationalist aspirations of the revolutionaries to the French and to Europe in general. Jefferson wanted to offer a positive characterization of Virginia and its peoples and to dispel some of the negative views about the American colonies then circulating in the ancien régime. Thus, he defends the legitimacy of not only the revolution but also the peoples and lands of the "New World" in a more general sense given that these were being regularly maligned by uninformed but influential French politicians and scientists, such as the famous, and famously racist, naturalist and geologist the Comte de Buffon (Shuffleton's introduction to the text in Jefferson [1785] 1999).

It is important to recall that *Notes on the State of Virginia* was a text that Jefferson initially wrote as a private document to submit to the French consul and which he had intended to share only with a few "learned" acquaintances in the new American Philosophical Society. His goal was to influence those who might be sitting on the fence, whose support for the revolution could make a difference. He did not desire a wider publication and was quite dismayed when a copy of the manuscript came into the hands of a French publisher intent to have it quickly translated for a general audience in France. Although Jefferson failed to limit its eventual circulation either in French or in its original English form, his plan to share it with only a small, trusted audience, and one that only included his peers, indicates to many

CRISIS OF WHITE IDENTITY   165

historians that this text represents his most sincere and unedited opinions.

When *Notes* was published in 1785 and quickly circulated in France, the work generated a surprising amount of public interest and suggested a keen curiosity about the lands across the Atlantic that were striving for independence from monarchic control. Jefferson provided a detailed description of the rivers, animals, natural resources, population counts, and climate variations of Virginia, with an assessment of its arable land and speculations about its geological history, and he also weighed in on the mystery of the huge animal bones that were being found in riverbeds, such as tusks and grinders. One might well wonder what a French audience or even a broader US audience found interesting in what is essentially a committee report, with its details on the most plentiful minerals (salt, flint, slate, sulphur, and "good mill stone, such as stands the fire"), its long lists of native plants and local animal species, as well as its lengthy critiques of nomenclature, the mistakes of previous geographers, and the controversial categorizations proposed by the Comte de Buffon. Jefferson's cataloguing of the native plants, using both popular names and those devised by Linnaeus, goes on for five pages. There are several pages that compare animal typologies in America with those found in Europe, based both on size and characteristics. He seems truly fascinated with the debate over whether elephants may have lived, or still live, in the Americas. He offers a long excursus on the climate, with extensive rain and temperature reports and even more detailed reports on wind direction. He writes at times like a surveyor, at times like a paleontologist, and often like an explorer who is also a farmer. What is clear is that this is a man who intends to settle this land and make it his home. And thus, today we can use this text to see how a particularly thoughtful white settler viewed his new world.

The popularity of this text is not really that mysterious. For one thing, it is written in an interesting style, with literary qualities that convey Jefferson's obvious marvel at the land. He gives a rhapsodic characterization of the way that the Patowmac (*sic*) River 'travels' a hundred miles along a mountain range, as if by intention, before it finds a space to unite with the Shenandoah River. There, he describes the force of the two rivers as effectively pummeling a mountain in

166 RACE AND RACISM

their path, reaching the sea, and thus redesigning the landscape. He engages in philosophical theories about the "Creator's" evident intentionality in placing animals only in environments that were hospitable to them, or whether perhaps the Creator invented the traits that allowed these animals to survive the terrain. Sometimes he seems to make a more naturalist argument, as when he writes, referring to the elephant and the mammoth, that "nature seems to have drawn a belt of separation between these two tremendous animals" (Jefferson [1785] 1999, 47).

These questions were not simply of scientific interest but part of larger debates with political implications concerning the comparison of the new world to the old. Was the former an immature, less developed model than the old, in its geography, its animals, and its peoples? Or was it its own distinct and fully mature entity which thus by implication merited its own distinct sovereignty and required thick local knowledge for an effective stewardship? From this text, then, we can read much more than the details of the landmass and its inhabitants, but also the way in which an eighteenth-century political thinker and settler is imagining the origin, value, history, and meaningfulness of the land from which he is making his living and, in fact, amassing his wealth. The laboring human beings on this land are also discussed in the *Notes* in some detail. Jefferson took the opportunity of this report not only to justify revolution against the British but also to develop his views of how to form and build the new society, not as an abstract republic but as a concrete entity in a very specific time and place, with a very specific population. This was surely another reason for the text's importance in its own time.

The anti-colonial theme that seems to be structuring the entirety of *Notes* motivates Jefferson's effort to highlight how both Virginia and America are distinct from Europe. This distinctiveness offers, as Shuffleton notes, both a naturalist and localist basis of settler claims to sovereignty. Jefferson takes pains to show that the place he is describing is not an offshoot of Europe and, indeed, is only deceptively similar. Many aspects of its geography as well as its living creatures were misnamed and significantly mischaracterized by Europeans, that is, non-settlers, based on hasty assumptions about the contiguity of mountain ranges or the typologies of certain animal species or hasty

CRISIS OF WHITE IDENTITY 167

speculations about the unvirtuous, underdeveloped character of the Native peoples. In regard to these negative mischaracterizations, Jefferson is prone to making a division between the local and the extant in a way that groups white settlers with the indigenous. This is seen in the following passage, which refers to the naming of the "Apalachian" (*sic*) mountains, a name he attributes to the fact that the "Indian nation" of Apalachees resided nearby:

> European geographers however extended the name northwardly as far as the mountains extended. . . . But the fact I believe is, that none of these ridges were ever known by that name to the inhabitants, either native or emigrant, but as they saw them so called in European maps. (Jefferson [1785] 1999, 20)

If the mountain range is named for the Appalachian people, he implies, why is it used to refer to mountains many hundreds of miles from their villages? Similarly, Jefferson takes issue with the commonalities assumed by some Europeans between animals in the Americas and animals from other continents. He emphasizes the unique characteristics of rabbits, squirrels, bees, and other living things in Virginia, marking them as so dissimilar from those found in Europe that he sometimes renames them. His overall emphasis is on the fact that European ideas about this land, including its geography, its animals, and its peoples, are often factually inadequate.

Jefferson, like many settlers, had continual contact with the native peoples of his region, since the time he was a child. His attitude toward them manifests what Walter Hixson, one of the major historians of settler colonialism, has called "colonial ambivalence," a combination of "fear and admiration, revulsion and desire, for indigenous people" (Hixson 2013, vii). White settlers lived with and amongst Native peoples, traded with them, walked the forest paths they had created, sometimes worshipped and raised children with them. They also learned many techniques that helped them adapt to these new lands, including the wearing of moccasins and leggings. "Newly arrived colonists," Hixson relates, "often expressed shock at the extent to which their 'civilized' European brethren had come to resemble the indigenes" (Hixson 2013, vii–viii).

168   RACE AND RACISM

In a letter that Jefferson wrote to John Adams on 11 June 1812, he described his relations with the local Native people:

In the very early part of my life, I was very familiar, and acquired impressions of attachment and commiseration for them that have never been obliterated. Before the Revolution, they were in the habit of coming often and in great numbers to the seat of our government, where I was very much with them. I knew much the great Ontassetè, the warrior and orator of the Cherokees; he was always the guest of my father.

As this indicates, the relations between indigenous groups and settlers was altogether different from relations with the enslaved, who were hardly allowed to visit "the seat of our government" in large groups or be received as guests in the homes of great landowners such as Jefferson's father. The relations Jefferson describes here appear to involve conditions of respect by the whites, sufficient to create the capacity to speak openly with one another and thus to learn something about their views and the conditions of life. Thus, it is not so surprising that there were multiple views among the US leaders about relations with native peoples, what the official policy should be, and whether treaties could carve out a form of peaceful coexistence.

The native peoples of the Americas come up for a spirited defense by Jefferson in *Notes*, particularly against charges that they are cowardly and in other ways inferior to Europeans in anatomy or character. He offers both first-personal accounts and accounts from sources he trusts to argue that the native peoples of the Americas are inordinately brave, have a healthy self-regard, and will suffer no disrespect. He wonders at how rare crime is among them even though, he believes, they have no system of laws. He defends their physical features and characteristics as similar to whites in fertility, reproductive capacity, and strength. He even argues that it is a mistake to assume they have less hair, since "with them it is disgraceful to be hairy on the body," so he hypothesizes that they pluck their hair out. He notes that native women are stronger and sturdier than European or white settler women but attributes this to the difficult physical labor they must engage in that develops their

CRISIS OF WHITE IDENTITY 169

bodies differently. He defends the possibility of genius among the indigenous, and offers this challenge

> to the whole orations of Demosthese and Cicero, and of any more eminent orato, if Europe has furnished any more eminent, to produce a single passage, superior to the speech of Logan, a Mingo chief, to Lord Dunmore, when governor of this state. (Jefferson [1785] 1999, 67)

Jefferson goes on to repeat the speech of Logan, whom he characterizes as a "chief celebrated in peace and war and long distinguished as the friend of the whites." Yet he also believes that the Native peoples are without letters, and thus theirs cannot in fairness be compared to the European forms of genius, based as they are on writing. Although he defends the Natives against what he considers to be unfair condemnation, he clarifies that "I do not mean to deny that there are varieties in the race of man, distinguished by their powers both of body and mind" (68). But he does deny that the Atlantic Ocean is a reliable or sufficient marker for differences of racial ranking and suggests, "there has been more eloquence than sound reasoning in support of this theory" (68). He also condemns the enslavement of Indians as an inhuman practice.

Jefferson's overall remarks on the native peoples of Virginia reveal many misperceptions and prejudices of his own. He cannot fathom that oral and pictographic methods of communication are simply a distinct form of literacy (e.g., Boone and Mignolo 1994). He assumes their gender arrangements are barbarous because women engage in so much physical labor, but this is using a European norm of judgment, and one that only applied to the upper classes. He likely favors the Mingo chief Logan because this particular chief was proud of having good relations with his white neighbors. And it is also likely that Jefferson misinterprets the story he discusses in the *Notes* of the Cherokee chief Sidouee. Jefferson is taken with the fact that this chief refused to execute a white man who had murdered several Cherokees, and he took this refusal to be motivated by friendship with the white man who was subject to a death sentence, rather than a general moral opposition to vengeful executions.

170   RACE AND RACISM

Nonetheless, from his lengthy descriptions of his Native neighbors, we can discern in Jefferson a respect that could engender an approach of peaceful coexistence rather than genocidal war. This seems a good case study of the sort of "colonial ambivalence" Hixson describes. And, as the historian Daniel Immerwahr relates, such an attitude was held by numerous US administrations, including Jefferson and Washington, through to the middle of the nineteenth century. The original thirteen colonies were considered sufficient unto themselves by many of the early white elites. They distrusted the rabble-rousing "frontiersmen" who were agitating for expansion, and Washington himself warned against "overspreading the Western country . . . by a parcel of banditti, who will bid defiance to all authority" (quoted in Immerwahr 2019, 27). Jefferson was intent to secure all Gulf Coast ports under the control of the United States, but he imagined this could be accomplished with an expansion of small settlements of white farmers who could live peaceably among the existing indigenous villages and towns (Immerwahr 2019, 32).

Thus, continental expansion enabled by genocide was far from a given in the early decades of the new nation. Some congressmen like Josiah Quincy argued that the racially mixed populations of the Louisiana territory were incapable by reason of nature to participate in shared self-government. Yet Andrew Jackson, serving as president from 1829 to 1837, put forward a plan to designate 46 percent of the continent as "Indian Country," to be "governed by a confederacy of Indian polities and given a delegate in Congress" (Immerwahr 2019, 39). They would not be part of the United States, but there could be peace and amiable relations.

The relevant point for our purposes is that those, like Jefferson, who imagined peaceful coexistence between whites and Native peoples thought it would occur between neighbors who each lived in their own political entity rather than co-citizens of a shared polity. Jefferson certainly did not propose that the United States incorporate Native peoples as individuals with rights of suffrage equal to property-owning whites. One of President Jackson's later proposals did include a limited incorporation, where the Natives of what he proposed to designate the "Western territory" would be allotted a permanent state that would be

CRISIS OF WHITE IDENTITY 171

part of the union. But this plan involved the removal and segregation of the entire Native population of the continent into an area smaller than Texas. None of Jackson's proposals imagined equal power, nor did he support true Native sovereignty, nor did he imagine Native peoples as individuals, with individual rights to live where they pleased. His was a clear example of Herrenvolk democracy.

Those who advocated for even a small degree of native representation in the US Congress were shot down using familiar racist arguments. The proposal to have Native representation was described as an attempt to "add to our Union men of blood and color alien to the people of the United States," thus signaling that the ethno-racial makeup of the nation was a politically relevant and, indeed, crucial fact. One member of Congress emotionally declared that "the thought of a 'full-blood savage' with a desk in the Capitol" was simply "too much" (Immerwahr 2019, 40).

Jackson's proposal to create and recognize a Western territory of Indian country was tabled, and new laws and policies developed that allowed an expansion of white settlements and a removal of Native peoples without representation or any sincere mechanism for peacefully negotiating land disputes. It remains unclear whether racial ranking drove this shift, or the strategic political and economic necessities of the white settler nation, that is, the need to give land to landless whites. What is clear is that Jefferson rejected the most odious versions of the racial ranking as it was applied to Native peoples and yet never contemplated a shared polity. This may have been based on his awareness that they already had their own forms of governance. It may also have been based on the limits of the phenomenon of "colonial ambivalence." Hixson explains that despite the willingness of some Europeans to accommodate local natives, and their authentic admiration for many aspects of native knowledge and cultural ways, the Europeans

> were not culturally equipped to accept Indians as their equals with legitimate claims to the land. They viewed 'heathen,' transient, hunting-based societies as inferior to Christian settler societies. (Hixson 2013, viii)

172 RACE AND RACISM

This modernist form of cultural racism, explored in the previous chapter, eventually overcame the tendency to view the Natives positively, until the ultimate policy of the US government, as with other settler nations around the world, became extermination, either through mass murder, forced removal to arid regions, or draconian practices of assimilation.

Jefferson's *Notes* is also where we find Jefferson's views about the African peoples who were enslaved in the Americas, and their relationship to the central rationale of an American polity and its quest for sovereign independence from British colonialism. He called slavery a hideous blot upon the new country and expressed pride that "in the very first session held under the republican government, the assembly passed a law for the perpetual prohibition of the importation of slaves," which he believed would "in some measure stop the increase of this great political and moral evil, while the minds of our citizens may be ripening for a complete emancipation of human nature" (94). Thus, Jefferson was unambivalent on the immorality of slavery, making this plain in both his speeches and his writing. He believed its end was inevitable but espoused a gradualist approach that would bring about its demise through democratic means while maintaining national stability.

Yet, as with the case of the indigenous, Jefferson could not fathom a multiracial government even in the distant future that would share power across diverse racial groups. His proposal was forcible emigration of the enslaved to another land, in which they would be assisted with material resources, declared free and equal, and *replaced* by "an equal number of white inhabitants" who would be imported from elsewhere to fill their previous jobs. When asked, "Why not retain and incorporate the blacks into the state," since this would save significant government expense incurred by their removal and replacement, he answered as follows:

> Deep-rooted prejudices entertained by the whites; ten thousand recollections, by the blacks, of the injuries they have sustained; new provocations; the real distinctions which nature has made; and many other circumstances, will divide us into parties, and produce

CRISIS OF WHITE IDENTITY   173

convulsions which will probably never end but in the extermination
of the one or the other race. (145)

Thus, Jefferson had multiple reasons for his rejection of enfran-
chisement: Black people are different, he believed, but they have also
been wronged by the nation, and have legitimate grievances. Directly
after this passage, he describes other objections that include their color
and appearance as well as distinctions in their physique (their need
for less sleep), their intellect (more "sensation than reflection"), and
their character (prone to amusement, which he takes as a failing). As a
sidenote, in just the last few decades, new genetic research on Jefferson
has confirmed that he had several children with an enslaved woman,
Sally Hemmings. The historian Winthrop Jordan ([1968] 2012) had
surmised this before such technology was available, by noting that
Jefferson was always in the household nine months before Hemmings
gave birth. It is possible that earlier white historians had similar ideas
but chose not to discuss them in writing, even though the speculation
about the timing of his visits home had already circulated in the public
domain, including newspapers, when Jefferson became president. The
family reunions held today on the Jefferson estate in Virginia are now
racially integrated affairs.

Despite his multiyear relationship with Hemmings, the true nature
of which we can only guess at, Jefferson's writings clearly indicate that
he believed Black people to be intellectually, morally, and aesthetically
inferior to whites; he calls this "fixed in nature." This was surely part
of what motivated his concern that the end of slavery would create a
political crisis that could only be solved by the forced return of African
peoples to Africa. But it was not the only motivation.

In his autobiography, published in 1821, Jefferson wrote, "Nothing
is more certainly written in the book of fate than that these people are
to be free, nor is it less certain that the two races, equally free, cannot
live in the same government." It is significant that he says they *cannot,*
not that they *must* not. In Jefferson's view, the "thousand recollections"
of grievance by formerly enslaved after abolition "will lead to
convulsions which will probably never end but in the extermination
of one or the other race." Such a conglomeration of peoples with such

174   RACE AND RACISM

disparate historical experiences of the nation simply could not recon-
vene a new democratic polity. People were after all enslaved by federal
law, and their inability to petition against the beatings and rape and
the forced separation of their families during slavery was sanctioned at
the national and not merely the state level. For this reason, he believed
they could not serve as the unencumbered creators of a new society, as
Crèvecoeur imagines of European immigrants.

For Jefferson, the legitimacy of the grievances that enslaved people
had is precisely what makes it impossible to give them citizenship. He
does not claim the grievances of the formerly enslaved are imagined,
or based in resentment, or manufactured by opportunistic leaders, the
sorts of arguments often used today against minority group claims.
Rather, it is because of their *legitimate* grievances against the United
States that formerly enslaved people will not be able to share power
with whites or cooperate in the task of collective self-invention and deliberation over shared common concerns.

Like Crèvecoeur, then, Jefferson holds the view that democracy is
feasible only under certain conditions. He does not consider the possibility that the grievances of the formerly enslaved may not be aimed
at all white settlers in equal measure: those indentured servants, landless tenant farmers, who did not serve as functionaries of the slave
system, are not considered in his analysis. The grievance he discusses
is a grievance against the United States as a constituted political entity
that sanctioned slavery.

And of course, such grievances might be held today just as in-
tensely in many parts of the world, and against many existing
governments. Jefferson's arguments about slavery are perfectly analogous to other colonizer-colonized relationships. Recall that for
Crèvecoeur, the grievances of European immigrants are against past
injustice in their former home countries. Such grievances are politically meaningless in the United States. Yet the grievances of many
immigrants to the Global North may involve the very nations they
are attempting to reach. Similar considerations beset many debates
over immigration as we speak: Will this group of immigrants be
loyal, or will they be susceptible to terrorism and sabotage? Will
they ever be trustworthy? Can they make common cause with white
populations? Beyond the question of whether they *can* assimilate,

CRISIS OF WHITE IDENTITY 175

there is the question of whether they will be *motivated* to. Will they be capable of loving their new country, and its people? Or rather, as the far right portends, will we be opening the door to a structurally caused chaos of conflicting interests and loyalties that can never be resolved because, as Jefferson recognized, it is based on legitimate grievances from the past?

It is notable that Jefferson does not explore the obligations the nation may owe to the formerly enslaved, or the way in which a new collective set of shared interests might be crafted through repairing past injustices and creating new policies and opportunities. Instead, he believes that, after the abolition of slavery, the US should pay their passage back to the continent of Africa, though he is surely aware that many will not know which precise location would count as a 'return.' But importantly, his argument for repatriation seems to be motivated by white needs more than Black interests.

Jefferson also maintains without discussion the right of European settlers to create a new political constitution that encompasses the North American lands they have claimed. I suggest that this makes his reasoning a more tribal form of territoriality than Crèvecoeur gave, a right somehow justifiable by simple possession. European settlers may hold this land until or unless another group unseats them. It is not their condition as immigrants but their unity as settlers that confers this right. Such arguments are common among Christian nationalists today, and motivate the effort to shore up unity by censoring school curriculum so as to keep the "inner energy" strong, and in this way, sovereignty claims intact.

Nationalism legitimated

The exploration of these two thinkers has been a useful exercise in comprehending contemporary nationalist ideas. Despite their differences, we should notice that both Jefferson and Crèvecoeur center history in their accounts of the feasibility of democracy, and both focus on the conditions that can make a democratic polity feasible. Crèvecoeur's is an epistemic argument, about how a new political subjectivity is being formed in the settlements, one that can engage

176 RACE AND RACISM

in rational debate over common interests. Jefferson's approach is more nakedly self-interested: that those with justifiable grievances simply need to be forced out. Both assume a historically specific majority-white citizenry, and both produce reasons to maintain this that are independent of biological racism.

Both also help us see the important role that history plays in forming our social identities, as discussed in chapter 1. For Jefferson and Crèvecoeur, it is historical events that set the stage for the success of democracy, or its failure, rather than simply well-organized institutions imagined in abstract, decontextualized conditions. In a sense, they both pursue the nonideal approach to political philosophy. If historical grievances can be set aside or removed from the equation by voluntary migration, forced return, or coercive assimilation, then, and only then, can a substantive deliberative democracy unfold. The result is a justification for a very particular Herrenvolk democracy, not democracy simpliciter, and a rationale for white exceptionalism based on their pride of place in crafting a feasible democracy.

The overall lessons Jefferson and Crèvecoeur offer is that group history matters, and that group-based internal grievances and divisiveness is a nonstarter for a feasible democracy. Their approaches center questions of feasibility rather than justice, which makes sense given how new and tenuous the concept of democracy was at the time.[3] But this focus is part of what explains their unapologetic defense of what today we call white nationalism.

Their arguments are also instructive in another way: that one does not need to hold that whites are superior in order to accept white nationalism. One can accept it as simply a pragmatic fact about how nations can stay strong, united, and sovereign.

---

[3] Feasibility can be a feature of legitimacy, but it is not itself coterminous with legitimacy. Feasibility and justice have distinct concerns or aims. The requirement of ethnic homogeneity, as one can find in, e.g., Carl Schmitt, is also parasitic on historical conditions: whites (men at least) can form a democracy, and white majorities are vital, because of the differential relationship to the historical founding of the nation. So, as we bring history rather than ethnicity to the fore, we may be able to answer why conservative nationalism can be multiracial: because anti-communist Cubans, Nicaraguans, Venezolanos, Vietnamese and Cambodians, etc., come to the United States very much as the Europeans of the eighteenth century did: happy to escape, and desiring to create themselves anew.

CRISIS OF WHITE IDENTITY   177

What is clear is that our intellectual traditions have not given us a sense of possibility for forging multiracial states in which whites can belong without leading.[4]

The result of Crèvecoeur's explanation of the feasibility conditions for democracy and Jefferson's prediction of the ineradicable disharmony that slavery's abolition would produce was that the political culture of the United States never set itself the agenda of creating a nation that could unite groups with such disparate experiences and histories. We have never had a political culture that set itself the task of acknowledging these divergent histories and developing reparative policies, with the brief exception of Reconstruction. We have never had a political class that took on the task of negotiating in a meaningful way the legacy of racial injustices in the nation's history. We have never had a state that understood itself as in need of moral reform. So the project of creating not simply a multicultural and multiethnic nation with some sphere of protections for minorities, but a nation that acknowledges that many millions of citizens have legitimate grievances against the state itself, as well as acknowledging that some portions of the population continue to benefit from ill-gotten gains that generated the legitimate grievances, has not been on the agenda. I suspect this is because there is widespread, Jeffersonian skepticism that such an agenda could ever succeed without tearing the nation apart. Hence, we have a public culture that attempts to sever its ties to the past and reframe our history in ways that neutralize its threat. Our leaders are still echoing Jefferson's reasoning.

History does matter

Despite the failures of states to engage substantively with the political implications of diverse public cultures, in the twentieth and

---

[4] We should beware the role that universalist principles sometimes play in this logic. In the Netherlands, for example, Jan William Duyvendak and Josip Kešić's research has shown that the criterion used to allow immigration is whether a given immigrant can "become" Dutch (Duyvendak and Kešić 2022). But Dutch identity is itself associated with liberal universalism, understood and interpreted, of course, in specific ways, such as the formal division between church and state, and the acceptance of a public/private distinction. Those found inadequately committed to these ideas can be legitimately excluded. Once again, white people are distinct; even if others follow their creed, whites will be the vanguard.

178 RACE AND RACISM

twenty-first centuries, nation-state legitimation has been based in images of a multiethnic and even multiracial harmony. Ethnic and racial diversity is now a sign of cultural superiority. But today, with the increasing diversification of academic scholarship and public culture, nations include not only *diverse peoples* but *competing narratives of national history* told from diverse immigrant points of view. These competing narratives are not welcomed by all, or given a chance to inform national policies.

As the historian Gary Okihiro (1994) argued, the resistance of non-whites and non-Europeans to their mistreatment and marginalization in the United States contributed in significant ways to the development of ideas concerning justice and democracy. Foregrounding these parts of our national histories can begin to displace white exceptionalism and the myth of the "West" as the source of all political progress. And it may also help produce a vision of a multiracial, multiethnic, collective identity in which whites themselves can belong as equal participants alongside others. Intensive focus on implicit racism is having the unfortunate effect of spreading pessimism about such a possibility. The rise of the far right and nationalist movements is not plausibly attributable to simple ignorance or to racism: these movements are fueled by the fear of a future in which whites will have no place, no status, and no respect unless they go it alone. And a future in which all whites will be tarred equally with the colonial brush.

Dominant historical narratives have created choice structures that divide our interests, as if we are in permanent competition. Elites have intentionally sowed distrust and opposition and sought to disable unifying movements that seek structural change, including labor, peace, environmentalism, economic justice, and racial justice. Whistleblowers lose their jobs, dissidents within the military are imprisoned, anti-fascists are surveilled, progressive politicians are doxxed, and our mainstream corporate media barely covers the actual agendas that fuel protest, more often focusing on tactics and disruptions. The securitized state apparatus grows ever more expansive.

Beyond external challenges, social movements face equally difficult internal challenges. Today, we cannot amalgamate a left movement under a generic banner of class, or a thin concept of humanity,

CRISIS OF WHITE IDENTITY 179

or even the claim that climate change will affect us all equally, without addressing the ways in which we have competed with one another and accepted unfair advantages. Movements today that are not honest about these histories erode the trust that is essential for coalition.

As I have argued, we must address our diverse historical experiences and fears and explore the actual sources of division, the important interests we yet have in common, as well as the common interests we may be able to build together. And, to pursue such an agenda, we must be able to talk about race and about whiteness. This means more than addressing white racism and unearned privilege: we need also to hear the legitimate grievances that millions of white people have about lost jobs, stagnant wage levels, dangerous work environments, police harassment, impossible housing markets, and simple, sheer, persistent, cross-generational poverty and financial insecurity. We must also reconfigure how we understand and define the achievable coalition willing to fight for an agenda of economic justice that will work for all. (Hint: it won't include all classes; there is a limit to the ability to create collective interests.)

The question of white identity is dividing our nations, but, in truth, as opinion polls and elections reveal, the division is mostly among white people themselves. Sometimes the division appears to map onto a rural and urban divide, or a generational divide, or an educational divide, but these can also be misleading (Denvir 2020; Zeskind 2009; Metzl 2019; for counterpoint, Traverso 2019). Today's far right is younger and more tech-savvy than the more established ultraconservative organizations, more focused on building its online presence than creating rural militias, although they continue to emphasize the purchase of guns and the right to appear in public heavily armed. This factor creates a climate of physical intimidation and should remind those of us from Latin America of the paramilitaries that are 'officially' independent of the state yet doing its bidding nonetheless. In countries with stronger controls on gun ownership, the far right can use fashion symbols to publicize their group identities, from florid shirts to Fred Perry logos, black flags, and Confederate flags. Without the deadly weapons, the style can seem harmless and even cool, a veritable youth movement with more than white followers. Some have adapted

180 RACE AND RACISM

a recognizably Brooklyn hipster aesthetic: these are called 'nipsters,' or Nazi hipsters.

Thus, the new versions of the far right in the West have rather brilliantly marketed white nationalism as edgy and courageous, as fighting the good fight against censorship, thought control, unfair prejudices against masculinity, and the coercive conformity of 'wokeness.' Conspiracy theories and the general rhetoric target elites of various sorts, some of whom deserve it. Putting forward non-white leaders, such as Enrique Tarrio from the Proud Boys, and having so many women in the conservative talk show limelight as well as the electoral arena, helps to render the look of the movement as up-to-date rather than passé. These are the sort of rhetorical moves that draw in young people and city dwellers who might not otherwise be attracted to such groups.

But the differences with the older far right, including Nazism, are largely superficial. Today's European far right, such as the AfD (Alternative für Deutschland) in Germany, spins its agenda as a defense of the West's universal values and cosmopolitanism, which they say are now under threat from Muslim and African immigrants. Their main priority continues to be border control and support for deportation as a means to achieve a more homogeneous national community. Their antisemitism is sometimes veiled by support for Israel, though the repeated suggestion that Jewish people in Europe should move to Israel reveals darker motives. As Kundnani (2023) points out, the European Union's regionalism has opened its arms to the countries of Eastern Europe that were formerly in the Soviet bloc, but not to the countries of Africa, the Middle East, or the Global South. That wall is kept secure. Those who wish to emigrate to the EU or the UK, even from countries that were colonized by European nations, find they have extra obstacles to overcome.

As my reading of Jefferson tried to show, we need not assume that racism is the singular driver behind conservative agendas. In his book *Eurowhiteness*, Hans Kundnani argues that racism is not always the central motivator for the political shifts occurring in Europe today, and he provides evidence that those who supported Brexit had a range of motivations that included a long-standing disidentification with continental Europe. And, he shows that "Britain's ethnic minority

CRISIS OF WHITE IDENTITY 181

population identified even less with Europe than its white population did" (2023, 10). This disidentification is a continuation of sentiments since the end of World War II, after which many from the UK felt both distrust and disdain for those Europeans who perpetrated maniacal wars.

Kundnani makes a further argument, however, about the thinly veiled racism in the European Union itself. Even before the EU's founding, European regionalism was touted as a form of civic cosmopolitanism, providing a means to overcome nationalist forms of allegiance and embrace liberal universalism, civic freedoms, and human rights through social policies such as a 'social market economy.' Collective unity within postwar Europe was portrayed as based on rational ideas about the common good and voluntary commitments rather than the older allegiances to 'blood and soil.' Yet such claims came off as hypocrisy to many peoples from the former colonies whose histories of brutal treatment still received little acknowledgment in the public culture and little attention in school curriculum. The EU has in recent years accepted ten new countries from the east while maintaining its hard border with the south at the cost of many lives. This is hardly a true cosmopolitanism.

Racism is clearly a large part of the equation but, like Kundnani, I would argue that we should avoid the tendency to oversimplify support for the far right as grounded only in racism. As I argued in regard to the Great Replacement Theory, the desire to live in a harmonious community with economic security and safety as well as shared values is defensible. What is not defensible, and has not really been tested, is the idea that such desires require racial, ethnic, and religious homogeneity. What if, instead, this desire were made the basis to create a new set of common interests across a diversity of racial, ethnic, and religious groups? We could then compete for influence with the far right, rather than writing off all of their supporters as 'deplorables.'

Jared Taylor and other far-right ideologues have suggested that liaisons between whites and non-whites will continue to produce mixed children, and that mixed children and mixed cultures will erase white traditions and ways of life. Continued integration together with immigration will decimate 'Western culture,' and similar claims are

182   RACE AND RACISM

made about 'French culture,' 'German culture,' even 'European culture.' But these claims deny the multiple influences that have played a significant role in the historical development of the West over the last half-millennium, as I argued in chapter 2. Ironically, it is the very history of settlements, of global colonialism, and of transnational empires that has produced the hybridized cultures that new histories are documenting today, facts that the far right persist in denying or minimizing.

The fact that some of the far right want a 'kinder, gentler' rhetorical style is an indication of the way they view at least a portion of their base, as people who reject Nazism and racism. This may well be sincere among some, but the attachment to a concept of 'Western culture' involves racial ranking. The denial of any significant 'outside' influence, especially in the spheres of science, technology, and intellectual traditions, suggests racism. And this does ground much far-right nationalism. The reason pure or unmixed whites must survive, according to 'intellectuals' such as Jared Taylor, is because European culture and values are superior to Muslim culture and values. Such a view is at odds with accepting the facts of transculturation.

So, for these thinkers, replacing whites would replace the greatest racial group on earth. Richard Spencer, one-time head of the National Policy Institute, makes this racial comparison clear: "We were not meant to beg for moral validation from some of the most despicable creatures to ever populate the planet," he has stated (quoted in Caldwell 2016; R. Spencer 2016). Daniel Denvir shows that this idea has been basic to Trumpism, that the spectre of immigrant political leaders with a lineage from the Global South is simply unintelligible to the right, so much so that criticisms of US policy from such leaders are portrayed as tantamount to treason (Denvir 2020, 253). The general assault on 'wokeness' and 'woke agendas' is similarly a form of ad hominem attack. No one need defend the mythic narratives that legitimate the dominance of white-majority nation states or engage in public debates with the critics.

The stakes today may be even higher than they were in 1933. We can no longer hold onto the illusion that simply protecting current liberal states will be sufficient. The awareness of our histories and the ongoing global economic injustices as well as climate crisis requires

CRISIS OF WHITE IDENTITY 183

a significant social transformation rather than a defense of the liberal status quo.

Some far-right leaders, such as Jason Kessler, the architect of the infamous 2017 Unite the Right demonstration in Charlottesville, Virginia, argue that their movements are not anti-anyone, but simply pro-white. And he defines being pro-white as being against "white genocide," which is the dissolution of nations that were made by and for white people. He is partially right on this latter claim, since one of the first laws passed in the newly formed United States after its separation from Britain concerned the criteria by which an individual could become a citizen. It stated that any alien can petition to become a citizen of the United States if and only if they are a "free white person of good character." We should note all of the qualifications that this law stipulates: whiteness was not sufficient unto itself. Those seeking citizenship could not be indentured, because then they would not be free, nor could they have a criminal record, for then they could not pass as a person "of good character." (Both requirements remain in place today: immigrants must show financial solvency and not have an arrest record.) Suffrage was also restricted in that period not only by gender but by the ownership of property. Many states excluded "paupers," where this meant persons who benefit from "poor relief," including the inmates of "poorhouses" (Steinfeld 1989).

So, all whites were not politically equal, nor have they ever been. Western nations have told origin stories to legitimize their rights to land, their forms of government, and their right to control their borders. These origin stories have been used to legitimate Herrenvolk democracies, but they have not been told truthfully even in regard to white immigrant settlers.

Appealing to whites

In his late work, the philosopher Michel Foucault spent a great deal of time developing an account of the 'how' of power. He was especially interested in how power works to legitimate and produce knowledges, practices, discourses or discursive formations, and through all of this, how power produces forms of subjectivity. He came to argue that in

184   RACE AND RACISM

the modern period, there was a significant shift from what he called sovereign power to biopolitical forms, or "biopower" (Foucault 1980, 2010). Whereas the prerogative of sovereigns or kings was to 'kill or let live,' the prerogative, and the task, of biopolitical forms of the state is to 'make live or let die.' In other words, kings were not caretakers of their people: to be a subject was to be subject to be killed, while otherwise, one was let to live, however one might. With the rise of constitutional states, governments have been legitimated most by their caretaking roles, and these have actually expanded their powers and their ability to manage and organize our daily lives.

The new biopolitical form of power focused on ensuring the survival, not of individuals, but of populations. Their life, health, flourishing, and capacity to reproduce became the provenance of state concern. These topics thus became the subject of expanding knowledge systems that developed mechanisms to monitor, and measure, a population's well-being, including their diet, rates of reproduction, and mortality rates. Today we can find recent statistics easily online that give such facts about national populations, and some racial, religious, and ethnic ones, all maintained by state-funded agencies.

Foucault also called this pastoral power. Just as a shepherd tends his flock, keeping an eye on emergent diseases, the health of each individual sheep or goat must be known and managed, but with an eye toward the health of the whole. This is a group-oriented form of institutional power, in which life is actively supported through practices of management and cultivation. Biopower thus legitimates jettisoning some diseased or otherwise dangerous individuals.

Biopower is a familiar form to many cultures, often instantiated in religious traditions that legitimate violence and rule on the basis of care, concern, even love. In the era of modern states, pastoral power has involved the production of a massive set of operations that go well beyond the state to involve a whole series of cooperating but decentralized apparatuses and technologies involving medicine, psychiatry, education, and the social sciences.

For those who are not part of the populations designated as the subject of the caring governance, there is a *passive nonresponse* to their poverty, malnutrition, disease, unemployment, and lack of shelter. Many groups are outside of the domain of concern of what Foucault

CRISIS OF WHITE IDENTITY   185

called "governmentality": the caring discourses and apparatuses of biopolitical power that restricts, regulates, and sometimes engages in war in order to protect the lives and flourishing of the population subject to biopolitical concern. The population of concern may be imagined to be the whole of the white race. Yet this has never actually been put into effect, and it is becoming less so.

Whites who are poor, who are identified as criminals, who come from undesirable areas such as southern and eastern Europe or internal colonies such as Ireland, who are disabled in some way or are nonheterosexual or trans, have been let to die in droves. Sometimes it is hard to make a clear distinction between the categories of 'kill' versus 'let die,' as when the AIDS epidemic first raged and governments attacked the victims ideologically, furthering their isolation and subsequent vulnerability to the disease. Yet Foucault's concept of biopower is useful in understanding the shift in legitimation claims: governments today claim a right to rule based on their provenance to manage the affairs of state in our collective interests.

Unemployed whites have not come in for much of this care and concern, ever, but in the last several decades white wage earners across Europe and North America have also lost ground in economic well-being. They have had their pensions cut, been forced to retire later, and experienced significant declines in real wages even while the cost of housing is soaring everywhere. There are national differences in regard to these issues, yet the rise of neoliberal economic policies has endangered the public infrastructures of health care, education, and transportation (upon which many wage workers depend for their livelihoods), affecting wage-earning whites in every country (Metzl 2019). The worsening mortality rates of white men in the United States particularly stand out, however: these have steadily declined since 1980, even while the US economy has quadrupled in magnitude. Things are of course getting bad for all of the poor and working people of Western nations, yet the point is that the white poor have not been shielded by their racial identity from the increasing death rates. As the historian Nell Painter (2010, 389) has put it, "whiteness is not what it used to be."

In the long history of the West, there have always been masses of white poor. But what is now happening is that the trend line has

186   RACE AND RACISM

changed, so that the conditions of the white poor and white working-class are declining as the national economies, ostensibly, get better (the top 10 percent has seen its wealth quadrupled, the top 1 percent by a factor of six, and the group defined as middle-income has had its wealth doubled). The gig economy forces people to compete in open deregulated markets, to work for less, and to work with less safety measures.

Thus, there are clear and obvious shared interests in regard to economic livelihoods that span racial and ethnic and national divides. These are not the only sorts of interests we have, nor are they always viewed as more important than every other interest we have. But like some dystopian movie, groups today compete over which will fall into the "let die" category of biopolitical regimes, some striving to secure their place against migrants and refugees, who are seen to be garnering more institutional support and public sympathy.

So, to repeat, we must begin where Jefferson refuses to go: to imagine the possibility of a democracy that is truly inclusive, including the families of the formerly enslaved, the aggrieved victims of the majority, and those whose land and children were stolen. This was the task Jefferson found unthinkable, and many today seem to agree. The Replacement Theory offers a narrative that supports Jefferson's approach: whites will lose everything, democracy will fail, 'they' will always hate us, 'they' will not have our back. A popular slogan in the US for some time has been "No Trump, no America."

Such a cynicism and pessimism has never had a consensus of support (e.g., Bouteldja 2016; Sonnie and Tracy 2011; Bush 2011; Wilkins 2022). Fanon himself said, in reference to Algeria, "It does not necessarily mean that the solution to a situation of colonial injustice is for the colonizers to simply pack up their bags and leave." He ends *Black Skin, White Masks* on the hopeful note that "I want the world to recognize, with me, the open door of every consciousness" (Fanon 1967b, 232). Yet Fanon is also clear about what is required to bring about a new order: the collective empowerment of the dispossessed.

There is a young philosopher in the United States, Olúfẹ́mi O. Táíwò, whose family is Yoruba from Nigeria, and who has articulated the idea of choosing one's ancestors (2022, 199–208). In his culture (he grew up in the Midwest, of all places, but in an immigrant community), as

CRISIS OF WHITE IDENTITY   187

he explains, "our ancestors are still here with us" (2022, 202). They put demands on us and steer us toward what we truly need. Táíwò explains that when speaking to an older person in the Yoruba language, one uses plural pronouns, and this seems to him a way of symbolizing the idea that when one speaks to an elder one is speaking to history "and all its attendant accumulations" (202). Those accumulations include all that we see and know in the present, not only the physical infrastructure of the world but our ways of life, our forms of interaction, our ways of being.

Although there is no choice in regard to the impact of history, or its legacy, there is a choice, Táíwò argues, in regard to who we honor and who we follow. Our predecessors did not all agree, and most all of us in the world today have a cultural, national, or familial inheritance that includes moral effort as well as atrocity. But we surely all have forebears who intended to contribute to a positive change that would not be met in their lifetime, who reached out across time and space to plant seeds that might bear fruit. In the present moment, we are in conversation with our forebears and with our own descendants, to decide whose outlook to accept and how to make a path for our descendants. The truth is that the Replacement Theory does not represent all whites. It does not represent those who intermarried, who joined Native tribes, who made peace with their neighbors, who refused to kill Vietnamese, who tried to stop the invasion of Afghanistan even after 9/11, who organize against fascism. The crisis of the historical narrative of whiteness will be solved not with a coherent story of alternative positivity but with a clear-eyed statement of the choice history has left in our laps.

Conclusion

In this book, I have argued that our current struggle with racism and racist ideas needs a shift in focus.

We need to understand social identities that have been given racial designations differently, not merely as imposed concepts or as a form of inaccurate labeling driven by racism. Rather, racial identities signify real social identities formed in the crucible of modern colonialism, not representing all of what we are but, certainly, a part of what we are, how we are seen, how we are judged, and how we ourselves engage in seeing and judging. The segregation and organization of peoples, of labor markets, and of geographical regions through the use of racial markers has played a role in forming all of us. We have been created under the historical conditions of modern colonialism, with modes of practice so habitual as to become invisible or misnamed as simple rationality or common sense. Racial identities are highly contextual and changeable, but understanding how they work is critical for an adequate self-understanding.

I have also argued that we need to emphasize the culturalist form that racism often takes, a form that is masked in the neutral language of 'development' and 'tradition' and 'advanced,' and even sometimes 'progressive.' Today, the public mainstream in the Global North judges groups mainly in the language of cultural differences—what people do, what they believe, how they live—rather than in the language of biological race. But the effects are astoundingly similar to the old racial ranking systems that invoked biological causes. Addressing cultural racism need not lead us down the path of relativism, and in fact such a claim is often a strategy to avoid the difficult task of collaborative learning necessary to understand group differences. But, addressing the ways in which racism hides behind cultural difference will also bring into view how multicultural our societies actually are, not just in the sense of different groups sharing an urban space but in the sense of

Race and Racism. Linda Martín Alcoff, Oxford University Press. © Oxford University Press 2025.
DOI: 10.1093/9780197796948.003.0004

CONCLUSION 189

the content of cultural groupings. Though it is sometimes unacknowledged, cultural influences have traveled in every direction to create what we think of as the "West" as well as the rest.

And I have named the identity crises besetting every society in the Global North as consisting in a narrative crisis and a legitimation crisis. White and European group histories, both national and regional, have long been mythologized but are today getting regularly pummeled by an avalanche of careful historical scholarship that is correcting the record. As mythic narratives fall away, this creates legitimation crises for nation-state formations and calls into question their claims to have an unqualified right to control their borders and maintain their existing demographic majorities as well as current wealth and global power. We also need to disaggregate the distinct experiences and interests among whites and find ways to enhance our common interests, especially with low-wage workers, who are also facing a lot of pummeling these days.

Racial concepts today have a very specific modern/colonial flavor, and it is this form that flows through our contemporary material and visible worlds. Racism is reenforced by what we see, hear, and read and is structured into our ways of living. To change these, we need more than psychology.

I remain hopeful that social movements and careful scholarship can create new approaches.

Let me bookmark these claims with two final examples, one drawn from the very beginning of the modern/colonial world era, and one taken from our current times, both of which should give us cause for hope.

In 1492, upon reaching land in a new world, Christopher Columbus described in his journals the people he encountered, in some surprising ways.[1] He wrote that "all the people [are] strong and brave." "They all go naked, men and women, as the day they were born . . . without any shame." He described with wonder that "they are without covetousness of another man's goods." He found them 'to be quite

---

[1] All of these passages can be found in the journal logs of his voyages, now translated and available online, or in published versions such as *The Log of Christopher Columbus*, published in 1987 by International Marine Publishers.

190 RACE AND RACISM

rational and of acute intelligence" as well as "very gentle and fearful." At one point, he expounded, "They are the best people in the world and the most peaceable" and "I do not believe that in all the world there are better men." And his admiration extends to the way they look: "They were all very well made, stout in body and very comely in countenance ... all of splendid appearance. They are very handsome people." Later he says, "In fact they were the handsomest men and the most beautiful women" whom he had encountered anywhere. "And the women have very pretty bodies."

Clearly, Columbus's first impressions were uniformly positive, as recounted extensively in these journals and confirmed by his compatriots. Despite marked differences in custom, dress, and physical appearance (he describes Carib peoples as "of the color of the Canary Islanders, neither black nor white"), Columbus is obviously quite taken with the peoples he encounters. He not only admires their looks but their character and intelligence.

This perception and attitude, as we know, did not last very long. Just one year later, on his second voyage, Columbus declares the Indians to be cowards and thieves. He still likes their appearance but directs his men to cut the ears and noses off the Indians who steal, since "those are the parts of the body that cannot be concealed." He never considers whether 'stealing' is an unintelligible concept for a people without the practice of private property, or how it squares with his initial perception of their lack of covetousness. He now manifests a complete indifference to the brutalization of the same people whom he had extolled on the first voyage, and he speaks of them more and more as recalcitrant bits of flora and fauna who need to be subdued.

How to understand this dramatic, and rapid, change of assessment and treatment? We can only make conjectures about what motivated his change of heart. Columbus had returned to Spain to face recriminations for the extensive debts his voyages had cost the Crown, and he was impressed with the need to find a way to pay for more of these exciting adventures. Perhaps he merely came back down to earth, back to the social conventions of his own culture, after a euphoric trip abroad. We cannot know for certain about Columbus's psychic state or internal reasoning, with five hundred years between us. All we can know is that he felt quite positively disposed toward the Native peoples

CONCLUSION 191

at first, but that soon afterward he came under pressure to repay his debts. All that we can say for certain, then, is that the context of a project of colonial plunder accompanied his change of heart.

Xenophobia, insofar as it is understood to be a fear of the foreign, is not an inevitable or uniform human response to the initial encounter of difference. The variable ways in which we find groups confronting each other are too great to justify a belief that our fears and animosities will always dominate or that dislike and contempt is the natural initial reaction. The Roman Empire was a brutal slave society, and yet their approach to imperialism was absorption rather than expulsion or genocide, and they tolerated the continuation of multiple religious and cultural practices. There was an amicable and productive trade between the British Isles and the west of Africa for several hundred years before colonialism and the slave trade commenced. We saw Jefferson describing long periods of peaceful relations between settlers and local Native groups. The Iberian Peninsula, 'Hispania,' famously carried on a pluri-religious, pluri-ethnic political and economic society before the Reconquista. There are innumerable such cases that defy the idea of a hardwired fear of all others who look, and live, differently.

Even the infamous Edward O. Wilson, the founder of sociobiology, and Steven Pinker, who tends toward overlarge transhistorical claims about human nature, agree on this point. Repulsion and fear must compete with attraction, curiosity, and delight as commonly observed responses to what is new and different. In our increasingly mixed-race world, the evidence is obvious. Many people are attracted beyond their own groups and also have some measure of trust as well as an interest in learning how the world looks to those unlike themselves.

So, xenophobia is not inevitable, but on the other hand, it appears to be ubiquitous as a potentiality. This can spur social policies and practices of exclusion and segregation, border walls and laws against exogamous marriages. This is not unique to Europeans, or to white people, nor is it manifest in uniform ways across these two categories. Xenophobic responses to difference can be overpowered by other forms of response that promote exchange and coexistence. To quote Said again, "far more than they fight, cultures coexist and interact fruitfully with each other" (2004, xvi). The modern/colonial world has been motivated to devise rationalizations of their violence and their

192   RACE AND RACISM

material extractions, to control the flow of information, the curricula of children, and the images most likely to be seen in publicly accessible spaces. It is this colonial context, still contemporary, to which anti-racists need to draw attention.

Thus, in those societies today that have persistent and systematic racism, we need to look at the contexts that engender and support the derogation to which Columbus turned. And that requires a historical understanding centered on modern colonialism. Columbus had to raise funds, and the initial prospects he found for precious metals were insufficient. He began to bring back peoples, and he began to argue for enslavement.

Although we are still living with the aftereffects of this *longue durée* of European colonialism, there is no simple story of the interactions it engendered, and things today have changed quite a bit. The following story of a more recent interaction, one that spanned death, holds a different lesson.

In one of the most famous novels of the twentieth century, *The Stranger*, Albert Camus—the Camus I began chapter 3 with—describes a murder intended to reveal the serious state of moral despair that his hero cannot shake. Meursault has lost his sense of the meaningfulness of human existence and commits a murder, apparently without any intelligible motive. This is the central act of the novel, the critical event that conveys Camus's idea that the human race is abandoned in an indifferent universe but that our much-valued existential freedom, the freedom to live or to kill, follows from this condition. And so, on the shore of a city in Algeria, Meursault, an ordinary Frenchman, kills an unnamed Arab without provocation, or remorse.

But does *this* act truly convey the human condition? Does it express something universal, independent of location, context, or the specific identities of the individuals involved? Meursault is himself described with careful detail in Camus's novel, and his malaise is given a context: he has just lost his mother, has a job he dislikes, no particular religious feelings, a preference for coffee, and casual female lovers. And the novel, written in the first person from Meursault's point of view, is replete with references to his sincere belief in the absurdity of life. He is moved neither by his mother's death nor her burial and remains uncurious and noncommittal about his own feelings and

CONCLUSION 193

actions. Going one way rather than another, having sex or not having sex, killing or not killing are all portrayed as subject to the accidents of mood. Until he faces his own execution, Meusault finds no event or act more important than any other. The reader thus gains a rich picture of Meursault's inner life, his thoughts and his responses to events. *The Stranger* admirably conveys the mental and emotional condition of Meursault, but only of Meursault.

The victim, on the other hand, is famously described quite sparely as "an Arab." This indifferent portrayal helps to convey Meursault's cold nonchalance, his inattentiveness to the humanity around him, his moral stupor. But we must notice that in his internal monologue, Meursault does not choose to identify his victim as "a man," and neither does Camus. Rather, he is identified as "an Arab." We know nothing about the man who is shot other than this aspect of his social identity, which in the twentieth century took on an ethno-racial cast, rendering one's nationality irrelevant. In 1942, when the novel first appeared, Meursault and his victim would have shared a nationality, yet the common basis of their relation is nowhere acknowledged.

In truth, identifying the victim simply as "an Arab" conveys an ocean of meaning to the reader, enlivening certain sensibilities, certain reactions, and not others, depending on the reader's own identity. The victim is othered, perhaps so that the reader (assumed to be mainly French, perhaps, as well as white or European) can intuit the distance Meursault felt existed between himself and the anonymous man he killed. One might as well step on an ant.

However, in 2013, over seventy years after *The Stranger* appeared in print, and more than fifty years after Camus's death, readers were finally able to discover the name of the nameless victim. Kamel Daoud, an Algerian novelist and journalist, published a novel entitled *The Meursault Investigation* (2015), in which he imagined the murder from the point of view of the victim's younger brother. And so, it is from him that the victim is now given a name, a family, and a history, and that readers can come to comprehend the impact of the death on more than Meursault. "The Arab" was named Musa, Daoud tells us, and his murder became the central event in the life of his family. Its significance for Musa's brother and mother is made clear throughout, and from this perspective, we see Meursault anew as a white French

194   RACE AND RACISM

Algerian, a *pied-noir*, and no longer as an abstraction standing in for all of humanity.

Camus's novel is focused on the fact of existential freedom, which involves not simply the freedom to act but to determine the meaning and significance of one's acts. The enigmatic ending of the novel shows Meursault happily awaiting execution, happy with the fact that he lived his life freely, happy with the thought that "on the day of my execution there should be a huge crowd of spectators and that they should greet me with howls of execration" (A. Camus 1942, 154). Daoud's novel follows the style of Camus's in many respects: it is a first-person monologue, given as if he is speaking to the reader directly, with a conversational, self-reflective, acerbic tone. Daoud's narrator conveys a bemused ambivalence toward the absurdities of life, as well as toward the political absurdities of French colonialism.

Daoud's novel is not an angry screed against colonialism or Camus, and in fact he has said that his novel is an homage to *The Stranger*. Instead of critique, Daoud provides an elaborate engagement with a famous, and famously problematic, novel that was set in his home country but told readers little about it. As a correction, Daoud provides a rumination on Algerian life and the legacies of French colonial power, but also, more generally, he ruminates on poverty and on the difficulty of losing a son, a brother, no matter one's religious or philosophical inclinations.

Most importantly, Daoud sets up a conversation between equals, between persons, and peoples, who are differently positioned in history and in political geography. Both protagonists created by Daoud and Camus share a skepticism toward religion, an acute awareness of the preposterousness of life, and a certain amount of misogyny, but they do not share an understanding of Algeria under French colonialism and of how colonialism affected the subjectivity of those who shared that space in markedly different ways. Meursault is willfully oblivious; Musa's brother cannot be.

At the end of *The Stranger*, Meursault has changed his mood, from morose to self-satisfied, even happy, as he awaits his fate. He has lived life without illusion, on what he believes to be his own terms, acting as he pleased rather than from some ill-advised faith in any sort of deontological absolutes. He has acted freely, and he supports others doing

CONCLUSION 195

the same, whether in concordance with his own desires or not. Thus, Meursault presents himself at the end as achieving a heightened self-awareness through the short period of time in which the novel takes place. He enacts a certain version of existential morality with a universalist application, and it is this achievement that improves his mood and justifies his confidence in his own self-understanding. The protagonist that Daoud presents raises doubts, however, about Meursault's self-understanding, suggesting that he is not quite as free as he thinks. Daoud does not simply flip the script, making Meursault into an anonymous "Frenchman," but renders both Meursault and Musa into human beings in a given context, richly drawn.

Thus, Daoud provides readers with an outstretched hand, with information about the side that is too often silent and speechless in fiction written from the colonial era. He offers the start of a conversation, set on equal terms, in which participants are identified by more than decontextualized abstractions, yet never reduced to our geopolitical particulars. These are the opportunities we have before us today.

References

Achebe, Chinua. 2009. *The Education of a British-Protected Child*. London: Penguin.

Alcoff, Linda Martín. 2006. *Visible Identities: Race, Gender and the Self*. New York: Oxford University Press.

Alcoff, Linda Martín. 2010. "Sotomayor's Reasoning." *Southern Journal of Philosophy*, vol. 48, no. 1 (March): 122–138.

Alcoff, Linda Martín. 2015. *The Future of Whiteness*. New York: Polity Press.

Alcoff, Linda Martín. 2018. *Rape and Resistance: Understanding the Complexity of Sexual Violation*. London: Polity Press.

Alcoff, Linda Martín. 2021a. "Critical Philosophy of Race." *Stanford Encyclopedia of Philosophy*. Stanford University, 1997–. Article published 15 September 2021. https://plato.stanford.edu/entries/critical-phil-race/.

Alcoff, Linda Martín. 2021b. "The Southern White Worker Question." In *Thinking from the South: Philosophy from Southern Standpoints*, edited by Shannon Sullivan, 17–34. Chicago: Northwestern University Press.

Alcoff, Linda Martín, 2022. "Is Conferralism Descriptively Adequate?" *European Journal of Philosophy* 31 (1): 289–296.

Allais, Lucy. 2016. "Problematising Western Philosophy as One Part of Africanising the Curriculum." *South African Journal of Philosophy* 35 (4): 537–545.

Allen, Danielle. 2004. *Talking to Strangers: Anxieties of Citizenship since Brown v. Board of Education*. Chicago: University of Chicago Press.

Allen, Theodore W. 1994. *The Invention of the White Race: Racial Oppression and Social Control, Volume One*. New York: Verso Books.

Allende, Isabel. 2003. *My Invented Country: A Memoir*. Translated by Margaret Sayers Peden. London: HarperCollins.

American Psychiatric Association. 2013. "Identity Disturbance." In *Diagnostic and Statistical Manual of Mental Disorders*, edited by American Psychiatric Association, 5th ed., 664, Washington, DC: American Psychiatric Association.

Anderson, Benedict. 1998. *The Spectre of Comparisons: Nationalism, Southeast Asia and the World*. New York: Verso.

Andreasen, R. O. 1998. "A New Perspective on the Race Debate." *British Journal for the Philosophy of Science*." 49 (2): 199–225.

Appiah, Kwame Anthony. 1992. *In My Father's House: Africa in the Philosophy of Culture*. New York: Oxford University Press.

Appiah, Kwame Anthony. 2005. *The Ethics of Identity*. Princeton, NJ: Princeton University Press.

Applebaum, Barbara. 2010. *Being White, Being Good: White Complicity, White Moral Responsibility, and Social Justice Pedagogy*. New York: Rowman and Littlefield.

198 REFERENCES

Ásta. 2018. *Categories We Live By: The Construction of Sex, Gender, Race, and Other Social Categories.* New York: Oxford University Press.

Augstein, H. F., ed. 1996. *Race: The Origins of an Idea, 1760–1850.* Bristol: Thoemmes Press.

Barber, Willam, II. 2016. *The Third Reconstruction: How a Moral Movement Is Overcoming the Politics of Division and Fear.* Boston: Beacon Press.

Barreiro, José, ed. 1992. *Indian Roots of American Democracy.* Ithaca, NY: AKWE:KON Press.

Bautman, Elif. 2023. "Novels of Empire: Rereading Russian Classics in the Shadow of the Ukraine War." *New Yorker,* 30 January 2023, 42–51.

Beltrán, Cristina. 2010. *The Trouble with Unity: Latino Politics and the Creation of Identity.* New York: Oxford University Press.

Beltrán, Cristina. 2020. *Cruelty as Citizenship: How Migrant Suffering Sustains White Democracy.* Minneapolis: University of Minnesota Press.

Bernasconi, Robert. 1995. "Sartre's Gaze Returned: The Transformation of the Phenomenology of Racism." *Graduate Faculty Philosophy Journal* 18 (2): 359–379.

Bernasconi, Robert. 2006. "The European Knows and Does Not Know: Fanon's Response to Sartre." In *Frantz Fanon's Black Skin, White Masks,* edited by Max Silverman, 100–111. Manchester: Manchester University Press.

Bernasconi, Robert. 2023. *Critical Philosophy of Race: Essays.* New York: Oxford University Press.

Bethencourt, Francisco. 2013. *Racisms: From the Crusades to the Twentieth Century.* Princeton, NJ: Princeton University Press.

Bilgrami, Akeel. 1995. "What Is a Muslim? Fundamental Commitment and Cultural Identity." In Identities, edited by Kwame Anthony Appiah and Henry Louis Gates, Jr., 198–219. Chicago: University of Chicago Press.

Bilgrami, Akeel, editor. 2016. *Beyond the Secular West.* New York: Columbia University Press.

Blackburn, Robin. 2024. *The Reckoning: From the Second Slavery to Abolition, 1776–1888.* New York: Verso Books.

Blackhawk, Ned. 2023. *The Rediscovery of America: Native Peoples and the Unmaking of U.S. History.* New Haven, CT: Yale University Press.

Blitzer, Jonathan. 2024. *Everyone Who Is Gone Is Here: The United States, Central America, and the Making of a Crisis.* New York: Penguin Press.

Blum, Lawrence. 2002. *I'm Not a Racist, but . . . : The Moral Quandary of Race.* Ithaca, NY: Cornell University Press.

Blum, Lawrence. 2020. "'Cultural Racism': Biology and Culture in Racist Thought." *Journal of Social Philosophy,* 54(3), 1–20.

Bobo, Lawrence D., and Camille Z. Charles. 2009. "Race in the American Mind: From the Moynihan Report to the Obama Candidacy." *Annals of the American Academy of Political and Social Science* 621 (1): 243–254.

Bogues, Anthony. 2005. "John Stuart Mill and 'The Negro Question': Race, Colonialism, and the Ladder of Civilization." In *Race and Racism in Modern Philosophy,* 150–168. edited by Andrew Valls. Ithaca, NY: Cornell University Press.

Boone, Elizabeth H., and Walter Mignolo, editors. 1994. *Writing without Words: Alternative Literacies in Mesoamerica and the Andes.* Durham, NC: Duke University Press.

REFERENCES   199

Bouteldja, Houria. 2016. *Whites, Jews, and Us: Toward a Politics of Revolutionary Love.* South Pasadena, CA: Semiotext(e).

Brenner, Y., and K. Ohlendorf. 2016a. "News after the Fact: Reporting on New Year's Eve in Cologne with Hindsight." *De Correspondent,* May 2, 2016. thecorrespondent.com/4403/news-after—the-reporting-on-new-years-eve-in-cologne-with-hindsight/740954526851-d527a047.

Brenner, Y., and K. Ohlendorf. 2016b. "Time for the Facts: What Do We Know about Cologne Four Months Later?" *De Correspondent,* 2 May 2016. thecorrespondent.com/4401/time-for-the-facts-what-do-we-know-about-cologne-four-momths-later/1073698080444-e20ada1b.

Brodkin, Karen. 1998. *How Jews Became White Folks and What That Says about Race in America.* Rutgers, NJ: Rutgers University Press.

Burkhart, Brian. 2019. *Indigenizing Philosophy through the Land: A Trickster Methodology for Decolonizing Ethics and Indigenous Futures.* Lansing: Michigan State University Press.

Burrough, Bryan, Chris Tomlinson, and Jason Stanford. 2022. *Forget the Alamo: The Rise and Fall of an American Myth.* New York: Penguin Books.

Bush, Melanie. 2011. *Everyday Forms of Whiteness: Understanding Race in a 'Post-racial' World.* 2nd ed. New York: Rowman and Littlefield.

Cabral, Amilcar. 1973. "Identity and Dignity in the Context of the National Liberation Struggle." In *Return to the Source: Selected Speeches of Amilcar Cabral,* 9–25. New York: Monthly Review Press.

Cabral, Amilcar. 2016. *Resistance and Decolonization.* Translated by Dan Wood. New York: Rowman and Littlefield.

Caldwell, Christopher. 2016. "What the Alt-Right Really Means." *New York Times,* December 2006.

Calhoun, Cheshire. 2000. *Feminism, the Family, and the Politics of the Closet: Lesbian and Gay Displacement.* New York: Oxford University Press.

Camus, Albert. 1942. *The Stranger.* Translated by Stuart Gilbert. New York: Random House.

Camus, Albert. 2023. *Travels in the Americas: Notes and Impressions of a New World.* Edited by Alice Kaplan. Translated by Ryan Bloom. Chicago: University of Chicago Press.

Camus, Renaud. 2018. *You Will Not Replace Us!* Paris: Chez l'auteur.

Candelaria, Ginetta. 2007. *Black Behind the Ears: Dominican Racial Identity from Museums to Beauty Shops.* Durham, NC: Duke University Press.

Cash, W. J. 1941. *The Mind of the South.* New York: Random House.

Castells, Manuel. 1997. *The Power of Identity.* Vol. 2, *The Information Age: Economy, Society and Culture.* Oxford: Blackwell Publishers.

Castro-Gómez, Santiago. 2021. *Zero-Point Hubris.* Translated by George Ciccariello-Maher and Don T. Deere. New York: Rowman and Littlefield.

Césaire, Aimé. 1972. *Discourse on Colonialism.* Translated by Joan Pinkham. New York: Monthly Review Press.

Chavez, Leo. 2008. *The Latino Threat: Constructing Immigrants, Citizens, and the Nation.* Palo Alto, CA: Stanford University Press.

Corlett, J. Angelo. 2003. *Race, Racism and Reparations.* Ithaca, NY: Cornell University Press.

Coronil, Fernando. 2019. *The Fernando Coronil Reader: The Struggle for Life Is the Matter.* Edited by Julie Skurski et al. Durham, NC: Duke University Press.

200 REFERENCES

Cowie, Jefferson. 2022. *Freedom's Dominion: A Saga of White Resistance to Federal Power*. New York: Basic Books.

Crèvecoeur, Hector St. John. (1782) 1981. *Letters from an American Farmer and Sketches of Eighteenth Century America*. New York: Penguin.

Currah, Paisley. 2022. *Sex Is as Sex Does: Governing Transgender Identity*. New York: New York University Press.

Daoud, Kamel. 2015. *The Meursault Investigation*. Translated by John Cullen. New York: Other Press.

Darby, Derrick. 2023. *A Realistic Blacktopia: Why We Must Unite to Fight*. New York: Oxford University Press.

de la Cadena, Marisol. 2015. *Earth Beings: Ecologies of Practice across Andean Worlds*. Durham, NC: Duke University Press.

de Sousa Santos, Boaventura. 2018. *The End of the Cognitive Empire: The Coming of Age of Epistemologies of the South*. Durham, NC: Duke University Press.

Denvir, Daniel. 2020. *All-American Nativism: How the Bipartisan War on Immigrants Explains Politics as We Know It*. New York: Verso.

Diaz, Kim. 2020. "Indigenism in Peru and Bolivia." In *Latin American and Latinx Philosophy: A Collaborative Introduction*. Edited by Robert Eli Sanchez, Jr., 180–197. New York: Routledge.

Dinges, John. 1991. *Our Man in Panama: The Shrewd Rise and Brutal Fall of Manual Noriega*. Revised ed. New York: Random House.

Dodds Pennock, Caroline. 2023. *On Savage Shores: How Indigenous Americans Discovered Europe*. New York: Knopf.

Dorfman, Ariel. 2023. "I Watched a Democracy Die. I Don't Want to Do It Again." *New York Times*, 10 September 2023.

Du Bois, W. E. B. 1903. *The Souls of Black Folk*. Chicago: A.C. McClurg and Co.

Du Bois, W. E. B. (1935) 1998. *Black Reconstruction in America, 1868–1880*. New York: Free Press.

Dunbar-Ortiz, Roxanne. 2021. *Not a Nation of Immigrants: Settler Colonialism, White Supremacy, and a History of Erasure and Exclusion*. Boston: Beacon Press.

Dupré, John. 2008. "What Genes Are and Why There Are no Genes for Race." In *Revisiting Race in a Genomic Age*, edited by Barbara A. Koenig, Sandra Soo-Jin Lee, and Sarah S. Richardson, 39–51. New Brunswick, NJ: Rutgers University Press.

Dussel, Enrique. 2013. *The Ethics of Liberation: In the Age of Globalization and Exclusion*. Edited by Alejandro Vallega. Translated by Eduardo Mendieta et al. Durham, NC: Duke University Press.

Duyvendak, Jan Willem, and Josip Kešić. 2022. *The Return of the Native: Can Liberalism Safeguard Us against Nativism?* New York: Oxford University Press.

Eliade, Mircea. 1961. *The Sacred and the Profane: The Nature of Religion*. Translated by Willard R. Trask. New York: Harper Torchbooks.

Eliade, Mircea. 1967. *Myth, Dreams and Mysteries*. Translated by Philip Mairet. New York: Harper and Row.

Elkins, Caroline, and Susan Pedersen. 2012. *Settler Colonialism in the Twentieth Century: Projects, Practices, Legacies*. New York: Routledge.

Escobar, Arturo. 2018. *Designs for the Pluriverse: Radical Independence, Autonomy, and the Making of Worlds*. Durham, NC: Duke University Press.

REFERENCES 201

Escobar, Arturo, and Mauricio Pardo. 2007. "Social Movements and Biodiversity on the Pacific Coast of Colombia." In *Another Knowledge Is Possible: Beyond Northern Epistemologies*, edited by Boaventura de Sousa Santos, 288–314. New York: Verso Press.

Espinosa-Miñoso, Yuderkys, María Lugones, and Nelson Maldonado-Torres, editors. 2024. *Decolonial Feminism in Abya Yala: Caribbean, Meso, and South American Contributions and Challenges.* New York: Rowman and Littlefield.

Eze, Emmanuel Chukwudi, editor. 1997. *Race and the Enlightenment: A Reader.* Cambridge, MA: Blackwell Publishers.

Fanon, Frantz. (1959) 1967a. *L'An V de la Révolution Algéienne.* Paris: Maspero; translated as *A Dying Colonialism*, by H. Chevalier. New York: Grove Press.

Fanon, Frantz. 1963. *The Wretched of the Earth.* Translated by Constance Farrington. New York: Grove Press.

Fanon, Frantz. 1964. *Toward the African Revolution.* Translated by Haakon Chevalier. New York: Grove Press.

Fanon, Frantz. 1967b. *Black Skin, White Masks.* Translated by Charles Lam Markmann. New York: Grove Press.

Farago, Jason. 2022. "The War in Ukraine Is the True Culture War." *New York Times*, 15 July 2022.

Foner, Eric. 1999. *The Story of American Freedom.* New York: W. W. Norton.

Foner, Eric. 2019. *The Second Founding: How the Civil War and Reconstruction Remade the Constitution.* New York: W. W. Norton.

Foucault, Michel. 1980. *Power/Knowledge: Selected Interviews and Other Writings by Michel Foucault, 1972–1977.* Edited by Colin Gordon. Translated by Colin Gordon et al. New York: Pantheon Books.

Foucault, Michel. 2010. *The Birth of Biopolitics: Lectures at the College de France, 1978–1979.* Edited by Michel Senellart. Translated by Guy Burchell. London: Picador.

Frank, Dana. 2018. *The Long Honduran Night: Resistance, Terror and the United States in the Aftermath of the Coup.* Chicago: Haymarket Books.

Frankenberg, Ruth, ed. 1997. *Displacing Whiteness: Essays in Social and Cultural Criticism.* Durham, NC: Duke University Press.

French, Howard W. 2021. *Born in Blackness: Africa, Africans and the Making of the Modern World, 1471 to the Second World War.* New York: W. W. Norton.

Gadamer, Hans-Georg. 1976. *Philosophical Hermeneutics.* Translated and edited by David E. Linge. Berkeley: University of California Press.

Gadamer, Hans-Georg. (1960) 1991. *Truth and Method.* 2nd edition. Translated by Joel Weinsheimer and Donald G. Marshall. New York: Crossroad Press.

Gallagher, Charles. 1994. "White Reconstruction in the University." *Socialist Review* 94 (1–2): 165–188.

Garcia, Jorge L. A. 1996. "The Heart of Racism." *Journal of Social Philosophy* 27, no. 1 (March): 5–46.

Garcilaso de la Vega (El Inca). 2006. *Royal Commentaries of the Incas and the General History of Peru.* Abridged. Translated by Harold V. Livermore. Indianapolis, IN: Hackett.

Getachew, Adom. 2019. *Worldmaking after Empire: The Rise and Fall of Self-Determination.* Princeton, NJ: Princeton University Press.

202 REFERENCES

Ghosh, Amitav. 2021. *The Nutmeg's Curse: Parables for a Planet in Crisis.* Chicago: University of Chicago Press.

Gilroy, Paul. 1993. *Small Acts: Thoughts on the Politics of Black Cultures.* London: Serpent's Tail.

Glasgow, Josh. 2009. *A Theory of Race.* New York: Routledge.

Glasgow, Josh, Sally Haslanger, Chike Jeffers, and Quayshawn Spencer. 2019. *What Is Race? Four Philosophical Views.* New York: Oxford University Press.

Glissant, Édouard. 1989. *Caribbean Discourse: Selected Essays.* Translated by J. Michael Dash. Charlottesville: University Press of Virginia.

Glissant, Édouard. 1997. *Poetics of Relation.* Translated by Betsy Wing. Ann Arbor: University of Michigan Press.

Goldberg, David Theo. 1993. *Racist Culture: Philosophy and the Politics of Meaning.* Hoboken, NJ: Blackwell Publishers.

Goldberg, David Theo. 1997. *Racial Subjects: Writings on Race in America.* New York: Routledge.

Gómez, Laura E. 2007. *Manifest Destinies: The Making of the Mexican American Race.* New York: New York University Press.

Gonzalez, Juan. 2011. *Harvest of Empire: A History of Latinos in America.* Revised ed. New York: Penguin Books.

Gooding-Williams, Robert. 1998. "Race, Multiculturalism, and Democracy." *Constellations* 5, no. 1 (March): 18–41.

Gordon, Jane Anna. 2014. *Creolizing Political Theory: Reading Rousseau through Fanon.* New York: Fordham University Press.

Gossett, Thomas F. 1965. *Race: The History of an Idea in America.* New York: Schocken Books.

Gracia, Jorge J. E. 2005. *Surviving Race, Ethnicity and Nationality: A Challenge for the Twenty-First Century.* Lanham, MD: Rowman and Littlefield.

Graeber, David, and David Wengrow. 2021. *The Dawn of Everything: A New History of Humanity.* New York: Farrar, Strauss, and Giroux.

Grandin, Greg. 2019. *The End of the Myth: From the Frontier to the Border Wall in the Mind of America.* New York: Henry Holt and Company.

Grinde, Donald A., Jr. 1992. "Iroquoian Political Concept and the Genesis of American Government." In *Indian Roots of American Democracy*, edited by José Barreiro, 47–66. Ithaca, NY: AKWE:KON Press.

Grosfoguel, Ramón. 1999. "'Cultural Racism' and Colonial Caribbean Migrants in Core Zones of the Capitalist World-Economy." *Review: Fernand Braudel Center* 22 (4): 409–434.

Guglielmo, Thomas G. 2003. *White on Arrival: Italians, Race, Color and Power in Chicago, 1890–1945.* New York: Oxford University Press.

Hacking, Ian. 2002. *Historical Ontology.* Cambridge, MA: Harvard University Press.

Hall, Stuart. 1996. "New Ethnicities." In *Stuart Hall: Critical Dialogues in Cultural Studies*, edited by David Morley and Kuan-Hsing Chen, 441–449. New York: Routledge.

Hall, Stuart. 1978. "Racism and Moral Panics in Post-war Britain." In *Five Views of Multi-racial Britain*, edited by Commission for Racial Equality. London: Commission for Racial Equality.

REFERENCES 203

Hall, Stuart, with Bill Schwarz. 2017. *Familiar Strangers: A Life between Two Islands.* Durham, NC: Duke University Press.

Hämäläinen, Pekka. 2022. *Indigenous Continent: The Epic Contest for North America.* London: W. W. Norton.

Hanchard, Michael G. 2018. *The Spectre of Race: How Discrimination Haunts Western Democracy.* Princeton, NJ: Princeton University Press.

Haney-López, Ian. 2006. *White by Law: The Legal Construction of Race.* Revised ed. New York: New York University Press.

Haney-López, Ian. 2019. *Merge Left: Fusing Race and Class, Winning Elections, and Saving America.* New York: New Press.

Hannaford, Ivan. 1996. *Race: The History of an Idea in the West.* Baltimore, MD: Johns Hopkins University Press.

Hardimon, Michael. 2017. *Rethinking Race: The Case for Deflationary Realism.* Cambridge, MA: Harvard University Press.

Harding, Sandra. 2015. *Objectivity and Diversity: Another Logic of Scientific Research.* Chicago: University of Chicago Press.

Harris, Leonard, ed. 1999. *Racism.* New York: Prometheus Books.

Haslanger, Sally. 2012. *Resisting Reality: Social Construction and Social Critique.* New York: Oxford University Press.

Haslanger, Sally. 2019. "Tracing the Sociopolitical Reality of Race." In *What Is Race? Four Philosophical Views*, by Joshua Glasgow, Sally Haslanger, Chike Jeffers, and Quayshawn Spencer, 4–37. New York: Oxford University Press.

Henry, Paget. 2000. *Caliban's Reason: Introducing Afro-Caribbean Philosophy.* New York: Routledge.

Hixson, Walter L. 2013. *American Settler Colonialism: A History.* New York: Palgrave Macmillan.

Hobsbawm, E. J. 1959. *Primitive Rebels: Studies in Archaic Forms of Social Movement in the 19th and 20th Centuries.* New York: W. W. Norton.

Hobsbawm, E. J. 1990. *Nations and Nationalism Since 1780: Programme, Myth, Reality.* Revised ed. Cambridge: Cambridge University Press.

Hooker, Juliet. 2009. *Race and the Politics of Solidarity.* New York: Oxford University Press.

Ignatiev, Noel, and John Garvey, editors. 1996. *Race Traitor.* New York: Routledge.

Immerwahr, Daniel. 2019. *How to Hide an Empire: A History of the Greater United States.* New York: Farrar, Strauss, Giroux.

Independent Commission of Inquiry on the U.S. Invasion of Panama. 1991. *The U.S. Invasion of Panama: The Truth behind Operation "Just Cause."* Boston: South End Press.

Jameson, Frederic. 2024. *Inventions of a Present: The Novel in Its Crisis of Globalization.* New York: Verso.

Jeffers, Chike. 2019. "Cultural Constructionism." In *What Is Race? Four Philosophical Views*, by Joshua Glasgow, Sally Haslanger, Chike Jeffers, and Quayshawn Spencer, 38–72. New York: Oxford University Press.

Jefferson, Thomas. (1785) 1999. *Notes on the State of Virginia.* Edited by Frank Shuffleton. New York: Penguin Books.

Jefferson, Thomas. 2021. *The Autobiography of Thomas Jefferson.* Overland Park, KS: Digireads.com Publishing.

204 REFERENCES

Jimeno, Myriam. 2014. *Juan Gregorio Palechor: The Story of My Life.* Translated by Andy Klatt. Durham, NC: Duke University Press.

Jordan, Winthrop. (1968) 2012. *White over Black: American Attitudes toward the Negro, 1550–1812.* Chapel Hill: University of North Carolina Press.

Kassab, Elizabeth Suzanne. 2009. *Contemporary Arab Thought: Cultural Critique in Comparative Perspective.* New York: Columbia University Press.

Kassab, Elizabeth Suzanne. 2019. *Enlightenment on the Eve of Revolution: The Egyptian and Syrian Debates.* New York: Columbia University Press.

Khader, Serene J. 2019. *Decolonizing Universalism: A Transnational Feminist Ethic.* New York: Oxford University Press.

Khalidi, Rashid. 2010. *Palestinian Identity: The Construction of Modern National Consciousness.* New York: Columbia University Press.

Khalidi, Rashid. 2020. *The Hundred Years War on Palestine: A History of Settler Colonialism and Resistance, 1917–2017.* Metropolitan Books.

Kim, David Haekwon. 1999. "Contempt and Ordinary Inequality." In *Racism and Philosophy,* edited by Susan Babbitt and Sue Campbell, 108–123. Ithaca, NY: Cornell University Press.

Kim, David Haekwon. 2015. "Shame and Self-Revision in Asian-American Assimilation." In *Living Alterities: Phenomenology, Embodiment, and Race,* edited by Emily S. Lee, 103–132. Albany: State University of New York Press.

Kitcher, Philip. 1999. "Race, Ethnicity, Biology, Culture." In *Racism: Key Concepts in Critical Theory,* edited by Leonard Harris, 87–117. Amherst, NY: Humanities Press.

Kitcher, Philip. 2007. "Does 'Race' Have a Future?" *Philosophy and Public Affairs* 35, no. 4 (Fall): 293–317.

Kompridis, Nikolas. 2006. *Critique and Disclosure: Critical Theory between Past and Future,* Boston: MIT Press.

Kotef, Hagar. 2020. "Violent Attachments." *Political Theory* 48 (1): 4–29.

Kundnani, Hans. 2023. *Eurowhiteness: Culture, Empire, and Race in the European Project.* London: Hurst and Company.

Lelie, Frans, Maurice Crul, and Jens Schneider. 2012. *The European Second Generation Compared: Does the Integration Context Matter?* Amsterdam: Amsterdam University Press.

Linebaugh, Peter, and Marcus Rediker. 2000. *The Many-Headed Hydra: Sailors, Slaves, Commoners and the Hidden History of the Revolutionary Atlantic.* Boston: Beacon Press.

Liu, Catherine. 2021. *Virtue Hoarders: The Case against the Professional Managerial Class.* Minneapolis: University of Minnesota Press.

Locke, Alain. 2012. *The Works of Alain Locke.* Edited by Charles Molesworth. New York: Oxford University Press.

Losurdo, Domenico. 2014. *Liberalism: A Counter-history.* New York: Verso.

Luiselli, Valeria. 2017. *Tell Me How It Ends: An Essay in 40 Questions.* Minneapolis: Coffee House Press.

MacIntyre, Alasdair. (1971) 1978. *Against the Self-Images of the Age: Essays on Ideology and Philosophy.* Notre Dame, IN: University of Notre Dame Press.

MacIntyre, Alasdair. 1984. *After Virtue: A Study in Moral Theory.* 2nd ed. Notre Dame, IN: University of Notre Dame Press.

Macpherson, C. B. 1966. *The Real World of Democracy.* Oxford: Clarendon Press.

REFERENCES   205

Maglo, K. 2011. "The Case against Biological Realism about Race: From Darwin to the Post-genomic Era." *Perspectives in Science* 19 (4): 361–390.

Maglo, Koffi N. 2010. "Genomics and the Conundrum of Race: Some Epistemic and Ethical Considerations." *Perspectives in Biology and Medicine* 53, no. 3 (Summer): 357–372.

Maher, Geo. 2022. *Anticolonial Eruptions: Racial Hubris and the Cunning of Resistance.* Oakland: University of California Press.

Marcano, Donna-Dale L. 2010. "The Difference that Difference Makes: Black Feminism and Philosophy." In *Convergences: Black Feminism and Continental Philosophy.* Edited by Maria del Guadalupe Davidson, Kathryn T. Gines, and Donna-Dale L. Marcano. Albany: State University of New York Press, 53–66.

Mariátegui, José Carlos. 1971. *Seven Interpretive Essays on Peruvian Reality.* Translated by Marjory Urquidi. Austin: University of Texas Press.

Mariátegui, José Carlos. 1996. *The Heroic and Creative Meaning of Socialism: Selected Essays of José Carlos Mariátegui.* Edited and translated by Michael Pearlman. Atlantic Highlands, NJ: Humanities Press.

Martí, José. 2002. *Jose Martí: Selected Writings.* Edited and translated by Esther Allen. New York: Penguin Books.

McDermott, Monica. 2020. *Whiteness in America.* New York: Polity Press.

McGary, Howard. 1999. *Race and Social Justice.* Malden, MA: Blackwell Publishers.

McGhee, Heather. 2021. *The Sum of Us: What Racism Costs Everyone and How We Can Prosper Together.* New York: One World Press.

McPherson, Lionel. 2015. "Deflating Race." *Journal of the American Philosophical Association* 1, no. 4: 674–693.

McPherson, Lionel. 2024. *The Afterlife of Race: An Informed Philosophical Search.* New York: Oxford University Press.

Metzl, Jonathan M. 2019. *Dying of Whiteness: How the Politics of Resentment Is Killing America's Heartland.* New York: Basic Books.

Mignolo, Walter. 1995. *The Darker Side of the Renaissance: Literacy, Territoriality, and Colonization.* Ann Arbor: University of Michigan Press.

Mignolo, Walter. 2005. *The Idea of Latin America.* Malden, MA: Blackwell Publishers.

Mignolo, Walter D. 2011. *The Darker Side of Western Modernity: Global Futures, Decolonial Options.* Durham, NC: Duke University Press.

Mignolo, Walter D. 2021. *The Politics of Decolonial Investigations.* Durham, NC: Duke University Press.

Mills, Charles. 1997. *The Racial Contract.* Ithaca, NY: Cornell University Press.

Mills, Charles W. 1998. *Blackness Visible: Essays on Philosophy and Race.* Ithaca, NY: Cornell University Press.

Mills, Charles W. 2017. *Black Rights / White Wrongs: The Critique of Racial Liberalism.* New York: Oxford University Press.

Mishra, Pankaj. 2024. "Memory Failure." *London Review of Books,* 4 January 2024, 11–12.

Mohawk, John. 1992. "The Indian Way Is a Thinking Tradition." In *Indian of American Democracy,* edited by José Barreiro, 20–29. Ithaca, NY: AKWE:KON Press.

Monahan, Michael J. 2011. *The Creolizing Subject: Race, Reason, and the Politics of Purity.* New York: Fordham University Press.

206 REFERENCES

Morgan, Edmund S. 2005. *American Slavery, American Freedom.* New York: W. W. Norton.

Morgan, Helen. 2021. *The Work of Whiteness: A Psychoanalytic Perspective.* New York: Routledge.

Morrison, Joseph L. 1967. *W. J. Cash: Southern Prophet; A Biography and Reader.* New York: Alfred A. Knopf.

Morrison, Toni. 1992. *Playing in the Dark: Whiteness and the Literary Imagination.* New York: Vintage.

Moses, Dirk. 2007. *German Intellectuals and the Nazi Past.* Cambridge: Cambridge University Press.

Mosley, Albert G. 1999. "Negritude, Nationalism, and Nativism: Racists or Racialists." In *Racism,* edited by Leonard Harris, 75–86. Amherst, NY: Humanity Books.

Myers, Ella. 2022. *The Gratifications of Whiteness: W. E. B. Du Bois and the Enduring Rewards of Anti-Blackness.* New York: Oxford University Press.

Narayan, Uma. 1998. *Dislocating Cultures: Identities, Tradition, and Third-World Feminisms.* New York: Routledge.

Nascimento, Amos, and Matthias Lutz-Bachmann, eds. 2018. *Human Dignity: Perspectives from a Critical Theory of Human Rights.* New York: Routledge.

Ndlovu-Gatsheni, Sabelo J. 2018. *Epistemic Freedom in Africa: Deprovincialization and Decolonization.* London: Routledge.

Ngai, Mae M. 2004. *Impossible Subjects: Illegal Aliens and the Making of Modern America.* Princeton, NJ: Princeton University Press.

Ngai, Mae M. 2021. *The Chinese Question: The Gold Rushes, Chinese Migration, and Global Politics.* New York: W. W. Norton.

Ngũgĩ Wa Thiong'o. 2023. *The Language of Languages.* Kolkata: Seagull Books.

Nguyen, Viet Thanh. 2023. *A Man of Two Faces: A Memoir, a History, a Memorial.* New York: Grove Press.

Norris, Michele. 2024. *Our Hidden Conversations: What Americans Really Think about Race and Identity.* New York: Simon and Schuster.

Okihiro, Gary Y. 1994. *Margins and Mainstreams: Asians in American History and Culture.* Seattle: University of Washington Press.

Olsen, Joel. 2004. *The Abolition of White Democracy.* Minneapolis: University of Minnesota Press.

Omi, Michael, and Howard Winant. 1994. *Racial Formation in the United States: From the 1960s to the 1990s.* 2nd edition. New York: Routledge Press.

Ortiz, Fernando. (1947) 1995. *Cuban Counterpoint: Tobacco and Sugar.* Translated by Harriet de Onís. Durham, NC: Duke University Press.

Otele, Olivette. 2020. *African Europeans: An Untold History.* London: Hurst.

Özyürek, Esra. 2023. *Subcontractors of Guilt: Holocaust Memory and Muslim Belonging in Postwar Germany.* Palo Alto, CA: Stanford University Press.

Painter, Nell Irvin. 2010. *The History of White People.* New York: W. W. Norton.

Paris, Roland. 2022. "Putin Has Been Redefining 'Sovereignty' in Dangerous Ways." *Washington Post,* 3 March 2022.

Pham, Quynh N., and Robbie Shilliam, eds. 2016. *Meanings of Bandung: Postcolonial Orders and Decolonial Visions.* New York: Rowman and Littlefield.

Pierce, Jeremy. 2014. *A Realist Metaphysics of Race: A Context-Sensitive, Short-Term Retentionist, Long-Term Revisionist Approach.* Lanham, MD: Lexington Books.

REFERENCES 207

Piper, Adrian. 1992–1993. "Xenophobia and Kantian Rationalism." *Philosophical Forum 24*, no. 1–3: 188–232.

Pitts, Andrea J. 2021. *Nos/Otras: Gloria E. Anzaldúa, Multipliciteus Agency and Resistance.* Albany: State University of New York Press.

Prashad, Vijay. 2001. *Everybody Was Kung Fu Fighting: Afro-Asian Connections and the Myth of Cultural Purity.* Boston: Beacon Press.

Pratt, Scott L. 2002. *Native Pragmatism: Rethinking the Roots of American Philosophy.* Bloomington: Indiana University Press.

Puchner, Martin. 2023. *Culture: The Story of Us, from Cave Art to K-Pop.* New York: W. W. Norton.

Quijano, Anibal. 1999. "Coloniality and Modernity/Rationality." In *Globalizations and Modernities: Experiences and Perspectives of Europe and Latin America,* edited by Göran Jan Teeland and Lise-Lotte Wallenius, 11–20. Stockholm: Forskn ngsrådsanämnden.

Quijano, Anibal. 2008. "Coloniality of Power, Eurocentrism, and Latin America." Translated by Michael Ennis. In *Coloniality at Large: Latin America and the Postcolonial Debate,* edited by Mabel Moraña, Enrique Dussel, and Carlos Jáuregui, 181–224. Durham, NC: Duke University Press.

Rana, Aziz. 2010. *The Two Faces of American Freedom.* Cambridge, MA: Harvard University Press.

Redecker, E. V. 2016. *"Anti-Genderismus* and right-wing hegemony." *Radical Philosophy,* no. *198,* 2–7.

Richeson, Jennifer A., and Sophie Trawaltar. 2008. "The Threat of Appearing Prejudiced and Race-Based Attentional Biases." *Psychological Science,* no. 19, 98–102.

Rivera, Omar. 2019. *Delimitations of Latin American Philosophy: Beyond Redemption.* Bloomington: Indiana University Press.

Robinson, Constance Noyes, ed. 1970. *Oneida Community: An Autobiography, 1851–1876.* Syracuse, NY: Oneida Community Mansion House / Syracuse University Press.

Rodo, José Enrique. 1988. *Ariel.* Translated by Margaret Sayers Peden. Austin: University of Texas Press.

Roediger, David. R. 1994. *Towards the Abolition of Whiteness: Essays on Race, Politics and Working Class History.* New York: Verso.

Roosevelt, Kermit, III. 2022. *The Nation That Never Was: Reconstructing America's Story.* Chicago: University of Chicago Press.

Said, Edward W. 1979. *Orientalism.* New York: Vintage Books.

Said, Edward W. 1993. *Culture and Imperialism.* New York: Alfred A. Knopf.

Said, Edward W. 2004. *Humanism and Democratic Criticism.* New York: Columbia University Press.

Sartre, Jean-Paul. (1948) 1995. *Anti-Semite and Jew: An Exploration of the Etiology of Hate.* Translated by George J. Becker. New York: Schocken Books.

Sartre, Jean-Paul. 2013. *We Have Only This Life to Live: The Selected Essays of Jean-Paul Sartre 1939–1975.* Edited by Ronald Aronson and Adrian Van Den Hoven. New York: New York Review Books.

Schutte, Ofelia. 1993. *Cultural Identity and Social Liberation in Latin American Thought.* Albany: State University of New York Press.

208 REFERENCES

Sealey, Kris. 2018. "The Composite Community: Thinking through Fanon's Critique of a Narrow Nationalism." *Critical Philosophy of Race* 6 (1): 27–57.

Sealey, Kris. 2020. *Creolizing the Nation*. Evanston, IL: Northwestern University Press.

Sharpley-Whiting, T. Denean. 2003. "*Tropiques* and Suzanne Césaire: The Expanse of Negritude and Surrealism." In *Race and Racism in Continental Philosophy*, edited by Robert Bernasconi with Sybol Cook, 115–128. Bloomington: Indiana University Press.

Shelby, Tommie. 2005. *We Who Are Dark: The Philosophical Foundations of Black Solidarity*. Cambridge, MA: Harvard University Press.

Shelby, Tommie. 2016. *Dark Ghettos: Injustice, Dissent and Reform*. Cambridge, MA: Harvard University Press.

Sheth, Falguni. 2009. *Toward a Political Philosophy of Race*. Albany: SUNY Press.

Sheth, Falguni. 2022. *Unruly Women: Race, Neocolonialism, and the Hijab*. New York: Oxford University Press.

Silva, Denise Ferreira da. 2007. *Toward a Global Idea of Race*. Minneapolis: University of Minnesota Press.

Simpson, Audra. 2014. *Mohawk Interruptus: Political Life across the Borders of Settler States*. Durham, NC: Duke University Press.

Sokol, Jason. 2007. *There Goes My Everything: White Southerners in the Age of Civil Rights, 1945–1975*. New York: Vintage Books.

Sonnie, Amy, and James Tracy. 2011. *Hillbilly Nationalists, Urban Race Rebels, and Black Power: Community Organizing in Radical Times*. Brooklyn, NY: Melville House.

Spencer, Quayshawn. 2012. "What 'Biological Racial Realism' Should Mean." *Philosophical Studies*, no. 159, 181–204.

Spencer, Quayshawn. 2014. "A Radical Solution to the Race Problem." *Philosophy of Science*, no. 81, 1025–1038.

Spencer, Quayshawn. 2018. "Racial Realism II: Are folk Races Real?" *Philosophical Compass* 13 (1). https://compass.onlinelibrary.wiley.com/doi/abs/10.1111/phc3.12467.

Spencer, Quayshawn. 2019. "Is Race an Illusion or a (Very) Basic Reality?" In *What Is Race: Four Philosophical Views*, by Joshua Glasgow, Sally Haslanger, Chike Jeffers, and Quayshawn Spencer, 111–149. New York: Oxford University Press.

Spencer, Richard, ed. 2016. *The Uprooting of European Identity*. Brooklyn, NY: Radix.

Spengler, Oswald. 2018. *The Decline of the West*. Vol. 1. New York: Alfred A. Knopf.

Steele, Claude M. 2010. *Whistling Vivaldi and Other Clues to How Stereotypes Affect Us*. New York: W.W. Norton.

Steinfeld, Robert. 1989. "Property and Suffrage in the Early American Republic." *Stanford Law Review* 41, no. 2 (January): 335–376.

Stewart, Jeffrey C. 1992. Introduction to *Race Contacts and Interracial Relations: Lectures on the Theory and Practice of Race*, by Alain LeRoy Locke, edited by Jeffrey C. Stewart, xix–lix. Washington, DC: Howard University Press.

Sullivan, Shannon. 2005. *Revealing Whiteness: The Unconscious Habits of White Privilege*. Bloomington: Indiana University Press.

Sullivan, Shannon. 2014. *Good White People: The Problem with Middle-Class Anti-racism*. Albany: State University of New York Press.

REFERENCES 209

Sveinsdóttir, Ásta. 2013. "The Social Construction of Human Kinds." *Hypatia* 28, no. 4 (Fall): 716–732.

Táíwò, Olúfẹ́mi. 2010. *How Colonialism Preempted Modernity in Africa*. Bloomington: Indiana University Press.

Táíwò, Olúfẹ́mi O. 2022. *Reconsidering Reparations*. New York: Oxford University Press.

Takaki, Ronald. 1998. *Strangers from a Different Shore: A History of Asian Americans*. Revised ed. New York: Little, Brown and Company.

Taylor, Charles. 1989. *Sources of the Self: The Making of Modern Identity*. Cambridge, MA: Harvard University Press.

Taylor, Charles. 1991. *The Ethics of Authenticity*. Cambridge, MA: Harvard University Press.

Taylor, Jared, editor. 1998. *The Real American Dilemma: Race, Immigration and the Future of America*. Oakton, VA: New Century Books.

Taylor, Keeanga-Yamahtta. 2016. *From #BlackLivesMatter to Black Liberation*. Chicago: Haymarket Books.

Taylor, Paul C. 2004. *Race: A Philosophical Introduction*. Second ed. Cambridge: Polity Press.

Taylor, Paul C. 2016. *Black Is Beautiful: A Philosophy of Black Aesthetics*. Malden, MA: Wiley Blackwell.

Telles, Edward E. 2006. *Race in Another America: The Significance of Skin Color in Brazil*. Princeton, NJ: Princeton University Press.

Teuton, Sean Kicummah. 2008. *Red Land, Red Power: Grounding Knowledge in the American Indian Novel*. Durham, NC: Duke University Press.

Tong, Michelle, and Samantha Artiga. 2021. "Use of Race in Clinical Diagnosis and Decision-Making: Overview and Implications." *KFF (online)*. https://www.kff.org/racial-equity-and-health-policy/issue-brief/use-of-race-in-clinical-diagnosis-and-decision-making-overview-and-implications/.

Torres-Saillant, Silvio. 1998. "The Tribulations of Blackness: Stages in Dominican Racial Identity." *Latin American Perspectives* 25 (3): 126–146.

Torres-Saillant, Silvio. 2013. *Caribbean Poetics: Towards an Aesthetic of West Indian Literature*. Revised ed. Leeds: Peepal Tree Press.

Traverso, Enzo. 2019. *The New Faces of Fascism: Populism and the Far Right*. New York: Verso.

Trouillot, Michel-Rolph. 1995. *Silencing the Past: Power and the Production of History*. Boston: Beacon Press.

Vallejo, César. (1931) 1988. *Tungsten*. Translated by Robert Mezey. Syracuse, NY: Syracuse University Press.

Vasconcelos, José. 1979. *The Cosmic Race*. Translated by Didier T. Jaén. London: Johns Hopkins University Press.

von Vacano, Diego A. 2014. *The Color of Citizenship: Race, Modernity and Latin American/Hispanic Political Thought*. New York: Oxford University Press.

Wallerstein, Immanuel. 2006. *European Universalism: The Rhetoric of Power*. New York: New Press.

Warnke, Georgia. 2007. *After Identity: Rethinking Race, Sex, and Gender*. Cambridge: Cambridge University Press.

Weir, Allison. 2013. *Identities and Freedom: Feminist Theory between Power and Connection*. New York: Oxford University Press.

210 REFERENCES

Whyte, Kyle. 2013. "On the Role of Traditional Ecological Knowledge as a Collaborative Concept: A Philosophical Study." *Ecological Processes* 2 (April): article 7.

Wilder, Gary. 2015. *Freedom Time: Negritude, Decolonization, and the Future of the World.* Durham, NC: Duke University Press.

Wilkins, Ben, ed. 2022. *Anne Braden Speaks: Selected Writings and Speeches 1960–2006.* New York: Monthly Review Press.

Williams, Bernard. 1995. "Identity and Identities." In *Identity*, edited by Henry Harris, 1–12. New York: Clarendon Press.

Williams, Patricia J. 1997. *Seeing a Color-Blind Future: The Paradox of Race.* New York: Farrar, Strauss, and Giroux.

Williams, Raymond. 1981. *The Sociology of Culture.* Chicago: University of Chicago Press.

Winn, Peter. 1986. *Weavers of the Revolution: The Yarur Workers and Chile's Road to Socialism.* New York: Oxford University Press.

Wittig, Monique. 1981. "One Is Not Born a Woman." *Feminist Issues* 1, no. 2 (Winter): 47–54.

Wolfe, Patrick. 1999. *Settler Colonialism and the Transformation of Anthropology: The Politics and Poetics of an Ethnographic Event.* New York: Continuum.

Zea, Leopoldo. 1986. "Essays on Philosophy of History." In *Latin American Philosophy in the Twentieth Century: Man, Values, and the Search for Philosophical Identity*, edited by Jorge J. E. Gracia, 219–230. Buffalo, NY: Prometheus Books.

Zea, Leopoldo. 1992. *The Role of the Americas in History*, edited by Amy Oliver. Translated by Sonja Karsen. Lanham, MD: Rowman and Littlefield.

Zeskind, Leonard. 2009. *Blood and Politics: The History of the White Nationalist Movement from the Margins to the Mainstream.* New York: Farrar, Strauss, Giroux.

Index

For the benefit of digital users, indexed terms that span two pages (e.g., 52–53) may, on occasion, appear on only one of those pages.

abortion, 142–43
Achebe, Chinua, 38n.5
Adams, John, 150, 168
Adorno, xvi, 37–38
advanced cultures, 70–71, 76, 80, 89, 93, 104
Allais, Lucy, 103
Allen, Danielle, 134–35, 136
Allen, Theodore W., 8, 9–10, 28
Allende, Isabel., 122, 131
Allende, Salvador., 121, 122, 123
Andean people, 62, 83, 85–86
Anderson, Benedict, 101–2
Andreasen, R. O., 3–4
antiracism, 61
antisemitism, xvi, 72, 142, 180
Appiah, Kwame Anthony 37–38
Arnold, Matthew, 74–75, 88–89, 96
assimilability, xx, 31–32, 65–66, 89–90, 105, 139–40, 174–75
assimilation, xx, 20–21, 30, 36–37, 38, 69, 72, 87, 89–90, 93, 96–97, 172, 176
Astá, 14–15
Augstein, H. F., 25
Aztec, 81, 107

Barreiro, José, 100, 148
Bautman, Elif, 84
Beltrán, Cristina, xviii, 9–10, 45, 48–50, 51–52, 59, 90, 139, 140, 146
Benjamin, Walter, 98
Bernasconi, Robert, 40, 45
Bethencourt, Francisco 26, 66–68, 70, 78–79

Bilgrami, Akeel, 18–19, 86
Blackhawk, Ned, 112–13
Blum, Lawrence, 2–3, 63
Boas, Franz, 96
Bobo, Lawrence, 63
Bogues, Anthony, 93
Bouteldja, Houria, 186
Brenner, Y., 72
Brodkin, Karen, 139–40
Burkhart, Brian, 33–34
Bush, Melanie, 186

Cabral, Amilcar, 42, 90, 94–95
Camus, Albert, 108–9, 110–11, 112–13, 192–94
Camus, Renaud, 138–39, 140–41, 142, 144
Candelaria, Ginetta, 3, 131
capitalism, xvi–xvii, 57, 70, 76–77, 123
-racial, 49–50, 70, 104
Castells, Manuel 21
Castro-Gómez, Santiago, 79, 80–81, 91–92
Césaire, Aimé, 36–37, 38–39, 42, 43
Césaire, Suzanne, 36–37, 38–39, 42, 43
Charles, Camille, 63
Chavez, Leo, 139
chief Logan, 169
Christian nationalism, 52, 104, 114, 145, 175
Christianity, xviii–xix, xxi–xxii 26, 27, 52, 53, 81–82, 104, 114, 115, 129, 131–32, 138–39, 140, 141, 145, 146, 171, 175

212 INDEX

citizenship, 22, 36, 56–57, 86–87, 115, 128, 145, 156, 174, 183
class, xxiv–xxv, 8, 15n.3, 20, 42, 54–55, 56–57, 61, 64–65, 74–76, 105–6, 108–9, 112, 132–33, 137–38, 145, 151, 155, 156–58, 169, 177, 178–79, 185–86
coloniality of power, 89–90
colonial matrix of power, 92–93
colorism, 1, 3, 17–18, 26, 78
Conquest of the Americas, 13, 31–32, 47, 57, 70, 91, 98–99, 103
Corlett, J. Angelo, 2–3
Coronil, Fernando, 45–46, 50, 96
Cowie, Jefferson, 55–57, 58, 59, 131–32
Creolité, 105–6
Crèvecoeur, Hector St. John, 147–48, 149–50, 151–56, 158, 161, 162–64, 173–76, 177
critical philosophy of race, 1, 28
cultural racism,
    definition of, 62, 64, 65, 66–67
culture, definition of, 64–65, 73, 88–94
    as apparatus (dispositif) 91–92, 93–94, 184–85
    as contextual, 74–75
    and identity formation, 42, 75–76
    and imperialism, 73–76, 77, 83, 84, 90
    political critique of, 73–74, 77–78
    as universal, 74–76
Currah, Paisely, 61

Darby, Derrick, 115
DEI, 93
De la Cadena, Marisol, 32, 33–34
democracy, xviii, 16, 28–29, 36–37, 39n.6, 114, 121, 127, 128, 139–40, 148–51, 152, 154, 155, 161, 174, 175–76, 176n.3, 177, 178, 186
    Herrenvolk Democracy, 51–52, 170–71
dewesternization, 93–94
Diaz, Kim, 158
Dodds Pennock, Caroline, 99
Dorfman, Ariel, 120, 121, 123, 127, 128
Du Bois, W.E.B., 18, 30, 33–34, 37–38, 39–40, 45

Dunbar-Ortiz, Roxanne, 158
Dupré, John, 3–4
Dussel, Enrique, 65, 100

education, 20, 30–31, 33, 36, 58–59, 85, 93, 113, 130, 142–43, 179–80, 184, 185
Eliade, Mircea, 68, 69–70, 87
Elkins, Caroline, xviii, 54–55
Escobar, Arturo, 85–86
ethnicity, ix–x, xix, 3–4, 12, 14, 17–18, 75–76, 92–93, 132–33, 140–41, 176n.3
ethno-nationalism, xviii, xxiii, 147–48
ethnorace, ix–x, 87, 112–13, 119–20, 128, 131–32, 143–44, 151, 171, 193
European Enlightenment, 37–38, 39n.6, 52, 99–100, 127
Eze, Emmanuel, 127

Falcon's Vine vaccine, 80–81
Fanon, Frantz, 40, 42, 59–60, 62, 63–65, 66, 70–71, 117–18, 122, 127, 134, 138–39, 186
Farago, Jason, 84
fascism, xvi, 87, 89–90, 128, 187
Frankenberg, Ruth, 127
Frankfurt School, xvi–xvii
French, Howard, 112–13, 158

Gadamer, Hans-Georg, 28, 40–41, 69–70
Garcia, Jorge, 2–3
Garcilaso de la Vega, El Inca, 31–32, 84, 99
gender based violence, 82
genetics, 3–5, 79, 81–82
Getachew, Adom, 36–37, 41–42
Ghosh, Amitav, 52–53
Gilroy, Paul, 88–90, 94–95
Glasgow, Josh, 27–28
Glissant, Édouard, 41, 106
Goldberg, David Theo, 2–3, 76
Gómez, Laura, 131

INDEX   213

Gonzalez, Juan, 123
Gooding-Williams, Robert, 21
Gordon, Jane Anna, 105–6
Gossett, Thomas F., 25
Gracia, Jorge J.E., 2–3
Graeber, Davis, 68, 79, 99, 100
Grandin, Greg, xviii, 112–13, 124
Grosfoguel Ramón, xiii, 62, 70
Guerra y Sanchez, Ramiro, 95
Guglielmo, Thomas, 3
gun violence, 82, 142–43, 179–80

Habermas, xvi
Hacking, Ian, 44–45
Hall, Stuart, 1, 6–7, 14–15, 28, 78,
    105–6, 116
Hämäläinen, Pekka, 99
Hamilton, Alexander, 156
Hanchard, Michael, 66
Haney-López, Ian, 3, 22, 131, 136,
    138n.2, 138–39
Hannaford, Ivan, 25
Hardimon, Michael, 5–7, 10, 16–17
Harding, Sandra, 43, 79–80
Harris, Leonard, 28, 35
Haslanger, Sally, 8–9, 27–28, 45
Haudenosaunee, 150–51
Henry, Paget, 32
Herder, 88–89
hermeneutic horizon, 28, 42–43, 117
    -pluritopic horizons, 41
Herrenvolk Democracy, 51–52, 148–49,
    170–71, 176, 183
Herrenvolk Republicanism, 51–52
historical formation of race defined,
    43–45, 47, 48–49
Hixson Walter L., 112–13, 167,
    170, 171
Hobbes, Thomas, 85
Hobsbawm, 112, 149–50
Hooker, Juliet, 32–33
Horkheimer, Max xvi
humanism, 73, 93–94, 106–7

identity, theories of, 12–25, 28–29, 30–
    31, 34, 41

Immerwahr, Daniel, xviii, 53–54, 163,
    169–71
immigration, 26–27, 56–57, 58, 72, 81–
    82, 85, 87, 89–90, 93–94, 101, 105,
    114, 136–37, 139, 140–41, 142–43,
    145, 161, 174–75, 177n.4, 181–82
Inca, 81, 84, 99
indigenous, 31–33, 107, 150
    "Indian", 33–34
    interpretation of, 171, 190
    treatment of, xix, 53–54, 55–56, 57, 76–
        77, 83–84, 150, 169, 170, 171
    'inner energy', 88
    integration, 77
Iroquois, 22, 150

Jeffers, Chike, 7–8, 29–30, 45–48
Jefferson, Thomas, xxiii–xxiv, 51, 54–55,
    87, 115–16, 147–50, 161, 162–71,
    172–77, 180–81, 186
Jews, xix, xxi–xxii, 129–30, 131, 138–39,
    140, 141, 146
Jimeno, Myriam, 32
Jordan, Winthrop, 49–50, 173

Khader, Serene, 65
Khalidi, Rashid, 53–54n.7, 140–41
Kim, David Haekwon, 87
Kitcher, Philip, 3–4
Kompridis, Nicolas, 105–6
Kotef, Hagar, 48–49
Kundnani, 52–53, 180–81

labor, 83–84
Latinos, 11, 22–23, 153–54
Lelie, Frans, 105
Linebaugh, Peter, 50–51, 149–50
Liu, Catherine, 137–38
Locke, Alain, 35
Locke, John, 153
Losurdo, Domenico, 52–53

MacIntyre, Alasdair, 118–19
Maglo, Koffi N., 4–5
Maher, Geo, 149–50
Marcano, Donna-Dale, 28–29

214 INDEX

Marcuse, xvi
Mariátegui, José Carlos, 30–33,
    38–39
Martí, José, xxiii–xxiv, 32–33, 38–
    39, 102–3
McDermott, Monica, 113–14
McGary, Howard, 2–3
McGhee, 114, 137–39, 138n.2
McPherson, Lionel, 40
Mestizahe, xvi, 30–31, 34, 41, 78,
    102–3
Mestizo, 30–31, 102–3
Métissage, 36, 38, 41, 42, 43
Metzl, Jonathan, 114, 179–80, 185
Mignolo, Walter, 70, 92–94, 169
Mill, John Stuart, 93
Mills, Charles, 24–25, 28, 29, 62
mixed race, 11, 14, 22, 78, 120, 170,
    181–82, 191
modern/colonial world system 65
Monahan, Michael, 51
Morant Bay Rebellion, 93
Morgan, Edmund, 49–50
Morgan, Helen, 39–40
Morrison, J., 157
Morrison, Toni, 125–26
Moses, Dirk, 125–26
Mosley, Albert, 35–36, 37–38
multiculturalism, 93
Muslims, xviii–xix, xxi–xxii, 18–19, 72–
    73n.1, 129–30, 140–41, 146

Narayan, Uma, 82
Nascimento, Amos, 105–6
nationalism, 94, 104
Nazis, 62, 70
Ndlovu-Gatsheni, Sabelo, 93–94
Negritude, 35–38, 40, 41–42
Ngai, Mae, 139–40
Ngugi Wa Thiong'o, 38n.5

Ohlendorf, K., 72
Okihiro, Gary, 65–66
Olsen, Joel, 59
Omi, Michael, 21, 29–30, 47, 50
orientalism, 88, 90–91

Ortiz, Fernando, xxi, 43, 94–99, 100–1,
    103, 105–6
Otele, Olivette, 102

Painter, Nell Irvin, 49–50, 185
Panama, xv–xvi, 121–23, 159–60
Pardo, M., 85–86
Paris, Roland, 85
Pierce, Jeremy, 4–5
Piper, Adrien, 2–3
pluralism, 73, 86
pluri-nationalism, 85–86
population genetics, 3–5
poverty, xvii, 22–23, 50–51, 58–59, 76–77,
    95, 104–5, 136–37, 156–57, 179,
    184–85, 194
Prashad, Vijay, 65
Pratt, Scott, 33–34
Puchner, Martin, 100
Putin, 84–85

Quijano, Anibal, 89–90, 92–93

race, ix, xvii, xviii, xix, 7–9, 16, 17–30
    cultural construction of, 45–47
    deflationary view of, 5, 7–8
    elimination of, 6–7, 8, 27–28,
        39–40, 42
    and ethnicity, ix
    history of the concept, 30–34
    minimalist view of, 5–6, 7, 8, 10
    political construction of, 45, 46, 47
    terms, 11
    and universals, 40, 42
racism,
    attitudinal, 61, 70–71, 72
    biological, 62–64, 76–77, 78–79, 82–
        83, 93
    changes in, 70–71
    definition of, 66–68
    environmental, 78–81, 82–83, 93
    geographical, 78–80, 81, 82–83
    inevitability of, 68
    scientific discrediting of, 63
rape as an alibi of racism, 72
Redecker, E.V., 72

INDEX 215

Rediker, M., 50–51, 149–50
religion, xx, xxiii–xxiv, 16–17, 18, 30, 68,
    75–76, 81–82, 85–86, 88, 92–93, 95,
    97, 102, 119, 120, 129, 140–41, 150,
    152–53, 158, 194
replacement theory, xi, xxi–xxii, 114, 127,
    129–30, 138–41, 142–43, 144–47,
    155, 181, 186, 187
resistance 71
Rivera, Omar, xxiii–xxiv, 31–32, 33
Rodo, Jose Enrique, 32–33, 95
Roediger, David, 51–52
Roma, 100
Roosevelt III, Kermit, 115–16, 149

Said, Edward, xxi, xxiv, 73–76, 77–78, 83,
    88, 90–91, 106–7, 191–92
Sartre, Jean-Paul, 28–29, 40, 41–42, 72
Scarouady, 150
Schutte, Ofelia, 33
Sealey, Kris, 41–42, 105–6
secular liberalism, 86
settlements, 53–54n.7, 57, 145, 147, 150,
    153–54, 170, 171, 175–76, 181–82
settlers, xix, xxiii–xxiv, 53–54n.7, 57, 80–
    81, 91–92, 100, 127, 145, 146, 150,
    151, 153–54, 155, 161, 166–67, 168,
    174, 175, 183, 191
    representation of, 80–81, 91–92
Shapiro, Ben, 81–82
Sharpley-Whiting, T. Denean, 36
Shelby, Tommie, 22–23, 29, 46–47
Sheth, Falguni, 53, 59, 140–41
Silva, Denise Ferreira da, 2–3
Sinti, 100
slavery, xxiii, 9–10, 12, 30, 32, 33–34, 36,
    42, 49–50, 51–52, 59, 71, 78, 81, 93,
    112–13, 114–16, 124, 128, 158, 162,
    163, 172, 173–75, 177
social construction of race, xviii, 7–12,
    24–25, 27–28, 29–30, 43–44, 45–
    47, 87–88
Sokol, Jason, 110–11
Sonnie Amy, 186
sovereignty, 84–87
Spencer, Quayshawn, 4–5

Spencer, Richard, 182
Spengler, Oswald 96, 106
Steele, Claude, 9–10, 135–36
Stewart, Jeffrey, 35
suffrage, 22, 26–27, 53–54, 148–49, 151,
    170–71, 183
Sullivan, Shannon, 39–40 135–36
Sveinsdóttir, Ásta, 14–15

Táíwo, Olúfémi, 39n.6, 69
Táíwo, Olúfémi O., 62, 124, 127, 186–87
Taylor Keeanga-Yahmatta, 61
Taylor, Paul C. 21, 67–68, 74–75, 98–99
Telles, Edward 78, 131
Teuton, Sean Kicummah, 33–34
Tong, Michelle, 4–5
Torres-Saillant, Silvio, 10–11, 75–76
Tracy, James, 186
traditional vs. historical cultures, 68–70, 76
transculturation, 73, 94–103
    and Europe, 101–2
    and religion, 97, 98
Troillot, Michel-Rolph, 69–70, 148
Trump, Donald, 81–82, 85

Ukraine, 84, 85

Valladolid debate, 76–77, 107
Vallejo, César, 83–84
Vasconcelos, José, 30–31, 32–33, 102–3
Von Vacano, Diego, 30–31

Wallerstein, Immanuel, xxiv
Warnke, Georgia, 16
Weber, M., 89
Weir, Allison, 22–24
Wengrow, D., 68, 79, 99, 100
white identity, xviii, xxii–xxiii, 8,
    24–25, 48–60, 109, 111, 113–16,
    117, 118–21, 124–25, 141, 142–46,
    152, 155–56, 158, 161, 172–73, 179–
    80, 181–82
    Internal diversity, 8, 59–60, 111, 183, 189
    White poor, 156–58, 171, 179, 185–86
White supremacy, 37–38, 78, 176–77,
    176n.3, 178

216 INDEX

white nationalism, 103–4, 105, 136–37, 145, 176, 180
Whyte, Kyle, 79–80
Wilder, Gary, 37–38
Williams, Bernard, 16–17, 47, 118
Williams, Patricia, 40

Williams, Raymond, xxi, 88–91, 92
Winant, Howard, 21, 29–30, 47, 50
Winn, Peter, 121
Wolfe, Patrick, 53–54n.7

Zea, Leopoldo, 33